The Fremantle Diary

THE
Fremantle Diary

Being the JOURNAL of Lieutenant Colonel
ARTHUR JAMES LYON FREMANTLE,
Coldstream Guards,
on his Three Months in the Southern States

EDITING AND COMMENTARY BY
Walter Lord

BURFORD BOOKS

Printed in the United States of America

10   9   8   7   6   5   4   3   2   1

Library of Congress Cataloging-in-Publication Data
Fremantle, Arthur James Lyon, Sir, 1835–1901.
    [Three months in the southern states]
    The Fremantle diary / by Walter Lord.
        p.   cm.
    Originally published: Three months in the southern states. 1864.
    ISBN 1-58080-085-8
    1. Confederate States of America — Description and travel.
    2. Fremantle, Arthur James Lyon, Sir, 1835–1901 — Journeys —
Confederate States of America.   3. United States — History — Civil
War, 1861–1865 — Personal narratives, British.   4. Fremantle, Arthur
James Lyon, Sir, 1835–1901 — Diaries.   5. British — Confederate
States of America — Diaries.   I. Lord, Walter, 1917–   . II. Title.
E487.F863 2001
973.7'092 — dc21

00-045543

Editor's Introduction

"Colonel Fremantle of England was ensconced in the forks of a tree not far off, with glass in constant use," recalled General John B. Hood. The occasion was the Confederate High Command's conference in a Gettysburg meadow early on the second day of the Civil War's climactic battle. General Hood was reminiscing some twelve years later in a letter to the Southern Historical Society, but he still remembered vividly the ubiquitous, oddly dressed Englishman who peered down from the tree with his spyglass as the Confederate leaders argued whether to attack the Union lines.

General Hood never said what he thought about the presence of this strange outsider, but he probably took it for granted. By that time, Lieutenant Colonel Arthur James Lyon Fremantle, H. M. Coldstream Guards, had become a familiar sight throughout the Confederacy.

He had arrived in Brownsville, Texas, three months earlier as a young man of twenty-eight on military leave from the British Army. He was traveling for pleasure, and, like the sailor who spends his shore leave rowing in the park, he naturally picked the only place where there was a war on. He had gone to the South instead of the North because he had the Victorian's sympathy for the underdog (except where England was concerned), but he had no deep convictions — his real reason was adventure, pure and simple.

Fremantle threw himself enthusiastically into his trip, moving gradually from Brownsville across Texas, Louisiana, Mississippi and Georgia to the headquarters of General Bragg's army in Tennessee. There he relaxed for a week and then moved on to

Editor's Introduction

Charleston, Richmond and finally joined General Lee's army on its march to Gettysburg. As the echoes of the great battle died away, he suddenly discovered that his leave was almost up. Hurriedly he crossed the lines; satisfied the puzzled Federals that he might be peculiar but he was no spy; and took the next boat home, where he resumed an impeccable but uneventful career in the British colonial armies.

In the course of his whirlwind tour, Fremantle probably covered the South more thoroughly than anybody else who lived through the Confederacy. Certainly he saw more people. As he traveled along, he quickly showed that he was a marvelous celebrity collector. He looked up everyone — Lee, Longstreet, Jeff Davis, Joe Johnston, Beauregard and all the rest. Remarkably enough, these meetings were rarely perfunctory. Fremantle charmed even the grumpiest Confederates, like Longstreet and Bragg. Invariably, he became a member of the family — whether he was sharing the only fork in Joe Johnston's mess or sharing Lee's confidences at Gettysburg. So when Fremantle finally went home, he had not only been everywhere, but he knew everybody.

Like the good tourist he was, Fremantle kept a diary, recording the places he went, the sights he saw and the people he met. His unique experiences, and his wonderful knack for describing them, made the diary an entrancing account of the South at war. Before the end of 1863, it was published in London and in the following year was reprinted in New York and Mobile, Alabama. The Mobile edition came at a time when the South was growing desperate for supplies and appeared bound in flowered wallpaper.

Everywhere the diary stirred enormous interest. People bought it in England because pro-Southern feeling was running high; they bought it in the North because of the hungry curiosity about conditions in the Confederacy; they bought it in the South because any token of an Englishman's sympathy helped keep alive the desperate hope for foreign intervention. All these interests disappeared when the war ended. People wanted only to forget, and the diary was buried with the past.

Today, the national mood has changed. Sectional bitterness has given way to a common pride in the glory and courage of both sides. With this new perspective, Fremantle's journal once again comes into its own. Nowhere is there a more revealing firsthand picture of the South at war. The sources of her strength and the seeds of her weakness parade by in a curiously contradictory pattern. We see disabled veterans given special work to stretch the last ounce of Southern manpower — while weak conscription and poor discipline simultaneously eat away the armies in the field. We see splendid resourcefulness in building from scratch an entire munitions industry — and we find it closed on Sundays, even as late as Gettysburg.

Nor is Fremantle only concerned with important problems. He's a master at painting in trivial details that bring the war and its personalities to life — General Magruder in a gay evening of amateur theatricals; General Bragg getting baptized; General Joe Johnston gathering wood for a locomotive; General Longstreet whittling on a stick at Gettysburg; General Beauregard getting gray hairs due not to lack of sleep but lack of hair tonic. Equally vivid are the pictures of unnamed and unsung heroes — Lee's veterans in tattered butternut; saucy Pennsylvania girls taunting the Confederate invaders.

Today, the appeal of Fremantle's journal extends far beyond the Civil War. It is one of the best contemporary accounts we have of American frontier life. Fremantle covers everything — how to address a mule team effectively; how to get first to a water hole; how to dodge tobacco juice; how polecat tastes. We meet rangers so tough *they* scalp the Indians — yet so gentle they show nothing but kindness to women, strangers and the weak. We see a riproaring community, where the locomotive engineer shoots his passenger, and the steamboat passengers shoot each other; yet a community so shy and bashful that the passengers pull down the stagecoach blinds every time they lose their clothes in a robbery.

Even more fascinating is the vivid picture Fremantle gives of America in its adolescent years. In a sense, our national voice was changing. We were neither out of pioneer days nor into modern times. The old was incongruously mixed with the new, and the new with the old, often when least expected. It's a world where one day, communication is limited to prairie schooner; the next, there's an exchange of playful telegrams worthy of a college sophomore. One day, there's an endless variety of elaborate cocktails to drink; the next, there's nothing but filthy water from a lonely mud-hole. Within a space of twenty-four hours, Fremantle is first forced to do his traveling by stagecoach, then has the luxury of a berth on a sleeping car.

Fremantle's diary plays another important role. It gives us a splendid portrait of that great institution of the nineteenth century, the British tourist. Serenely oblivious to the uproar around him, yet always ready to try anything, Fremantle is a superb example of the Old Breed.

Sometimes he is almost a caricature. He dutifully records all toasts to the Queen. He refuses to go to a party without his evening clothes. He searches in vain for a good old-fashioned cavalry charge with drawn sabers. He's dismayed by the inability of the Confederate infantry to form a hollow square. He proudly reports each occasion when he has succeeded in burying his instincts and has managed to shake hands with somebody. On trains, he is always happy to take a seat in the ladies' car, until he discovers, to his indignation, that "one is liable to be ousted by a female."

Yet behind this stiff façade is a man of character. While undoubtedly maintaining his "standards" to the end, Fremantle simultaneously threw himself into the spirit of the times. He clearly grew to enjoy fighting for a train seat, gulping a dinner in seven minutes flat, dancing the "American Cotillion," trading wisecracks on the stagecoach, and even going to bed with his boots on. There's no greater proof of his true quality than the warmth and affection he generated wherever he went. He was the pet of everybody, from General Longstreet to Mr. Sargent, the tough mule driver on the trip across Texas.

For all these reasons, Fremantle's diary becomes a fascinating mirror of the whole period — its courage, its weakness, its nobility and its dreary prejudices. All blend together to form a picture of not a lost cause but a lost era.

WALTER LORD

New York
January 1954

Contents

Contents

Contents

Contents

[xiv   ]

Contents

The Fremantle Diary

Preface

At the outbreak of the American war, in common with many of my countrymen, I felt very indifferent as to which side might win; but if I had any bias, my sympathies were rather in favor of the North, on account of the dislike which an Englishman naturally feels at the idea of slavery.

But soon a sentiment of great admiration for the gallantry and determination of the Southerners, together with the unhappy contrast afforded by the foolish bullying conduct of the Northerners, caused a complete revulsion in my feelings, and I was unable to repress a strong wish to go to America and see something of this wonderful struggle.

Having successfully accomplished my design, I returned to England, and found amongst all my friends an extreme desire to know the truth of what was going on in the South; for, in consequence of the blockade, the truth can with difficulty be arrived at, as intelligence coming mainly through Northern sources is not believed; and, in fact, nowhere is the ignorance of what is passing in the South more profound than it is in the Northern States.

In consequence of a desire often expressed, I now publish the Diary which I endeavored, as well as I could, to keep up day by day during my travels throughout the Confederate States.

I have not attempted to conceal any of the peculiarities or defects of the Southern people. Many persons will doubtless highly disapprove of some of their customs and habits in the wilder portion of the country; but I think no generous man, whatever may be his political opinions, can do otherwise than admire the courage, energy, and patriotism of the whole population, and the skill of its leaders, in this struggle against great odds.

And I am also of the opinion that many will agree with me in thinking that a people in which all ranks and both sexes display a unanimity and a heroism which can never have been surpassed in the history of the world is destined, sooner or later, to become a great and independent nation.

CHAPTER 1

At the Mouth of the Rio Grande

I Fall in with H.M.'s Frigate Immortalité *— Lynch Law Three Hours After Reaching America — Visits Across the Mexican Border — Cocktails in the Most Scientific Manner — At the Grand Fandango — The 3d Texas Infantry on Review — General Bee Hides His Pistols at a Dance — Mexican Girls Are a Badly Painted Lot — The Texan Rangers Sing "God Save the Queen!" — I Am Now Comparatively Reconciled to Shaking Hands with Everyone*

2d March, 1863 — I left England in the royal mail steamer *Atrato,* and arrived at St. Thomas on the 17th.

22d March — Anchored at Havana at 6:15 A. M., where I fell in with my old friend, H. M.'s frigate *Immortalité.* Captain Hancock not only volunteered to take me as his guest to Matamoros, but also to take a Texan merchant, whose acquaintance I had made in the *Atrato.* This gentleman's name is M'Carthy. He is of Irish birth — an excellent fellow, and a good companion; and when he understood my wish to see the "South," he had most good-naturedly volunteered to pilot me over part of the Texan deserts. I owe much to Captain Hancock's kindness.

23d March — Left Havana in H. M. S. *Immortalité,* at 11 A. M. Knocked off steam when outside the harbor.

* * *

1st April — Anchored at 8:30 P. M., three miles from the mouth of the Rio Grande, or Rio Bravo del Norte, which is, I believe, its more correct name, in the midst of about seventy merchant vessels.

2d April — The Texan and I left the *Immortalité*, in her cutter, at 10 A. M., and crossed the bar in fine style. The cutter was steered by Mr. Johnston, the master, and having a fair wind, we passed in like a flash of lightning and landed at the miserable village of Bagdad, on the Mexican bank of the Rio Grande.[1]

The bar was luckily in capital order — 3½ feet of water, and smooth. It is often impassable for ten or twelve days together: the depth of water varying from 2 to 5 feet. It is very dangerous, from the heavy surf and undercurrent. Sharks also abound. Boats are frequently capsized in crossing it, and the *Orlando* lost a man on it about a month ago.

Seventy vessels are constantly at anchor outside the bar; their cotton cargoes being brought to them, with very great delays, by two small steamers from Bagdad. These steamers draw only 3 feet of water, and realize an enormous profit.

Bagdad consists of a few miserable wooden shanties, which have sprung into existence since the war began. For an immense distance endless bales of cotton are to be seen.

Immediately we landed, M'Carthy was greeted by his brother merchants. He introduced me to Mr. Ituria, a Mexican, who promised to take me in his buggy to Brownsville, on the Texan bank of the river opposite Matamoros. M'Carthy was to follow in the evening to Matamoros.

The Rio Grande is very tortuous and shallow. The distance by river to Matamoros is sixty-five miles, and it is navigated by steamers, which sometimes perform the trip in twelve hours, but more often take twenty-four, so constantly do they get aground.

The distance from Bagdad to Matamoros by land is thirty-five miles; on the Texan side to Brownsville, twenty-six miles.

I crossed the river from Bagdad with Mr. Ituria, at 11 o'clock; and, as I had no pass, I was taken before half-a-dozen Confederate officers, who were seated round a fire contemplating a tin of potatoes. These officers belonged to Duff's cavalry (Duff being my Texan's partner). Their dress consisted simply of flannel shirts, very ancient trousers, jack boots with enormous spurs, and black felt hats ornamented with the "lone star of Texas." They looked rough and dirty, but were extremely civil to me.[2]

The captain was rather a boaster, and kept on remarking, "We've given 'em h——ll on the Mississippi, h——ll on the Sabine" [pronounced Sabeen], "and h——ll in various other places."

He explained to me that he couldn't cross the river to see M'Carthy, as he with some of his men had made a raid over there three weeks ago and carried away some *renegados*, one of whom, named Mongomery, they had *left* on the road to Brownsville. By the smiles of the other officers, I could easily guess that something very disagreeable must have happened to Mongomery. He introduced me to a skipper, who had just run his schooner, laden with cotton, from Galveston, and who was much elated in consequence. The cotton had cost 6 cents a pound in Galveston, and is worth 36 here.

Mr. Ituria and I left for Brownsville at noon. A buggy is a light gig on four high wheels.

The road is a natural one — the country quite flat, and much covered with mesquite trees, very like pepper trees. Every person

[7]

we met carried a six-shooter, although it is very seldom necessary to use them.

After we had proceeded about nine miles we met General Bee, who commands the troops at Brownsville. He was traveling to Boca del Rio in an ambulance,* with his quartermaster general, Major Russell.[3] I gave him my letter of introduction to General Magruder, and told him who I was.

He thereupon descended from his ambulance and regaled me with beef and beer in the open. He is brother to the General Bee who was killed at Manassas.[4] We talked politics and fraternized very amicably for more than an hour. He said the Mongomery affair was against his sanction, and he was sorry for it. He said that Davis, another *renegado*, would also have been put to death had it not been for the intercession of his wife. General Bee had restored Davis to the Mexicans.

Half an hour after parting company with General Bee we came to the spot where Mongomery had been *left*; and sure enough, about two hundred yards to the left of the road, we found him.

He had been slightly buried, but his head and arms were above the ground, his arms tied together, the rope still round his neck, but part of it still dangling from quite a small mesquite tree. Dogs or wolves had probably scraped the earth from the body, and there was no flesh on the bones. I obtained this my first experience of lynch law within three hours of landing in America.

I understand that this Mongomery was a man of very bad character, and that, confiding in the neutrality of the Mexican soil, he was in the habit of calling the Confederates all sorts of insulting

---

* An ambulance is a light wagon, and generally has two springs behind, and one transverse one in front. The seats can be so arranged that two or even three persons may lie at full length.

[8]

epithets from the Bagdad bank of the river; and a party of his *renegados* had also crossed over and killed some unarmed cotton teamsters, which had roused the fury of the Confederates.

About three miles beyond this we came to Colonel Duff's encampment. He is a fine-looking, handsome Scotchman, and received me with much hospitality. His regiment consisted of newly raised volunteers — a very fine body of young men, who were drilling in squads. They were dressed in every variety of costume, many of them without coats, but all wore the high black felt hat.

Notwithstanding the peculiarity of their attire, there was nothing ridiculous or contemptible in the appearance of these men, who all looked thoroughly like "business." Colonel Duff told me that many of the privates owned vast tracts of country, with above a hundred slaves, and were extremely well off. They were all most civil to me.[5]

Their horses were rather rawboned animals, but hardy and fast. The saddles they used were nearly like the Mexican. Colonel Duff confessed that the Mongomery affair was wrong, but he added that his boys *"meant well."*

We reached Brownsville at 5:30 P. M., and Mr. Ituria kindly insisted on my sleeping at his house instead of going to the crowded hotel.

3d April (Good Friday) — At 8 A. M. I got a military pass to cross the Rio Grande into Mexico, which I presented to the sentry, who then allowed me to cross in the ferryboat.

Carriages are not permitted to run on Good Friday in Mexico, so I had a hot dusty walk of more than a mile into Matamoros.

Mr. Zorn, the acting British Consul, and Mr. Behnsen, his partner, invited me to live at the Consulate during my stay at Matamoros, and I accepted their offer with much gratitude.

I was introduced to Mr. Colville, a Manchester man; to Mr. Maloney, one of the principal merchants; to Mr. Bennet, an Englishman, one of the owners of the *Peterhoff*, who seemed rather elated than otherwise when he heard of the capture of his vessel, as he said the case was such a gross one that our government would be obliged to take it up.[6] I was also presented to the *gobernador*, rather a rough.

After dining with Mr. Zorn, I walked back to the Rio Grande, which I was allowed to cross on presenting Mr. Colville's pass to the Mexican soldiers, and I slept at Mr. Ituria's again.

Brownsville is a straggling town of about 3000 inhabitants; most of its houses are wooden ones, and its streets are long, broad, and straight. There are about 4000 troops under General Bee in its immediate vicinity. Its prosperity was much injured when Matamoros was declared a free port.

After crossing the Rio Grande, a wide dusty road, about a mile in length, leads to Matamoros, which is a Mexican city of about 9000 inhabitants. Its houses are not much better than those at Brownsville, and they bear many marks of the numerous revolutions which are continually taking place there. Even the British Consulate is riddled with the bullets fired in 1861–1862.

The Mexicans look very much like their Indian forefathers, their faces being extremely dark and their hair black and straight. They wear hats with the most enormous brims, and delight in covering their jackets and leather breeches with embroidery.

Some of the women are rather good-looking, but they plaster their heads with grease and paint their faces too much. Their dress is rather like the Andalusian. When I went to the cathedral

I found it crammed with kneeling women. An effigy of our Saviour was being taken down from the cross and put into a golden coffin, the priest haranguing all the time about His sufferings, and all the women howling most dismally as if they were being beaten.

Matamoros suffers much from drought, and there had been no rain to speak of for eleven months.

I am told that it is a common thing in Mexico for the diligence to arrive at its destination with the blinds down. This is a sure sign that the travelers, both male and female, have been stripped by robbers nearly to the skin. A certain quantity of clothing is then, as a matter of course, thrown in at the window, to enable them to descend. Mr. Behnsen and Mr. Maloney told me they had seen this happen several times; and Mr. Oetling declared that he himself, with three ladies, arrived at the city of Mexico in this predicament.

4th April (Saturday) — I crossed the river at 9 A. M., and got a carriage at the Mexican side to take my baggage and myself to the Consulate at Matamoros. The driver ill-treated his half-starved animals most cruelly. The Mexicans are even worse than the Spaniards in this respect.

I called on Mr. Oetling, the Prussian Consul, who is one of the richest and most prosperous merchants in Matamoros, and a very nice fellow.

After dinner we went to a fandango, or open-air fête. About 1500 people were gambling, and dancing bad imitations of European dances.

5th April (Sunday) — Mr. Zorn, or Don Pablo as he is called here, Her Majesty's Acting Vice-Consul, is a quaint and most

[11]

good-natured little man — a Prussian by birth. He is overwhelmed by the sudden importance he has acquired from his office, and by the amount of work (for which he gets no pay) entailed by it — the office of British Consul having been a comparative sinecure before the war.

Mr. Behnsen is head of the leading firm. The principal place of business is at San Luis Potosi, a considerable city in the interior of Mexico. All these foreign merchants complain bitterly of the persecutions and extortion they have to endure from the government, which are doubtless most annoying; but nevertheless they appear to fatten on the Mexican soil.

I crossed to Brownsville to see General Bee, but he had not returned from Boca del Rio.

I dined with Mr. Oetling. We were about fourteen at dinner, principally Germans, a very merry party. Mr. Oetling is supposed to have made a million of dollars for his firm, by bold cotton speculations, since the war.

We all went to the theater afterwards. The piece was an attack upon the French and upon Southern institutions.[7]

6th April (Monday) — Mr. Behnsen and Mr. Colville left for Bagdad this morning, in a very swell ambulance drawn by four gay mules.

At noon I crossed to Brownsville and visited Captain Lynch, a quartermaster, who broke open a great box, and presented me with a Confederate felt hat to travel in. He then took me to the garrison, and introduced me to Colonel Buchel of the 3d Texas regiment, who is by birth a German, but had served in the French Army. He then prepared cocktails in the most scientific manner.[8] I returned to Matamoros at 2:30 P. M.

At the Mouth of the Rio Grande

Captain Hancock and Mr. Anderson (the paymaster) arrived from Bagdad in a most miserable vehicle, at 4 P. M. They were a mass of dust, and had been seven hours on the road, after having been very nearly capsized on the bar.

There was a great firing of guns and squibs in the afternoon, in consequence of the news of a total defeat of the French at Puebla, with a loss of 800 prisoners and 70 pieces of cannon.

Don Pablo, who had innocently hoisted his British flag in honor of Captain Hancock, was accused by his brother merchants of making a demonstration against the French.

After dinner we called on Mr. Maloney, whose house is gorgeously furnished, and who has a pretty wife.

7th April (Tuesday) — Mr. Maloney sent us his carriage to conduct Captain Hancock, Mr. Anderson, and myself to Brownsville.

We first called on Colonels Luckett and Buchel. The former is a handsome man, a doctor by profession, well informed and agreeable, but most bitter against the Yankees.

We sat for an hour and a half talking with these officers and drinking endless cocktails, which were rather good, and required five or six different liquids to make them.

We then adjourned to General Bee's, with whom we had another long talk, and with whom we discussed more cocktails.

At the General's we were introduced to a well-dressed goodlooking Englishman, Mr. ——, who, however, announced to us that he had abjured his nationality until Great Britain rendered justice to the South.* Two years since, this individual had his house burnt down; and a few days ago, happening to hear that one of the incendiaries was on the Mexican bank of the river,

* It seems he has been dreadfully "riled" by the late *Peterhoff* affair.

[13]

boasting of the exploit, he rowed himself across, shot his man, and then rowed back.

I was told afterwards that, notwithstanding the sentiments he had given out before us, Mr. —— is a stanch Britisher, always ready to produce his six-shooter at a moment's notice, at any insult to the Queen or to England.

We were afterwards presented to ——, rather a sinister-looking party, with long yellow hair down to his shoulders. This is the man who is supposed to have hanged Mongomery.

We were treated by all the officers with the greatest consideration, and conducted to the place of embarkation with much ceremony. Colonel Luckett declared I should not leave Brownsville until General Magruder arrives. He is expected every day.

Mr. Maloney afterwards told us that these officers, having given up everything for their country, were many of them in great poverty. He doubted whether —— had a second pair of boots in the world; but he added that, to do honor to British officers, they would scour Brownsville for the materials for cocktails.[9]

At 3 P. M. we dined with Mr. Maloney, who is one of the principal and most enterprising British merchants at Matamoros, and enjoyed his hospitality till 9:30. His wine was good, and he made us drink a good deal of it. Mr. Oetling was there, and his stories of highway robberies, and of his journeys *en chemise* were most amusing.

At 10 P. M. Mr. Oetling conducted us to the grand fandango given in honor of the reported victory over the French.

A Mexican fandango resembles a French *ducasse*, with the additional excitement of gambling. It commences at 9:30 and continues till daylight. The scene is lit up by numerous paper lanterns of various colors. A number of benches are placed so as to form a large square, in the center of which the dancing goes on, the men and women gravely smoking all the time. Outside the benches is the promenade bounded by the gambling tables and drinking booths. On this occasion there must have been thirty or forty gambling tables, some of the smaller ones presided over by old women, and others by small boys.

Monté is the favorite game, and the smallest silver coin can be staked, or a handful of doubloons. Most of these tables were patronized by crowds of all classes intent on gambling, with grave, serious faces under their enormous hats. They never moved a muscle, whether they won or lost.

Although the number of people at these fandangos is very great, yet the whole affair is conducted with an order and regularity not to be equalled in an assembly of a much higher class in Europe. If there ever is a row, it is invariably caused by Texans from Brownsville. These turbulent spirits are at once seized and cooled in the calaboose.

8th April (Wednesday) — Poor Don Pablo was "taken ill" at breakfast, and was obliged to go to bed. We were all much distressed at his illness, which was brought on by overanxiety connected with his official duties; and the way he is bothered by English and "Bluenose" * skippers is enough to try any one.[10]

Mr. Behnsen and Mr. Colville returned from Bagdad this afternoon, much disgusted with the attractions of that city.

General Bee's orderly was assaulted in Matamoros yesterday by a *renegado* with a six-shooter. This circumstance prevented the General from coming to Matamoros as he had intended.

At 5 P. M. Captain Hancock and I crossed over to Brownsville,

* Nova Scotian.

[15]

and were conducted in a very smart ambulance to General Bee's quarters, and afterwards to see a dress parade of the 3d Texas infantry.

Lieutenant colonel Buchel is the *working man* of the corps, as he is a professional soldier. The men were well clothed, though great variety existed in their uniforms. Some companies wore blue, some gray, some had French *képis*, others wide-awakes and Mexican hats. They were a fine body of men, and really drilled uncommonly well. They went through a sort of guard-mounting parade in a most creditable manner. About a hundred out of a thousand were conscripts.*

After the parade, we adjourned to Colonel Luckett's to drink prosperity to the 3d regiment.

We afterwards had a very agreeable dinner with General Bee; Colonels Luckett and Buchel dined also. The latter is a regular soldier of fortune. He served in the French and Turkish armies, as also in the Carlist and the Mexican wars, and I was told he had been a principal in many affairs of honor. But he is a quiet and unassuming little man, and although a sincere Southerner, is not nearly so violent against the Yankees as Luckett.

At 10 P. M. Captain Hancock and myself went to a ball given by the authorities of the "*Heroica y invicta ciudad de Matamoros*" (as they choose to call it), in honor of the French defeat. General Bee and Colonel Luckett also went to this fête, the invitation being the first civility they had received since the violation of the Mexican soil in the Davis-Mongomery affair. They were dressed in plain clothes, and carried pistols concealed in case of accidents.

---

* During all my travels in the South I never saw a regiment so well clothed or so well drilled as this one, which has never been in action, or been exposed to much hardship.

At the Mouth of the Rio Grande

We all drove together from Brownsville to the Consulate, and entered the ballroom en masse.

The outside of the municipal hall was lit up with some splendor, and it was graced by a big placard, on which was written the amiable sentiment, *"Muera Napoleon — viva Méjico!"* Semisuccessful squibs and crackers were let off at intervals. In the square also was a triumphal arch, with an inscription to the effect that "the effete nations of Europe might tremble."

I made great friends with the *gobernador* and *administrador*, who endeavored to entice me into dancing, but I excused myself by saying that Europeans were unable to dance in the graceful Mexican fashion. Captain Hancock was much horrified when this greasy-faced *gobernador* (who keeps a small shop) stated his intention of visiting the *Immortalité* with six of his friends, and sleeping on board for a night or two.

The dances were a sort of slow valse, and between the dances the girls were planted up against the wall, and not allowed to be spoken to by any one. They were mostly a plain-headed, badly painted lot, and ridiculously dressed.

9th April (Thursday) — Captain Hancock and Mr. Anderson left for Bagdad in Mr. Behnsen's carriage at noon.

I crossed over to Brownsville at 11:30, and dined with Colonels Luckett, Buchel, and Duff, at about one o'clock. As we were all colonels, and as every one called the other colonel *tout court*, it was difficult to make out which was meant. They were obliged to confess that Brownsville was about the rowdiest town of Texas, which was the most lawless state in the Confederacy. But they declared they had never seen an inoffensive man subjected to insult or annoyance, although the shooting-down and stringing-up sys-

[17]

tems are much in vogue, being almost a necessity in a thinly populated state much frequented by desperadoes driven away from more civilized countries.

Colonel Luckett gave me a letter to General Van Dorn, whom they considered the *beau ideal* of a cavalry soldier. They said from time immemorial the Yankees had been despised by the Southerners as a race inferior to themselves in courage and in honorable sentiments.[11]

At 3 P. M. Colonel Buchel and I rode to Colonel Duff's camp, distant about thirteen miles. I was given a Mexican saddle, in which one is forced to sit almost in a standing position. The stirrups are very long, and right underneath you, which throws back the feet.

Duff's regiment is called the Partisan Rangers. Although a fine lot of men, they don't look well at a foot parade, on account of the small amount of drill they have undergone, and the extreme disorder of their clothing. They are armed with carbines and six-shooters.

I saw some men come in from a scouting expedition against the Indians, 300 miles off. They told me they were usually in the habit of scalping an Indian when they caught him, and that they never spared one, as they were such an untamable and ferocious race. Another habit which they have learned from the Indians is to squat on their heels in a most peculiar manner. It has an absurd and extraordinary effect to see a quantity of them so squatting in a row or in a circle.

The regiment had been employed in quelling a counterrevolution of Unionists in Texas. Nothing could exceed the rancor with which they spoke of these *renegados*, as they called them, who were principally Germans.[12]

At the Mouth of the Rio Grande

When I suggested to some of the Texans that they might as well bury the body of Mongomery a little better, they did not at all agree with me, but said it ought not to have been buried at all, but left hanging as a warning to other evildoers.

With regard to the contentment of their slaves, Colonel Duff pointed out a good number they had with them, who had only to cross the river for freedom if they wished it.

Colonel Buchel and I slept in Colonel Duff's tent, and at night we were *serenaded*. The officers and men really sang uncommonly well, and they finished with "God Save the Queen!"

Colonel Duff comes from Perth. He was one of the leading characters in the secession of Texas; and he said his brother was a banker in Dunkeld.

10*th April* (Friday) — We roused up at daylight, and soon afterwards Colonel Duff paraded some of his best men, to show off the Texan horsemanship, of which they are very proud.

I saw them lasso cattle, and catch them by the tail at full gallop, and throw them by slewing them around. This is called tailing. They pick small objects off the ground when at full tilt, and, in their peculiar fashion, are beautiful riders; but they confessed to me they could not ride in an English saddle, and Colonel Duff told me that they could not jump a fence at all. They were all extremely anxious to hear what I thought of the performance, and their thorough good opinion of themselves was most amusing.

At 9 o'clock Colonel Buchel and I rode back to Brownsville; but as we lost our way twice, and were enveloped in clouds of dust, it was not a very satisfactory ride. Poor Captain Hancock must be luxuriating at Bagdad; for with this wind the bar must be impassable to the boldest mariner.

[19]

In the evening, a Mr. ——, a Texan Unionist, or *renegado*, gave us his sentiments at the Consulate, and drank a deal of brandy. He finished, however, by the toast, "Them as wants to fight, let 'em fight — I don't."

11*th April* (Saturday) — Mr. ——, the Unionist, came to me this morning, and said, in a contrite manner, "I hope, Kernel, that in the fumes of brandy I didn't say anything offensive last night." I assured him that he hadn't.

I have now become comparatively accustomed and reconciled to the necessity of shaking hands and drinking brandy with everyone.*

The ambulance returned from Bagdad today. Captain Hancock had managed to cross the bar in Mr. Oetling's steamer or lighter, but was very nearly capsized.

I went to a grand supper, given by Mr. Oetling in honor of Mr. Hill's departure for the city of Mexico. This, it appears, is the custom of the country.

12*th April* (Sunday) — I took an affectionate leave of Don Pablo, Behnsen, Oetling & Co., all of whom were in rather weak health on account of last night's supper.

The excellent Maloney insisted on providing me with preserved meats and brandy for my arduous journey through Texas. I feel extremely grateful for the kindness of all these gentlemen, who rendered my stay in Matamoros very agreeable. The hotel would have been intolerable.

I crossed to Brownsville at 3 P. M., where I was hospitably received by my friend Ituria, who confesses to having made a deal

* This necessity does not exist except in Texas.

of money lately by cotton speculations. I attended evening parade, and saw General Bee, Colonels Luckett, Buchel, Duff, and ——. The latter (who hanged Mongomery) improves on acquaintance.

General Bee took me for a drive in his ambulance, and introduced me to Major Leon Smith, who captured the *Harriet Lane*. The latter pressed me most vehemently to wait until General Magruder's arrival, and he promised, if I did so, that I should be sent to San Antonio in a first-rate ambulance. Major Leon Smith is a seafaring man by profession, and was put by General Magruder in command of one of the small steamers which captured the *Harriet Lane* at Galveston, the crews of the steamers being composed of Texan cavalry soldiers. He told me that the resistance offered after boarding was feeble; and he declared that had not the remainder of the Yankee vessels escaped unfairly under flag of truce they would likewise have been taken.[18]

After the *Harriet Lane* had been captured, she was fired into by the other ships; and Major Smith told me that, his blood being up, he sent the ex-master of the *Harriet Lane* to Commodore Renshaw with a message that unless the firing was stopped he would massaCREE the captured crew. After hearing this, Commodore Renshaw blew up his ship, with himself in her, after having given an order to the remainder, *sauve quipeut*.

From Brownsville to San Antonio

Hiring a Judge for Assistant Mule Driver — Wild Hogs Breathing in My Face — Rat Ranches — Encountering General Magruder — A Theatrical Evening with the General — Mule Driving Is an Art — A Violent Storm — Stopping at King's Ranch — Scorpions, Prairie Wolves and Rattlesnakes — Well-Cooked Polecat Is As Tasty As a Pig — How Texan Females Take Their Snuff — Fighting for a Mudhole — I Am Called a "Right Good Companion for the Road"

13th *April* (Monday) — I breakfasted with General Bee, and took leave of all my Brownsville friends.

M'Carthy is to give me four times the value of my gold in Confederate notes.* ¹

We left Brownsville for San Antonio at 11 A. M. Our vehicle was a roomy, but rather overloaded, four-wheel carriage, with a canvas roof, and four mules. Besides M'Carthy, there was a third passenger, a young Jewish merchant. Two horses were to join us, to help us through the deep sand.

The country, on leaving Brownsville, is quite flat. The road is a natural one, sandy and very dusty, and there are many small trees, principally mesquites. After we had proceeded seven miles, we halted to water the mules.

---

* The value of Confederate paper has since decreased. At Charleston I was offered six to one for my gold, and at Richmond eight to one.

At 2 P. M. a new character appeared upon the scene, in the shape of an elderly, rough-faced, dirty-looking man, who rode up, mounted on a sorry nag. To my surprise he was addressed by M'Carthy with the title of "Judge," and asked what he had done with our other horse. The Judge replied that it had already broken down, and had been left behind.

M'Carthy informs me that this worthy really is a magistrate or sort of judge in his own district; but he now appears in the capacity of assistant mule driver, and is to make himself generally useful. I could not help feeling immensely amused at this specimen of a Texan judge.[2]

We started again about 3 P. M., and soon emerged from the mesquite bushes into an open prairie eight miles long, quite desolate, and producing nothing but a sort of rush. After this, we entered a chaparral, or thick covert of mesquite trees and high prickly pears. These border the track and are covered with bits of cotton torn from the endless trains of cotton wagons. We met several of these wagons. Generally there were ten oxen or six mules to a wagon carrying ten bales, but in deep sand more animals are necessary. They journey very slowly towards Brownsville, from places in the interior of Texas at least five hundred miles distant. Want of water and other causes make the drivers and animals undergo much hardship.

The Judge rides on in front of us on his "Rosinante," to encourage the mules. His back view reminds one in a ludicrous manner of the pictures of Dr. Syntax.

Mr. Sargent, our portly driver, cheers his animals by the continual repetition of the sentence, "Get up, now, you great long-eared G—d d—d son of a —."

At 5 P. M. we reached a well, with a farm or ranch close to it.

Here we halted for the night. A cotton train was encamped close to us, and a lugubrious half-naked teamster informed us that three of his oxen had been stolen last night.

In order to make a fire, we were forced to enter the chaparral for wood, and in doing so, we ran many prickles into our legs, which caused us great annoyance afterwards, as they fester, if not immediately pulled out.

The water at this well was very salt, and made very indifferent coffee. M'Carthy called it the "meanest halting place we shall have."

At 8 p. m. M'Carthy spread a bullock rug on the sand near the carriage, on which we should have slept very comfortably had it not been for the prickles, the activity of many fleas, and the incursions of wild hogs. Mr. Sargent and the Judge, with much presence of mind, had encamped seventy yards off, and left to us the duty of driving away these hogs. I was twice awoke by one of these unclean animals breathing in my face.

We did about twenty-one miles today.

14th April (Tuesday) — When we roused up at 4 A. M. we found our clothes saturated with the heavy dew; also that, notwithstanding our exertions, the hogs had devoured the greatest part of our pet kid, our only fresh meat.

After feeding our mules upon the Indian corn we had brought with us, and drinking a little more salt-water coffee, the Judge "hitched in," and we got under way at 5:30 A. M. The country just the same as yesterday — a dead level of sand, mesquite trees, and prickly pears.

At 7:30 A. M. we reached "Leatham's ranch," and watered our mules. As the water was tolerable, we refilled our water barrels. I also washed my face, during which operation Mr. Sargent expressed great astonishment, not unmingled with contempt.

At Leatham's we met a wealthy Texan speculator and contractor, called Major or Judge Hart.

I find that *our* Judge is also an M. P., and that, in his capacity as a member of the Texan legislature, he is entitled to be styled the Honorable ——.

· At 9 A. M. we halted in the middle of a prairie, on which there was a little grass for the mules, and we prepared to eat. In the midst of our cooking, two deer came up quite close to us, and could easily have been killed with rifles.

We saw quantities of rat ranches, which are big sort of mole-hills, composed of cow-dung, sticks, and earth, built by the rats.

Mr. Sargent, our conductor, is a very rough customer — a fat, middle-aged man, who never opens his mouth without an oath, strictly American in its character. He and the Judge are always snarling at one another, and both are much addicted to liquor.

We live principally on bacon and coffee, but as the water and the bacon are both very salt, this is very inconvenient. We have, however, got some claret, and plenty of brandy.

During the midday halts, Mr. Sargent is in the habit of cooling himself by removing his trousers (or pants), and, having gorged himself, he lies down and issues his edicts to the Judge as to the treatment of the mules.

At 2:30 the M. P. hitched in again, and at 2:45 we reached a salt-water arm of the sea called the "Aroyo del Colorado," about eighty yards broad, which we crossed in a ferryboat. Half an hour later we "struck water" again, which, being superior to Leatham's, we filled up.

We are continually passing cotton trains going to Brownsville, also government wagons with stores for the interior. Near every well is a small farm or ranch, a miserable little wooden edifice surrounded by a little cultivation. The natives all speak Spanish, and wear the Mexican dress.

M'Carthy is very proud of his knowledge of the country, in spite of which he is often out in his calculations. The different tracks are so similar to one another, they are easily mistaken.

At 4:45 P. M. we halted at a much better place than yesterday. We are obliged to halt where a little grass can be found for our mules.

Soon after we had unpacked for the night, six Texan Rangers, of Wood's regiment, rode up to us. They were very picturesque fellows: tall, thin, and ragged, but quite gentlemanlike in their manners.

We are always to sleep in the open until we arrive at San Antonio, and I find my Turkish lantern most useful at night.*

15*th April* (Wednesday) — I slept well last night in spite of the ticks and fleas, and we started at 5:30 P. M. After passing a dead rattlesnake eight feet long, we reached water at 7 A. M.

At 9 A. M. we espied the cavalcade of General Magruder passing us by a parallel track about half a mile distant. M'Carthy and I jumped out of the carriage, and I ran across the prairie to cut him off, which I just succeeded in doing by borrowing the spare horse of the last man in the train.

I galloped up to the front, and found the General riding with a lady who was introduced to me as Mrs. ——, an undeniably pretty woman, wife to an officer on Magruder's staff. She is nat-

* A lantern for a candle, made of white linen and wire, which collapses when not in use. They are always used in the streets of Constantinople. The Texans admired it immensely.

urally the object of intense attention to all the good-looking officers who accompany the General through this desert.[3]

General Magruder, who commands in Texas, is a fine soldierlike
man, of about fifty-five, with broad shoulders, a florid complexion,
and bright eyes. He wears his whiskers and mustaches in the English fashion, and he was dressed in the Confederate gray uniform.[4]

He was kind enough to beg that I would turn back and accompany him in his tour through Texas. He had heard of my arrival, and was fully determined I should do this. He asked after
several officers of my regiment whom he had known when he was
on the Canadian frontier. He is a Virginian, a great talker, and
has always been a great ally of English officers.

He insisted that M'Carthy and I should turn and dine with
him, promising to provide us with horses to catch up to Mr. Sargent.

After we had agreed to do this, I had a long and agreeable conversation with the General, who spoke of the Puritans with intense disgust, and of the first importation of them as "that pestifer-
ous crew of the *Mayflower*"; but he is by no means rancorous
against individual Yankees. He spoke very favorably of M'Clellan,
whom he knew to be a gentleman, clever, and personally brave,
though he might lack moral courage to face responsibility.[5]

Magruder had commanded the Confederate troops at Yorktown
which opposed M'Clellan's advance. He told me the different
dodges he had resorted to, to blind and deceive the latter as to his
(Magruder's) strength. He spoke of the intense relief and amusement with which he had at length seen M'Clellan with his magnificent army begin to break ground before miserable earthworks,
defended only by 8000 men.[6]

Hooker was in his regiment, and was "essentially a mean man

and a liar." Of Lee and Longstreet he spoke in terms of the highest admiration.

Magruder was an artilleryman, and has been a good deal in Europe; and having been much stationed on the Canadian frontier, he became acquainted with many British officers, particularly those in the 7th Hussars and Guards.

He had gained much credit from his recent successes at Galveston and Sabine Pass, in which he had the temerity to attack heavily armed vessels of war with wretched river steamers manned by Texan cavalrymen.

His principal reason for visiting Brownsville was to settle about the cotton trade. He had issued an edict that half the value of cotton exported must be imported in goods for the benefit of the country (government stores). The President had condemned this order as illegal and despotic.

The officers on Magruder's staff are a very good-looking, gentlemanlike set of men. Their names are — Major Pendleton, Major Wray, Captain De Ponté, Captain Alston, Captain Turner, Lieutenant Colonel M'Neil, Captain Dwyer, Dr. Benien, Lieutenant Stanard, Lieutenant Yancy, and Major Magruder. The latter is nephew to the General, and is a particularly good-looking young fellow. They all live with their chief on an extremely agreeable footing, and form a very pleasant society.

At dinner I was put in the post of honor, which is always fought for with much acrimony — viz., the right of Mrs. ——.

After dinner we had numerous songs. Both the General and his nephew sang. So also did Captain Alston, whose corpulent frame, however, was too much for the feeble camp stool, which caused his sudden disappearance in the midst of a song with a loud crash. Captain Dwyer played the fiddle very well, and an aged and slightly elevated militia general brewed the punch and made several "elegant" speeches. The latter was a rough-faced old hero, and gloried in the name of M'Guffin. On these festive occasions General Magruder wears a red woollen cap, and fills the president's chair with great aptitude.

It was 11:30 before I could tear myself away from this agreeable party; but at length I effected my exit amidst a profusion of kind expressions, and laden with heaps of letters of introduction.[7]

16th April (Thursday) — Now our troubles commenced. Seated in Mexican saddles, and mounted on rawboned mustangs, whose energy had been a good deal impaired by a month's steady traveling on bad food, M'Carthy and I left the hospitable mess tent about midnight, and started in search of Mr. Sargent and his vehicle. We were under the guidance of two Texan Rangers.

About daylight we hove in sight of Los Animos, a desolate farmhouse, in the neighborhood of which Mr. Sargent was supposed to be encamped; but nowhere could we find any traces of him.

We had now reached the confines of a dreary region, sixty miles in extent, called "The Sands," in comparison with which the prairie and chaparral were luxurious.

The sand being deep and the wind high, we could not trace the carriage; but we soon acquired a certainty that our perfidious Jehu had decamped, leaving us behind.

We floundered about in the sand, cursing our bad luck, cursing Mr. Sargent, and even the good Magruder, as the indirect cause of our wretchedness. Our situation, indeed, was sufficiently deplorable. We were without food or water in the midst of a desert: so were our horses, which were nearly done up. Our bones ached

from the Mexican saddles; and, to complete our misery, the two
Rangers began to turn restive and talk of returning with the horses.
At this, the climax of our misfortunes, I luckily hit upon a Mexican, who gave us intelligence of our carriage; and with renewed
spirits, but very groggy horses, we gave chase.

But never did Mr. Sargent's mules walk at such a pace; and it
was 9 A. M. before we overtook them. My animal had been twice
on his head, and M'Carthy was green in the face with fatigue and
rage. Mr. Sargent received us with the greatest affability, and we
were sensible enough not to quarrel with him, although M'Carthy
had made many allusions as to the advisability of shooting him.

We had been nine and a half hours in the saddle, and were a
good deal exhausted. Our sulky Texan guides were appeased with
bacon, coffee, and $5 in coin.

We halted till 2 P. M., and then renewed our struggle through
the deep sandy wilderness; but though the services of the Judge's
horse were put into requisition, we couldn't progress faster than
two miles an hour.

Mule driving is an art of itself, and Mr. Sargent is justly considered a *professor* at it.

He is always yelling — generally imprecations of a seriocomic
character. He rarely flogs his mules; but when one of them rouses
his indignation by extraordinary laziness, he roars out, "Come here,
Judge, with a big club, and give him h—ll." While the animal is
receiving such discipline as comes up to the Judge's idea of the infernal regions, Mr. Sargent generally remarks, "I wish you was
Uncle Abe, I'd make you move, you G—d d—n son of a —." His
idea of perfect happiness seems to be to have Messrs. Lincoln and
Seward in the shafts.

Mules travel much better when other mules are in front of

them; and another dodge to which Mr. Sargent continually re-sorts is to beat the top of the carriage and kick the footboard. This makes a noise and gratifies the mules quite as much as licking them. Mr. Sargent accounts for his humanity by saying, "It's the worst plan in the world licking niggers or mules, because the more you licks 'em, the more they wants it."

We reached or "struck" water at 5:30 P. M.; but, in spite of its good reputation, it was so salt as to be scarcely drinkable. A num-ber of cotton wagons, and three carriages belonging to Mr. Ward, were also encamped with us.

We have only made sixteen miles today.

17th April (Friday) — Having spent last night in a Mexican saddle, our bullock rug in the sand appeared to me a most lux-urious bed.

We hitched in at 5 A. M., and struck water at 9 A. M., which, though muddy in appearance, was not so bad to drink.

I walked ahead with the Judge, who, when sober, is a well-informed and sensible man. Mr. Sargent and I are great friends, and, rough as he is, we get on capitally together.

A Mr. Ward, with three vehicles — a rival of Mr. Sargent's — is traveling in our company. He drove his buggy against a tree and knocked its top off, to the intense delight of the latter.

We breakfasted under difficulties. The wind being high, it drove up the sand in clouds and spoiled our food.

We went on again at 2 P. M. I had a long talk with a big mu-latto slave woman, who was driving one of Ward's wagons. She told me she had been raised in Tennessee, and that three years ago she had been taken from her mistress for a bad debt, to their mutual sorrow. "Both," she said, "cried bitterly at parting." [8] She doesn't like San Antonio at all. "Too much hanging and murdering for me," she said. She had seen a man hanged in the middle of the day, just in front of her door. .

Mr. Sargent bought two chickens and some eggs at a ranch, but one of the chickens got up a tree, and was caught and eaten by the Ward faction. Our camp tonight looks very pretty by the light of the fires.

18*th April* (Saturday) — At daylight we discovered, to our horror, that three of our mules were absent; but after an hour's search they were brought back in triumph by the Judge.

This delayed our start till 6:30 A. M.

I walked ahead again with the Judge, who explained to me that he was a "senator," or member of the Upper House of Texas — "just like your House of Lords," he said. He gets $5 a day whilst sitting, and is elected for four years.*

We struck water at 8:30 A. M., and bought a lamb for a dollar. We also bought some beef, which in this country is dried in strips by the sun, after being cut off the bullock. It keeps good for any length of time. To cook it, the strips are thrown for a few minutes on hot embers.

One of our mules was kicked last night. Mr. Sargent rubbed the wound with brandy, which did it much good.

Soon after leaving this well, Mr. Sargent discovered that, by following the track of Mr. Ward's wagons, he had lost the way. He swore dreadfully, and solaced himself with so much gin that when we arrived at Sulphur Creek at 12:30 both he and the Judge were, by their own confession, *quite tight.*

---

* I was afterwards told that the Judge's term of service had expired. El Paso was his district.

We halted, ate some salt meat, and bathed in this creek, which is about forty yards broad and three feet deep.

Mr. Sargent's extreme "tightness" caused him to fall asleep on the box when we started again, but the more seasoned Judge drove the mules.

The signs of getting out of the sands now began to be apparent; and at 5 P. M. we were able to halt at a very decent place with grass, but *no* water. We suffered here for want of water, our stock being very nearly expended.

Mr. Sargent, who was now comparatively sober, killed the sheep most scientifically at 5:30 P. M. At 6:30 we were actually devouring it, and found it very good. Mr. Sargent cooked it by the simple process of stewing junks of it in a frying pan, but we had only just enough water to do this.

19*th April* (Sunday) — At 1 A. M. this morning our slumbers on the bullock rug were disturbed by a sudden and most violent thunderstorm. M'Carthy and I had only just time to rush into the carriage, and hustle our traps underneath it, when the rain began to descend in torrents.

We got inside with the young Jew, whilst Mr. Sargent and the Judge crept underneath.

The rain lasted two hours; and at daylight we were able to refresh ourselves by drinking the water from the puddles, and effect a start.

But fate seemed adverse to our progress. No sooner had we escaped from the sand than we fell into the mud, which was still worse.

We toiled on till 11:30 A. M., at which hour we reached King's Ranch. For several days I had heard this spoken of as a sort of

Elysium, marking as it does the termination of the sands, and the commencement of comparative civilization.

We halted in front of the house, and after cooking and eating, I walked up to the "ranch," which is a comfortable, well-furnished wooden building.

Mr. and Mrs. King had gone to Brownsville; but we were received by Mrs. Bee, the wife of the Brownsville general, who had heard I was on the road.

She is a nice lively little woman, a red-hot Southerner, glorying in the facts that she has no Northern relations or friends, and that she is a member of the Church of England.

Mr. King first came to Texas as a steamboat captain, but now owns an immense tract of country, with 16,000 head of cattle, situated, however, in a wild and almost uninhabited district. King's Ranch is distant from Brownsville only 125 miles, and we have been six days in reaching it.

After drying our clothes and our food after the rain of last night, we started again at 2:30 P. M.

We now entered a boundless and most fertile prairie, upon which, as far as the eye could reach, cattle were feeding.

Bulls and cows, horses and mares came to stare at us as we passed. They all seemed sleek and in good condition, yet they get nothing but what they can pick up on the prairie.

I saw a man on horseback kill a rabbit with his revolver. I also saw a scorpion for the first time.

We halted at 5:30 P. M., and had to make our fire principally of cow-dung, as wood is very scarce on this prairie.

We gave up the Judge's horse at King's Ranch. The lawgiver now rides on the box with Mr. Sargent.

*   *   *

20th April (Monday) — I slept well last night in spite of the numerous prairie wolves which surrounded us, making a most dismal noise.

The Jew was ill again, but both Mr. Sargent and the Judge were very kind to him; so also was M'Carthy, who declared that a person incapable of protecting himself is always sure of kind treatment and compassion, even from the wildest Texans.

We started at 5 A. M., and had to get through some dreadful mud — Mr. Sargent in an awful bad humor, and using terrific language.

We were much delayed by this unfortunate rain, which had converted a good road into a quagmire. We detected a rattlesnake crawling along this morning, but there are not nearly so many of them in this country as there used to be.

We halted at 9 A. M., and, to make a fire for cooking, we set a rat ranch alight. This answered very well; but one big rat, annoyed by our proceedings, emerged hastily from his den, and very nearly jumped into the frying pan.

Two Texan Rangers, belonging to Taylor's regiment, rode up to us whilst we were at breakfast. These Rangers all wear the most enormous spurs I ever saw.

We resumed our journey at 12:30, and reached a creek* called "Agua Dulce" at 2 P. M. M'Carthy and I got out before crossing, to forage at some huts close by. We got two dozen eggs and some lard; but, on returning to the road, we found that Mr. Sargent had pursued his usual plan of leaving us in the lurch.

I luckily was able to get hold of a Mexican boy, and rode across the creek *en croupe*. M'Carthy dismounted a Negro, and so got over.

* All streams or rivers are called creeks, and pronounced "criks."

We halted at 5 P. M.

After dark M'Carthy crossed the prairie to visit some friends who were encamped half a mile distant. He lost his way in returning, and wandered about for several hours. The Judge, with great presence of mind, kept the fire up, and he found us at last.

The heat from nine to two is pretty severe; but in Texas there is generally a cool sea-breeze, which makes it bearable.

21st April (Tuesday) — We started at 5 A. M., and reached a hamlet called "Casa Blanca" at 6. We procured a kid, some Indian corn, and two fowls in this neighborhood.

We had now quitted the flat country, and entered an undulating or "rolling" country, full of live oaks of very respectable size, and we had also got out of the mud.

Mr. Sargent and the Judge got drunk again about 8 A. M., which, however, had a beneficial effect upon the speed. We descended the hills at a terrific pace — or, as Mr. Sargent expressed it, "*Going like h—ll a-beating tan bark.*"

We "nooned it" at a small creek; and after unhitching, Mr. Sargent and the Judge had a row with one another, after which Mr. Sargent killed and cooked the goat, using my knife for these operations. With all his faults he certainly is a capital butcher, cook, and mule driver. He takes great care of his animals, and is careful to inform us that the increased pace we have been going at is not attributable to gin.

He was very complimentary to me, because I acted as assistant cook and butcher.

Mr. Ward's party passed us about 1 P. M. The front wheels of his buggy having now smashed, it is hitched in the rear of one of the wagons.

We made a pretty good afternoon's drive through a wood of post oaks, where we saw another rattlesnake, which we tried to shoot. We halted at Spring creek at 6:30 P. M.; water rather brackish, and no grass for the mules.

The Judge gave us some of his experiences as a filibuster.[9] He declares that a well-cooked polecat is as good to eat as a pig, and that stewed rattlesnake is not so bad as might be supposed. The Texans call the Mexicans "greasers," the latter retort by the name "gringo."

We are now living luxuriously upon eggs and goat's flesh; and I think we have made about thirty-two miles today.

22d *April* (Wednesday) — We got under way at 5 A. M., the mules looking rather mean for want of grass.

At 8 A. M. we reached the Nueces River, the banks of which are very steep, and are bordered with a beautiful belt of live-oak trees, covered with mustang grapes.

On the other side of the Nueces is Oakville, a miserable settlement, consisting of about twenty wooden huts. We bought some butter there, and caught up Ward's wagons. The women at Oakville were most anxious to buy snuff. It appears that the Texan females are in the habit of dipping snuff — which means putting it into their mouths instead of their noses. They rub it against their teeth with a blunted stick.

We reached grass about 10 A. M., and nooned it, the weather being very trying — very sultry, without sun or wind.

We hitched in at 1:15 — Ward's wagons in our front, and a Frenchman's four-horse team in our rear. At 4 P. M. we reached the Weedy, a creek which, to our sorrow, was perfectly dry. We drove on till 7 P. M., and halted at some good grass.

There being a report of water in the neighborhood, Mr. Sargent, the Judge, Ward, and the Frenchman started to explore; and when, at length, they did discover a wretched little mudhole, it appears that a desperate conflict for the water ensued, for the Judge returned to us a mass of mud, and presenting a very crestfallen appearance. Shortly after, Mr. Sargent appeared, in such a bad humor that he declined to cook, to eat, to drink, or do anything but swear vehemently.

Deprived by this contretemps of our goat's flesh, we had recourse to an old ham and very stale bread.

We met many cotton trains and government wagons today, and I think we have progressed about thirty-four miles.

23d April (Thursday) — The wily Mr. Sargent drove the animals down to the mudhole in the middle of last night, and so stole a march upon Ward.

Our goat's flesh having spoiled, it had to be thrown away this morning. We started at 5:30 A. M., and reached Rocky at 7:30; but before this two of Ward's horses had "caved in," which completely restored our driver's good humor.

Rocky consists of two huts in the midst of a stony country; and about a mile beyond it we reached a pond, watered our mules, and filled our barrels. The water was very muddy to look at, but not bad to drink.

The mules were lazy today; and Mr. Sargent was forced to fill his bucket with stones, and pelt the leaders occasionally.

At 8 A. M. we reached an open, undulating prairie, and halted at 10:30. Mr. Sargent and I killed and cooked the two chickens.

He has done me the honor to call me a "right good companion for the road." He also told me that at one time he kept a hotel at El Paso — a sort of halfway house on the overland route to California — and was rapidly making his fortune when the war totally ruined him. This accounts for his animosity to "Uncle Abe."*

We hitched in again at 3 P. M., and after pushing through some deepish sand, we halted for the night only twenty-four miles from San Antonio. No corn or water, but plenty of grass; our food, also, was now entirely expended. Mr. Ward struggled up at 8:15, making a desperate effort to keep up with us, and this rivalry between Sargent and him was of great service.

This was our last night of camping out, and I felt almost sorry for it, for I have enjoyed the journey in spite of the hardships. The country through which I have passed would be most fertile and productive (at least the last 150 miles) were it not for the great irregularity of the seasons. Sometimes there is hardly any rain for two and three years together.

24th April (Friday) — We made a start at 4:15 A. M., and with the assistance of M'Carthy, we managed to lose our way; but at 6:15 a loud cheer from the box, of "Hoorraw for h—ll! who's afraid of fire?" proclaimed that Mr. Sargent had come in sight of Grey's ranch.

After buying some eggs and Indian corn there, we crossed the deep bed of the river San Antonio. Its banks are very steep and picturesque.

We halted immediately beyond to allow the mules to feed for an hour. A woman was murdered at a ranch close by some time

---

* General Longstreet remembered both Sargent and the Judge perfectly, and he was much amused by my experiences with these worthies. General Longstreet had been quartered on the Texan frontiers a long time when he was in the old army — August, 1863.

ago, and five bad characters were put to death at San Antonio by the vigilance committee on suspicion.

We crossed the Selado river at 11, and nooned it in its neighborhood.

Mr. Sargent and the Judge finished the gin; and the former, being rather drunk, entertained us with a detailed description of his treatment of a refractory Negro girl, which, by his own account, must have been very severe. M'Carthy was much disgusted at the story.*

After bathing in the Selado, Mr. Sargent, being determined to beat Ward, pushed on for San Antonio; and we drew up before Menger's hotel at 3 P. M., our mules dead beat — our driver having fulfilled his promise of "making his long-eared horses howl."

Later in the day I walked through the streets with M'Carthy to his store, which is a very large building, but now desolate, everything having been sold off. He was of course greeted by his numerous friends, and among others I saw a Negro come up to him, shake hands, and welcome him back.

I was introduced to Colonel Duff's brother, who is also a very good-looking man; but he has not thrown off his British nationality and become a "citizen."

The distance from Brownsville to San Antonio is 330 miles, and we have been 11 days and 4 hours en route.

* However happy and well off the slaves may be as a general rule, yet there must be many instances (like that of Mr. Sargent) of ill-treatment and cruelty. Mr. Sargent is a Northerner by birth, and is without any of the kind feeling which is nearly always felt by Southerners for Negroes — July, 1863.

CHAPTER 3

From San Antonio to Houston

Sight-seeing in San Antonio — Auctioning off Some Excess Luggage — Confederate Officers Nearly Always Propose the Queen's Health — Off by Stage to Alleyton — Dodging Tobacco Juice — Pot Shots at Jack Rabbits — The Spitting Gets a Little Wild — Eighteen People in One Stagecoach — My First Experience with Texas Railroads — Houston Is Better Than I Expected — Getting to Know an "Aristocratic Negro" — An Encounter with Sam Houston — Inspecting Galveston's Defenses — I Dance an American Cotillion

25th April (Saturday) — San Antonio is prettily situated on both banks of the river of the same name. It should contain about 10,000 inhabitants, and is the largest place in Texas, except Galveston.

The houses are well built of stone, and they are generally only one or two stories high. All have verandas in front.

Before the war San Antonio was very prosperous, and rapidly increasing in size; but trade is now almost at a complete standstill. All the male population under forty are in the military service, and many necessary articles are at famine prices. Coffee costs $7 a pound.

Menger's hotel is a large and imposing edifice, but its proprietor (a civil German) was on the point of shutting it up for the present.

During the morning I visited Colonel Bankhead, a tall, gentle-manlike Virginian, who was commanding officer of the troops here. He told me a great deal about the Texan history, the Jesuit missions, and the Louisiana purchase, &c. He alarmed me by doubting whether I should be able to cross the Mississippi if Banks had taken Alexandria.

I also made the acquaintance of Major Minter, another Virginian, who told me he had served in the 2d cavalry in the old United States Army. The following officers in the Confederate Army were in the same regiment — viz., General A. S. Johnson (killed at Shiloh), General Lee, General Van Dorn, General Hardee, General Kirby Smith, and General Hood.*

By the advice of M'Carthy, I sent my portmanteau and some of my heavy things to be sold by auction, as I could not possibly carry them with me.

I took my place by the stage for Alleyton (Houston): it cost $40; in old times it was $13.[1]

I dined with M'Carthy and young Duff at 3 P. M. The latter would not hear of my paying my share of the expenses of the journey from Brownsville. Mrs. M'Carthy was thrown into a great state of agitation and delight by receiving a letter from her mother, who is in Yankeedom. Texas is so cut off that she only hears once in many months.

Colonel and Mrs. Bankhead called for me in their ambulance at 5 P. M., and they drove me to see the source of the San Antonio, which is the most beautiful clear spring I ever saw. We also saw the extensive foundations for a tannery now being built by the Confederate government.

The country is very pretty, and is irrigated in an ingenious man-

* Also the Federal Generals Thomas and Stoneman.

[42]

ner by ditches cut from the river in all directions. It is thus in a great degree rendered independent of rain.

At San Antonio spring we were entertained by a Major Young, a queer little naval officer — why a major I couldn't discover.

Mrs. Bankhead is a violent Southerner. She was twice ordered out of Memphis by the Federals on account of her husband's principles; but she says that she was treated with courtesy and kindness by the Federal General Sherman, who carried out the orders of his government with regret.

None of the Southern people with whom I have spoken entertain any hopes of a speedy termination of the war. They say it must last all Lincoln's presidency, and perhaps a good deal longer.

In the neighborhood of San Antonio, one third of the population is German, and many of them were at first by no means loyal to the Confederate cause. They objected much to the conscription, and some even resisted by force of arms; but these were soon settled by Duff's regiment, and it is said they are now reconciled to the new regime.

My portmanteau, with what was in it — for I gave away part of my things — sold for $323. Its value in England couldn't have been more than £8 or £9. The portmanteau itself, which was an old one, fetched $51; a very old pair of butcher boots, $32; five shirts, $42; an old overcoat, $25.

26th April (Sunday) — At 11:30 A. M., M'Carthy drove me in his buggy to see the San Pedro spring, which is inferior in beauty to the San Antonio spring. A troop of Texan cavalry was bivouacked there.

We afterwards drove to the "missions" of San José and San Juan, six and nine miles from the town. These were fortified con-

vents for the conversion of the Indians, and were built by the
Jesuits about one hundred and seventy years ago. They are now
ruins, and the architecture is of the heavy Castilian style, elabo-
rately ornamented. These missions are very interesting, and there
are two more of them, which I did not see.

In the afternoon I saw many Negroes and Negresses parading about in their Sunday clothes — silks and crinolines — much
smarter than their mistresses.

At 5 P. M. I dined with Colonel Bankhead, who gave an entertainment, which in these hard times must have cost a mint of
money. About fourteen of the principal officers were invited. One
of them was Captain Mason `(cousin to the London commis-
sioner), who had served under Stonewall Jackson in Virginia. He
said that officer was by no means popular *at first*.

I spent a very agreeable evening, and heard many anecdotes of
the war. One of the officers sang the abolition song, "John Brown,"
together with its parody, "I'm bound to be a soldier in the army of
the South," a Confederate marching song, and another parody,
which is a Yankee marching song, "We'll hang Jeff Davis on a
sour-apple tree." [2]

Whenever I have dined with Confederate officers, they have
nearly always proposed the Queen's health, and never failed to
pass the highest eulogiums upon her majesty.

27th April (Monday) — Colonel Bankhead has given me letters
of introduction to General Bragg, to General Leonidas Polk, and
several others.

At 2 P. M. I called on Mrs. Bankhead to say good-by. She told
me that her husband had two brothers in the Northern service —
one in the army and the other in the navy. The two army brothers

were both in the battles of Shiloh and Perryville, on opposite sides. The naval Bankhead commanded the *Monitor* when she sank.

—— introduced me to a German militia general in a beerhouse this afternoon. These two had a slight dispute, as the latter spoke strongly in disapproval of "secret or night lynching."

The recent escapade of Captain Peñaloso seems to have been much condemned in San Antonio. This individual (formerly a butcher) hanged one of his soldiers a short time ago, on his own responsibility, for desertion and stealing a musket. This event came off at 12 o'clock noon, in the principal plaza of the city. The tree has been cut down, to show the feelings of the citizens.

There can be no doubt that the enforcement of the conscription has, as a general rule, been extremely easy throughout the Confederacy (except among the Germans); but I hear of many persons evading it, by getting into some sort of government employment — such as contractors, agents, or teamsters to the Rio Grande.[3]

To my extreme regret, I took leave of my friend M'Carthy this evening, whose hospitality and kindness I shall never forget.

I left San Antonio by stage for Alleyton at 9 P. M. The stage was an old coach, into the interior of which nine persons were crammed on three transverse seats, besides many others on the roof. I was placed on the center seat, which was extremely narrow, and I had nothing but a strap to support my back. An enormously fat German was my *vis-à-vis*, and a long-legged Confederate officer was in my rear. Our first team consisted of four mules; we afterwards got horses.

My fellow travelers were all either military men, or connected with the government.

Only five out of nine chewed tobacco during the night; but they aimed at the windows with great accuracy, and didn't *splash* me. The amount of sleep I got, however, was naturally very trifling.

28th April (Tuesday) — We crossed the river Guadalupe at 5 A. M., and got a change of horses.

We got a very fair breakfast at Seguin, at 7 A. M., which was beginning to be a well-to-do little place when the war dried it up. It commenced to rain at Seguin, which made the road very woolly, and annoyed the outsiders a good deal.

The conversation turned a good deal upon military subjects, and all agreed that the system of election of officers had proved to be a great mistake. According to their own accounts, discipline must have been extremely lax at first, but was now improving.[4]

They were most anxious to hear what was thought of their cause in Europe; and none of them seemed aware of the great sympathy which their gallantry and determination had gained for them in England in spite of slavery. We dined at a little wooden hamlet called Belmont, and changed horses again there.

The country through which we had been traveling was a good deal cultivated, and there were numerous farms. I saw cotton fields for the first time.

We amused ourselves by taking shots with our revolvers at the enormous jack rabbits which came to stare at the coach.

In the afternoon tobacco-chewing became universal, and the spitting was sometimes a little wild.

It was the custom for the outsiders to sit round the top of the carriage, with their legs dangling over (like mutes on a hearse returning from a funeral). This practice rendered it dangerous to put one's head out of the window, for fear of a back kick from the heels, or of a shower of tobacco juice from the mouths of the Southern chivalry on the roof.

In spite of their peculiar habits of hanging, shooting, &c., which seemed to be natural to people living in a wild and thinly populated country, there was much to like in my fellow travelers. They all had a sort of bon-hommie honesty and straightforwardness, a natural courtesy and extreme good nature, which was very agreeable. Although they were all very anxious to talk to a European — who, in these blockaded times, is a *rara avis* — yet their inquisitiveness was never offensive or disagreeable.

Any doubts as to my personal safety, which may have been roused by my early insight into lynch law, were soon completely set at rest. I soon perceived that if any one were to annoy me the remainder would stand by me as a point of honor.

We supped at a little town called Gonzales at 6:30.

We left it at 8 p. m. in another coach with six horses — big, strong animals.

The roads, being all natural ones, were much injured by the rains.

We were all rather disgusted by the bad news we heard at Gonzales of the continued advance of Banks, and of the probable fall of Alexandria.

The squeezing was really quite awful, but I did not suffer so much as the fat or long-legged ones. They all bore their trials in the most jovial good-humored manner.

My fat *vis-à-vis* (in despair) changed places with me, my two bench-fellows being rather thinner than his, and I benefited much by the change into a back seat.

* * *

29th *April* (Wednesday) — Exhausted as I was, I managed to sleep wonderfully well last night. We breakfasted at a place called Hallettsville at 7 A. M., and changed carriages again.

Here we took in four more Confederate soldiers as outsiders, and we were now eighteen in all. Nowhere but in this country would such a thing be permitted.

Owing to the great top weight, the coach swayed about like a ship in a heavy sea, and the escapes of a capsize were almost miraculous. It is said that at the end of a Texan journey the question asked is not, "Have you been upset?" but, "How many times have you been upset?"

The value of the Negroes working in the fields was constantly appraised by my fellow travelers; and it appeared that, in Texas, an able-bodied male fetched $2500, whilst a well-skilled seamstress was worth $3500.

Two of my companions served through the late severe campaign in New Mexico, but they considered forty-eight hours in a closely packed stage a greater hardship than any of their military experiences.

We passed many cotton fields and beautiful Indian corn, but much of the latter had been damaged by the hail.

I was told that one third of the land formerly devoted to cotton is still sown with that article, the remainder being corn, &c.* [5]

We also passed through some very pretty country, full of fine post-oak and cotton trees, and we met many Mexican cotton teams — some of the wagons with fourteen oxen or twelve mules, which were being cruelly ill-treated by their drivers.

We crossed several rivers with steep and difficult banks, and dined at a farmhouse at 2:30 P. M.

* It is only in Texas that so much cotton is still grown.

[48   ]

I have already discovered that, directly the bell rings, it is necessary to rush at one's food and bolt it as quickly as possible, without any ceremony or delay. Otherwise it all disappears, so rapacious and so voracious are the natives at their meals whilst traveling. Dinner, on such occasions, in no case lasts more than seven minutes.

We reached Columbus at 6 P. M., and got rid of half our passengers there. These Texan towns generally consist of one large plaza, with a well-built courthouse on one side and a hotel opposite, the other two sides being filled up with wooden stores. All their budding prosperity has been completely checked by the war; but every one anticipates a great immigration into Texas after the peace.

We crossed the Colorado River, and reached Alleyton, our destination, at 7 P. M.

This little wooden village has sprung into existence during the last three years, owing to its being the present terminus to the railroad. It was crammed full of travelers and cotton speculators; but, as an especial favor, the fat German and I were given a bed *between us.* I threw myself on the bed with my clothes on (*bien entendu*), and was fast asleep in five minutes. In the same room there were three other beds, each with two occupants.

The distance from San Antonio to Alleyton is 140 miles — time, forty-six hours.

30th April (Thursday) — I have today acquired my first experience of Texan railroads.[6]

In this country, where every white man is as good as another (by theory), and every white female is by courtesy a lady, there is only one class. The train from Alleyton consisted of two long cars, each holding about fifty persons. Their interior is like the aisle of a church, twelve seats on either side, each for two persons. The seats are comfortably stuffed, and seemed luxurious after the stage.

Before starting, the engine gives two preliminary snorts, which, with a yell from the official of "all aboard," warn the passengers to hold on; for they are closely followed by a tremendous jerk, which sets the cars in motion.

Every passenger is allowed to use his own discretion about breaking his arm, neck, or leg, without interference by the railway officials.

People are continually jumping on and off whilst the train is in motion, and larking from one car to the other. There is no sort of fence or other obstacle to prevent "humans" or cattle from getting on the line.

We left Alleyton at 8 A. M., and got a miserable meal at Richmond at 12:30. At this little town I was introduced to a seedy-looking man, in rusty black clothes and a broken-down "stove-pipe" hat. This was Judge Stockdale, who will probably be the next governor of Texas. He is an agreeable man, and his conversation is far superior to his clothing.

The rival candidate is General Chambers (I think), who has become very popular by the following sentence in his manifesto: "I am of opinion that married soldiers should be given the opportunity of embracing their families at least once a year, their places in the ranks being taken by unmarried men. The population must not be allowed to suffer."

Richmond is on the Brazos River, which is crossed in a peculiar manner. A steep inclined plane leads to a low, rickety, trestle bridge, and a similar inclined plane is cut in the opposite bank.

The engine cracks on all steam, and gets sufficient impetus in going down the first incline to shoot across the bridge and up the second incline. But even in Texas, this method of crossing a river is considered rather unsafe.

After crossing the river in this manner, the rail traverses some very fertile land, part of which forms the estate of the late Colonel Terry. There are more than two hundred Negroes on the plantation. Some of the fields were planted with cotton and Indian corn mixed, three rows of the former between two of the latter. I saw also fields of cotton and sugar mixed.

We changed carriages at Harrisburg, and I completed my journey to Houston on a cotton truck.

The country near Houston is very pretty, and is studded with white wooden villas, which are raised off the ground on blocks like haystacks. I reached Houston at 4:30 P. M., and drove to the Fannin House hotel.

Houston is a much better place than I expected. The main street can boast of many well-built brick and iron houses. It was very full, as it now contained all the refugees from the deserted town of Galveston.

After an extremely mild supper, I was introduced to Lieutenant Lee, a wounded hero who lost his leg at Shiloh; also to Colonel Pyron, a distinguished officer who commands the regiment named after him.

The fat German, Mr. Lee, and myself went to the theater afterwards.

As a great favor, my British prejudices were respected, and I was allowed a bed to myself; but the four other beds in the room had two occupants each. A captain, whose acquaintance I had made in the cars, slept in the next bed to me. Directly after we had got into bed a Negro came in, who, squatting down between our beds, began to clean our boots. The Southerner pointed at the slave, and thus held forth:

"Well, Kernel, I reckon you've got servants in your country, but not of that color. Now, sir, this is a real genuine African. He's as happy as the day's long; and if he was on a sugar plantation he'd be dancing half the night; but if you was to collect a thousand of them together, and fire one bomb in amongst them, they'd all run like h—ll." The Negro grinned, and seemed quite flattered.

1st May (Friday) — I called on General Scurry, and found him suffering from severe ophthalmia. When I presented General Magruder's letter, he insisted that I should come and live with him so long as I remained here. He also telegraphed to Galveston for a steamer to take me there and back.

We dined at 4 P. M. The party consisted of Colonel and Judge Terrill (a clever and agreeable man), Colonel Pyron, Captain Wharton, quartermaster general, Major Watkins (a handsome fellow, and hero of the Sabine Pass affair), and Colonel Cook, commanding the artillery at Galveston (late of the U. S. Navy, who enjoys the reputation of being a zealous Methodist preacher and a daring officer). The latter told me he could hardly understand how I could be an Englishman, as I pronounced my h's all right.

General Scurry himself is very amusing, and is an admirable mimic. His numerous anecdotes of the war were very interesting. In peace times he is a lawyer. He was a volunteer major in the Mexican War, and distinguished himself very much in the late campaigns in New Mexico and Arizona, and at the recapture of Galveston.[7]

After dinner, the Queen's health was proposed; and the party expressed the greatest admiration for Her Majesty, and respect for the British Constitution. They all said that universal suffrage did not produce such deplorable results in the South as in the North; because the population in the South is so very scattered, and the whites being the superior race, they form a sort of aristocracy.

They all wanted me to put off going to Galveston till Monday, in order that some ladies might go; but I was inexorable, as it must now be my object to cross the Mississippi without delay. All these officers despised sabers, and considered double-barreled shotguns and revolvers the best arms for cavalry.

2d May (Saturday) — As the steamer had not arrived in the morning, I left by railroad for Galveston. General Scurry insisted upon sending his servant to wait upon me, in order that I might become acquainted with "an aristocratic Negro." "John" was a very smart fellow, and at first sight nearly as white as myself.

In the cars I was introduced to General Samuel Houston, the founder of Texan independence. He told me he was born in Virginia seventy years ago, that he was United States senator at thirty, and governor of Tennessee at thirty-six. He emigrated into Texas in 1832; headed the revolt of Texas, and defeated the Mexicans at San Jacinto in 1836. He then became President of the Republic of Texas, which he annexed to the United States in 1845. As governor of the state in 1860, he had opposed the secession movement, and was *deposed*. Though evidently a remarkable and clever man, he is extremely egotistical and vain, and much disappointed at having to subside from his former grandeur. The town of Houston is named after him. In appearance he is a tall, handsome old man, much given to chewing tobacco, and blowing his nose with his fingers.* [8]

I was also introduced to another "character," Captain Chubb, who told me he was a Yankee by birth, and served as coxswain to the United States ship *Java* in 1827. He was afterwards imprisoned at Boston on suspicion of being engaged in the slave trade; but he escaped. At the beginning of this war he was captured by the Yankees, when he was in command of the Confederate States steamer *Royal Yacht*, and taken to New York in chains, where he was condemned to be hung as a pirate; but he was eventually exchanged. I was afterwards told that the slave-trading escapade of which he was accused consisted in his having hired a colored crew at Boston, and then coolly *selling* them at Galveston.

At 1 p. m. we arrived at Virginia Point, a *tête-de-pont* at the extremity of the mainland. Here Bates's battalion was encamped — called also the "swamp angels," on account of the marshy nature of their quarters, and of their predatory and irregular habits.

The railroad then traverses a shallow lagoon (called Galveston Bay) on a trestle bridge two miles long; this leads to another *tête-de-pont* on Galveston island, and in a few minutes the city is reached.

In the train I had received the following message by telegraph from Colonel Debray, who commands at Galveston: WILL COL. FREMANTLE SLEEP TONIGHT AT THE HOUSE OF A BLOCKADED REBEL? I answered: DELIGHTED; and was received at the terminus by Captain Foster of the staff, who conducted me in an ambulance to headquarters, which were at the house of the Roman Catholic bishop. I was received there by Colonel Debray and two very gentlemanlike French priests.

* He is reported to have died in August, 1863.

We sat down to dinner at 2 P. M., but were soon interrupted by an indignant drayman, who came to complain of a military outrage. It appeared that immediately after I had left the cars, a semi-drunken Texan of Pyron's regiment had desired this drayman to stop, and upon the latter declining to do so, the Texan fired five shots at him from his six-shooter, and the last shot killed the drayman's horse. Captain Foster (who is a Louisianian, and very sarcastic about Texas) said that the regiment would probably hang the soldier for being such a *disgraceful bad shot*.

After dinner Colonel Debray took me into the observatory, which commands a good view of the city, bay, and gulf.

Galveston is situated near the eastern end of an island thirty miles long by three and a half wide. Its houses are well built; its streets are long, straight, and shaded with trees; but the city was now desolate, blockaded, and under military law. Most of the houses were empty, and bore many marks of the ill-directed fire of the Federal ships during the night of the 1st of January last.

The whole of Galveston Bay is very shallow, except a narrow channel of about a hundred yards immediately in front of the now deserted wharves. The entrance to this channel is at the north-eastern extremity of the island, and is defended by the new works which are now in progress there. It is also blocked up with piles, torpedoes, and other obstacles.

The blockaders were plainly visible about four miles from land. They consisted of three gunboats and an ugly paddle steamer, also two supply vessels.

The wreck of the Confederate cotton steamer *Neptune* (destroyed in her attack on the *Harriet Lane*) was close off one of the wharves. That of the *Westfield* (blown up by the Yankee Commodore) was off Pelican Island.

[55   ]

In the night of the 1st of January, General Magruder suddenly entered Galveston, placed his fieldpieces along the line of wharves, and unexpectedly opened fire in the dark upon the Yankee war vessels at a range of about one hundred yards. But so heavy (though badly directed) was the reply from the ships that the fieldpieces had to be withdrawn. The attack by Colonel Cook upon a Massachusetts regiment, fortified at the end of a wharf, also failed, and the Confederates thought themselves "badly whipped." But after daylight the fortunate surrender of the *Harriet Lane* to the cotton boat *Bayou City*, and the extraordinary conduct of Commodore Renshaw, converted a Confederate disaster into the recapture of Galveston.

General Magruder certainly deserves immense credit for his boldness in attacking a heavily armed naval squadron with a few fieldpieces and two river steamers protected with cotton bales and manned with Texan cavalry soldiers.

I rode with Colonel Debray to examine Forts Scurry, Magruder, Bankhead, and Point. These works have been ingeniously designed by Colonel Sulokowski (formerly in the Austrian Army), and they were being very well constructed by one hundred and fifty whites and six hundred blacks under that officer's superintendence, the blacks being lent by the neighboring planters.

Although the blockaders can easily approach to within three miles of the works, and although one shell could easily start a stampede, yet they have not thrown any for a long time.

Colonel Debray is a broad-shouldered Frenchman, and is a very good fellow. He told me that he emigrated to America in 1848. He raised a company in 1861, in which he was only a private. He was next appointed aid-de-camp to the governor of Texas, with the rank of brigadier general. He then descended to a major of infantry, afterwards rose to a lieutenant colonel of cavalry, and is now colonel.

Captain Foster is properly on Magruder's staff, and is very good company. His property at New Orleans had been destroyed by the Yankees.

In the evening we went to a dance given by Colonel Manly, which was great fun. I danced an American cotillion with Mrs. Manly. It was very violent exercise, and not the least like anything I had seen before. A gentleman stands by shouting out the different figures to be performed, and every one obeys his orders with much gravity and energy.[9]

Colonel Manly is a very gentlemanlike Carolinian. The ladies were pretty, and, considering the blockade, they were very well dressed. Six deserters from Banks's army arrived here today. Banks seems to be advancing steadily, and overcoming the opposition offered by the handful of Confederates in the Teche country.

Banks himself is much despised as a soldier, and is always called by the Confederates Mr. Commissary Banks, on account of the efficient manner in which he performed the duties of that office for "Stonewall" Jackson in Virginia. The officer who is supposed *really* to command the advancing Federals is Weitzel. He is acknowledged by all here to be an able man, a good soldier, and well acquainted with the country in which he is maneuvering.[10]

3d May (Sunday) — I paid a long visit this morning to Mr. Lynn the British Consul, who told me that he had great difficulty in communicating with the outer world, and had seen no British man-of-war since the *Immortalité.*

At 1:30 I saw Pyron's regiment embark for Niblitt's Bluff to meet Banks. This corps is now dismounted cavalry, and the pro-

cession was a droll one. First came eight or ten instruments bray-
ing discordantly, then an enormous Confederate flag, followed by
about four hundred men moving by fours — dressed in every variety of costume, and armed with every variety of weapon. About
sixty had Enfield rifles; the remainder carried shotguns (fowling
pieces), carbines, or long rifles of a peculiar and antiquated manufacture. None had swords or bayonets — all had six-shooters and
bowie knives.

The men were a fine, determined-looking lot; and I saw among
them a short stout boy of fourteen, who had served through the
Arizona campaign. I saw many of the soldiers take off their hats
to the French priests, who seemed much respected in Galveston.
This regiment is considered down here to be a very good one, and
its colonel is spoken of as one of the bravest officers in the army.
The regiment was to be harangued by Old Houston before it embarked.*

In getting into the cars to return to Houston, I was nearly
forced to step over the dead body of the horse shot by the soldier
yesterday, and which the authorities had not thought necessary to
remove.

I got back to General Scurry's house at Houston at 4:30 P. M.

The general took me out for a drive in his ambulance, and I saw
innumerable Negroes and Negresses parading about the streets in
the most outrageously grand costumes — silks, satins, crinolines,
hats with feathers, lace mantles, &c., forming an absurd contrast
to the simple dresses of their mistresses. Many were driving about
in their master's carriages, or riding on horses which are often lent

* At the outbreak of the war it was found very difficult to raise infantry in
Texas, as no Texan walks a yard if he can help it. Many mounted regiments
were therefore organized, and afterwards dismounted.

to them on Sunday afternoons. All seemed intensely happy and satisfied with themselves.

—— told me that old Sam Houston lived for several years amongst the Cherokee Indians, who used to call him "the Raven" or the "Big Drunk." He married an Indian squaw when he was with them.

Colonel Ives, aid-de-camp to the President, has just arrived from Richmond, and he seems a very well-informed and agreeable man.

I have settled to take the route to Shreveport tomorrow, as it seems doubtful whether Alexandria will or will not fall.

CHAPTER 4

From Houston to Natchez

I Make a Present of My Evening Clothes — En Route on the Shreveport Stage — Wearing Boots to Bed — Northwestern Federal Troops Are Best — My Fellow Travelers Talk about Slavery — Brief Halt at Shreveport — Crayfishing with General Kirby Smith's Wife — Confusion at Monroe — The Yankees Close at Hand — By Sternwheeler to Harrisonburg — Sneaking along the Mississippi — Dodging Snakes, Alligators and Gunboats — I Get the Immense Luxury of a Bed to Myself

4th May (Monday) — General Scurry's servant John had been most attentive since he had been told off to me. I made him a present of my evening clothes, which gratified him immensely; and I shook hands with him at parting, which seems to be quite the custom.[1] The Southern gentlemen are certainly able to treat their slaves with extraordinary familiarity and kindness. John told me that the General would let him buy his freedom whenever he chose. He is a barber by trade, and was earning much money when he insisted on rejoining his master and going to the wars.

I left Houston by train for Navasoto at 10 A. M. A Captain Andrews accompanied me thus far. He was going with a troop of cavalry to impress one fourth of the Negroes on the plantations for the government works at Galveston, the planters having been backward in coming forward with their darkies.

Arrived at Navasoto (70 miles) at 4 P. M., where I took a stage for Shreveport (250 miles). I started at 4:30 P. M., after having had a little dispute with a man for a corner seat, and beating him.

It was the same sort of vehicle as the San Antonio one — eight people inside. During the night there was a thunderstorm.

5th May (Tuesday) — We breakfasted at Huntsville at 5:30 A. M. The Federal officers captured in the *Harriet Lane* are confined in the penitentiary there, and are not treated as prisoners of war. This seems to be the system now with regard to officers since the enlistment of Negroes by the Northerners.

My fellow travelers were mostly elderly planters or legislators, and there was one judge from Louisiana. One of them produced a pair of boots which had cost him $100; another showed me a common wide-awake hat which had cost him $40. In Houston, I myself saw an English regulation infantry sword exposed for sale for $225 (£45).

As the military element did not predominate, my companions united in speaking with horror of the depredations committed in this part of the country by their own troops on a line of march.

We passed through a well-wooded country — pines and post-oaks — the road bad. Crossed the river Trinity at 12 noon, and dined at the house of a disreputable-looking individual, called a Campbellite minister, at 4:30 P. M. The food consisted almost invariably of bacon, corn bread, and buttermilk: a meal costing a dollar.

Arrived at Crockett at 9:30 P. M., where we halted for a few hours. A *filthy bed* was given to the Louisianian Judge and myself. The Judge, following my example, took to it boots and all, remarking, as he did so, to the attendant Negro, that "they were a d—d sight cleaner than the bed."

Before reaching Crockett, we passed through the encampment of Phillipps's regiment of Texas Rangers, and we underwent much chaff.[2] They were en route to resist Banks.

6th May (Wednesday) — We left all the passengers at Crockett except the Louisianian Judge, a government agent, and the ex-boatswain of the *Harriet Lane*. This vessel had been manned by the Confederates after her capture; but she had since been dismantled, and her crew were being marched to Shreveport to man the ironclad *Missouri*, which was being built there.

The food we get on the road is sufficient, and good enough to support life. It consists of pork or bacon, bread made with Indian corn, and a peculiar mixture called Confederate coffee, made of rye, meal, Indian corn, or sweet potatoes. The loss of coffee afflicts the Confederates even more than the loss of spirits; and they exercise their ingenuity in devising substitutes, which are not generally very successful.

The same sort of country as yesterday — large forests of pines and post-oaks, and occasional Indian corn fields, the trees having been killed by cutting a circle near the roots. At 3 P. M., we took in four more passengers. One of them was a Major ——, brother-in-law to ——, who hanged Mongomery at Brownsville. He spoke of the exploit of his relative with some pride. He told me that his three brothers had lost an arm apiece in the war.

We arrived at Rusk at 6:30 P. M., and spent a few hours there; but notwithstanding the boasted splendor of the beds at the Cherokee Hotel, and although by Major ——'s influence I got one to myself, yet I did not consider its aspect sufficiently inviting to induce me to remove my clothes.

*   *   *

[62   ]

7th May (Thursday) — We started again at 1:30 A. M., in a smaller coach, but luckily with reduced numbers — the Louisianian Judge (who is also a legislator), a Mississippi planter, the boatswain, the government agent, and a Captain Williams, of the Texas Rangers.

Before the day broke we reached a bridge over a stream called Mud Creek, which was in such a dilapidated condition that all hands had to get out and cover over the biggest holes with planks.

The government agent informed us that he still held a commission as adjutant general to ——. The latter, it appears, is a cross between a guerrilla and a horse thief, and even by his adjutant general's account, he seems to be equally adept at both professions. The accounts of his forays in Arkansas were highly amusing, but rather strongly seasoned for a legitimate soldier.

The Judge was a very gentlemanlike nice old man. Both he and the adjutant general were much knocked up by the journey; but I revived the former with the last of the *Immortalité* rum. The latter was in very weak health, and doesn't expect to live long; but he ardently hoped to destroy a few more "bluebellies" * before he "goes under."

The Mississippi planter had abandoned his estate near Vicksburg, and withdrawn with the remnant of his slaves into Texas. The Judge also had lost all his property in New Orleans. In fact, every other man one meets has been more or less ruined since the war, but all speak of their losses with the greatest equanimity. Captain Williams was a tall, cadaverous backwoodsman, who had lost his health in the war. He spoke of the Federal General Rosecrans

* The Union soldiers are called "bluebellies" on account of their blue uniforms. These often call the Confederates "graybacks."

with great respect.³ He also passed the following high encomium upon the Northwestern troops, under Rosecrans's command:

"They're reg'lar great big h—llsnorters, the same breed as ourselves. They don't want no running after — they don't. They ain't no Dutch cavalry — * you bet!"

To my surprise all the party were willing to agree that, a few years ago, most educated men in the South regarded slavery as a misfortune and not justifiable, though necessary under the circumstances. But the meddling, coercive conduct of the detested and despised abolitionists had caused the bonds to be drawn much tighter.

My fellow travelers of all classes are much given to talk to me about their "peculiar institution." They are most anxious that I should see as much of it as possible, in order that I may be convinced that it is not so bad as has been represented, and that they are not all "Legrees," although they do not attempt to deny that there are many instances of cruelty. But they say a man who is known to ill-treat his Negroes is hated by all the rest of the community. They declare that Yankees make the worst masters when they settle in the South. All seem to be perfectly aware that slavery, which they did not invent but inherited from us English, is and always will be the great bar to the sympathy of the civilized world. I have heard these words used over and over again.

All the villages through which we passed were deserted except by women and very old men. Their aspect was most melancholy. The country is sandy, and the land not fertile, but the timber is fine.

We met several planters on the road, who with their families

* German dragoons, much despised by the Texans on account of their style of riding.

and Negroes were taking refuge in Texas, after having abandoned their plantations in Louisiana on the approach of Banks. One of them had as many as sixty slaves with him of all ages and sizes.

At 7 P. M. we received an unwelcome addition to our party, in the shape of three huge, long-legged, unwashed, odoriferous Texan soldiers, and we passed a wretched night in consequence. The Texans are certainly not prone to take offense where they see none is intended. When this irruption took place, I couldn't help remarking to the Judge, with regard to the most obnoxious man who was occupying the center seat to our mutual discomfort — "I say, Judge, this gentleman has the longest legs I ever saw." "Has he?" replied the Judge; "and he has got the d—dest, longest, hardest back I ever felt." The Texan was highly amused by these remarks upon his personal appearance, and apologized for his peculiarities. Crossed the Sabine river at 11:30 P. M.

8th May (Friday) — We reached Marshall at 3 A. M., and got four hours' sleep there. We then got into a railroad for sixteen miles, after which we were crammed into another stage.

Crossed the frontier into Louisiana at 11 A. M. I have therefore been nearly a month getting through the single state of Texas. Reached Shreveport at 3 P. M.; and, after washing for the first time in five days, I called on General Kirby Smith, who commands the whole country on this side of the Mississippi.

He is a Floridian by birth, was educated at West Point, and served in the United States Cavalry. He is only thirty-eight years old. He owes his rapid rise to a lieutenant general to the fortunate fact of his having fallen, just at the very nick of time, upon the Yankee flank at the first battle of Manassas.*

* Called by the Yankees "Bull Run."

[65]

He is a remarkably active man, and of very agreeable manners. He wears big spectacles and a black beard.

His wife is an extremely pretty woman from Baltimore, but she had cut her hair quite short like a man's. In the evening she proposed that we should go down to the river and fish for crayfish. We did so, and were most successful, the General displaying much energy on the occasion.[4]

He told me that M'Clellan might probably have destroyed the Southern army with the greatest ease during the first winter, and without running much risk to himself. The Southerners were so much overelated by their easy triumph at Manassas that their army had dwindled away.

I was introduced to Governor More, of Louisiana, to Lieutenant Governor Hyams, and also to the exiled governor of Missouri, Reynolds.

Governor Moore told me he had been on the Red River since 1824, from which date until 1840 it had been very unhealthy. He thinks that Dickens must have intended Shreveport by "Eden." *

Governor Reynolds, of Missouri, told me he found himself in the unfortunate condition of a potentate exiled from his dominions; but he showed me an address which he had issued to his Missourians, promising to be with them at the head of an army to deliver them from their oppressors.

Shreveport is rather a decent-looking place on the Red River. It contains about 3000 inhabitants, and is at present the seat of the Louisianian Legislature instead of Baton Rouge. But only twenty-eight members of the Lower House had arrived as yet, and business could not be commenced with less than fifty.

* I believe this is a mistake of Governor Moore. I have always understood Cairo was Eden.[5]

[66]

The river now is broad and rapid, and it is navigated by large steamers; its banks are low and very fertile, but reputed to be very unhealthy.

General Kirby Smith advised me to go to Monroe, and try to cross the Mississippi from there. He was so uncertain as to Alexandria that he was afraid to send a steamer so far.

I heard much talk at his house about the late Federal raid into the Mississippi,* which seems to be a copy of John Morgan's operations, except that the Federal raid was made in a thinly populated country, bereft of its male inhabitants.

9th May (Saturday) — Started again by stage for Monroe at 4:30 A. M. My companions were the Mississippi planter, a mad dentist from New Orleans (called by courtesy, doctor), an old man from Matagorda, buying slaves cheap in Louisiana, a wounded officer, and a wounded soldier.

The soldier was a very intelligent young Missourian, who told me (as others have) that at the commencement of these troubles, both he and his family were strong Unionists. But the Lincolnites, by using coercion, had forced them to take one side or the other — and there are now no more bitter Secessionists than these people.

This soldier (Mr. Douglas) was on his way to rejoin Bragg's army. A Confederate soldier when wounded is not given his discharge, but is employed at such work as he is competent to perform. Mr. Douglas was quite lame; but will be employed at mounted duties or at writing.

We passed several large and fertile plantations. The Negro quarters formed little villages, and seemed comfortable. Some of them held 150 or 200 hands. We afterwards drove through some

* Grierson's raid.

beautiful pine forests, and were ferried across a beautiful shallow lake full of cypresses, but not the least like European cypress trees.

We met a number more planters driving their families, their slaves, and furniture, towards Texas — in fact, everything that they could save from the ruin that had befallen them on the approach of the Federal troops.

At 5 P. M. we reached a charming little town called Mindon, where I met an English mechanic who deplored to me that he had been such a fool as to naturalize himself, as he was in hourly dread of the conscription.

I have at length become quite callous to many of the horrors of stage traveling. I no longer shrink at every random shower of tobacco juice; nor do I shudder when good-naturedly offered a quid. I eat voraciously of the bacon that is provided for my sustenance, and I am invariably treated by my fellow travelers of all grades with the greatest consideration and kindness. Sometimes a man remarks that it is rather "mean" of England not to recognize the South; but I can always shut him up by saying that a nation which deserves its independence should fight and earn it for itself — a sentiment which is invariably agreed to by all.[6]

10*th May* (Sunday) — I spent a very rough night in consequence of the badness of the road, the jolting of the carriage, and having to occupy a center seat.

In the morning we received news from everyone we met of the fall of Alexandria.

The road today was alive with Negroes, who are being "run" into Texas out of Banks's way. We must have met hundreds of them, and many families of planters, who were much to be pitied, especially the ladies.

On approaching Monroe, we passed through the camp of Walker's division (8000 strong). It was on the march from Arkansas to meet Banks. The division had embarked in steamers, and had already started down the Ouachita towards the Red River, when the news arrived of the fall of Alexandria, and of the presence of Federal gunboats in or near the Ouachita itself. This caused the precipitate return and disembarkation of Walker's division. The men were well armed with rifles and bayonets, but they were dressed in ragged civilian clothes. The old Matagorda man recognized his son in one of these regiments — a perfect boy.

Monroe is on the Ouachita (pronounced Washtaw), which is a very pretty and wide stream. After crossing it we arrived at the hotel after dark.

Universal confusion reigned there; it was full of officers and soldiers of Walker's division, and no person would take the slightest notice of us.

In desperation I called on General Hebert, who commanded the post. I told him who I was, and gave him a letter of introduction, which I had fortunately brought from Kirby Smith. I stated my hard case and besought an asylum for the night, which he immediately accorded me in his own house.

The difficulty of crossing the Mississippi appeared to increase the nearer I got to it, and General Hebert told me that it was very doubtful whether I could cross at all at this point. The Yankee gunboats, which had forced their way past Vicksburg and Port Hudson, were roaming about the Mississippi and Red River. Some of them were reported at the entrance of the Ouachita itself, a small fort at Harrisonburg being the only impediment to their appearance in front of Monroe.

On another side, the enemy's forces were close to Delhi, only forty miles distant.

There were forty or fifty Yankee deserters here from the army besieging Vicksburg. These Yankee deserters, on being asked their reasons for deserting, generally reply — "Our government has broken faith with us. We enlisted to fight for the Union, and not to liberate slaves." Vicksburg is distant from this place about eighty miles.

The news of General Lee's victory at Chancellorsville had just arrived here. Every one received it very coolly. People seemed to take it quite as a matter of course; but the wound of Stonewall Jackson was universally deplored.[7]

11*th May* (Monday) — General Hebert is a good-looking creole.* He was a West-Pointer, and served in the old army, but afterwards became a wealthy sugar planter. He used to hold Magruder's position as commander in chief in Texas, but he has now been shelved at Monroe, where he expects to be taken prisoner any day. From the present gloomy aspect of affairs about here, it seems extremely probable that he will not be disappointed in his expectations. He is extremely down upon England for not recognizing the South.†

He gave me a passage down the river in a steamer, which was to try to take provisions to Harrisonburg. At the same time, he

* The descendants of the French colonists in Louisiana are called Creoles; most of them talk French, and I have often met Louisianian regiments talking that language.

† General Hebert is the only man of education I met in the whole of my travels who spoke disagreeably about England in this respect. Most people say they think we are quite right to keep out of it as long as we can; but others think our government is foolish to miss such a splendid chance of "smashing the Yankees," with whom we must have a row sooner or later.

informed me that she might very probably be captured by a Yankee gunboat.

At 1 P. M. I embarked for Harrisonburg, which is distant from Monroe by water 150 miles, and by land 75 miles. It is fortified, and offers what was considered a weak obstruction to the passage of the gunboats up the river to Monroe.

The steamer was one of the curious American river boats which rise to a tremendous height out of the water, like great wooden castles. She was steered from a box at the very top of all, and this particular one was propelled by one wheel at her stern.

The river is quite beautiful; it is from 200 to 300 yards broad, very deep and tortuous, and the large trees grow right down to the very edge of the water.

Our captain at starting expressed in very plain terms his extreme disgust at the expedition, and said he fully expected to run against a gunboat at any turn of the river.

Soon after leaving Monroe, we passed a large plantation. The Negro quarters were larger than a great many Texan towns, and they held three hundred hands.

After we had proceeded about half an hour, we were stopped by a mounted orderly (called a courier). From the bank, he roared out the pleasing information, "They're a-fighting at Harrisonburg." The captain, on hearing this, turned quite green in the face, and remarked that he'd be "dogged" if he liked running into the jaws of a lion, and he proposed to turn back. But he was jeered by my fellow travelers, who were all either officers or soldiers, wishing to cross the Mississippi to rejoin their regiments in the different Confederate armies.

One pleasant fellow, more warlike than the rest, suggested that as we had some Enfields on board, we should make "a little bit

of a fight," or at least "make one butt at a gunboat." I was relieved to find that these insane proposals were not received with
any enthusiasm by the majority.

The plantations, as we went further down the river, looked very
prosperous; but signs of preparations for immediate skedaddling
were visible in most of them. I fear they are all destined to be soon
desolate and destroyed.

We came to a courier picket every sixteen miles. At one of them
we got the information, "Gunboats drove back." At this there was
great rejoicing, and the captain, recovering his spirits, became quite
jocose, and volunteered to give me letters of introduction to a
"particular friend of his about here, called Mr. Farragut." But the
next news, "Still a-fightin'," caused us to tie ourselves to a tree at
8 p. m., off a little village called Columbia, which is halfway between Monroe and Harrisonburg.

We then lit a large fire, round which all the passengers squatted
on their heels in Texan fashion, each man whittling a piece of
wood, and discussing the merits of the different Yankee prisons
at New Orleans or Chicago. One of them, seeing me, called out,
"I reckon, Kernel, if the Yankees catch you with us, they'll say
you're in d—d bad company"; which sally caused universal hilarity.

12th *May* (Tuesday) — Shortly after daylight three Negroes
arrived from Harrisonburg, and they described the fight as still
going on. They said they were "dreadful skeered." One of them
told me he would "rather be a slave to his master all his life, than
a white man and a soldier."

During the morning some of the officers and soldiers left the
boat, and determined to cut across country to Harrisonburg, but

I would not abandon the scanty remains of my baggage until I was forced to do so.

During the morning twelve more Negroes arrived from Harrisonburg. It appears that three hundred of them — the property of neighboring planters — had been engaged working on the fortifications, but they all with one accord bolted when the first shell was fired. Their only idea and hope at present seemed to be to get back to their masters. All spoke of the Yankees with great detestation, and expressed wishes to have nothing to do with such "bad people."

Our captain coolly employed them in tearing down the fences, and carrying the wood away on board the steamer for firewood.

We did nothing but this all day long, the captain being afraid to go on, and unwilling to return. In the evening a new alarm seized him — viz., that the Federal cavalry had cut off the Confederate line of couriers. During the night we remained in the same position as last night, head up stream, and ready to be off at a moment's notice.*

13th May (Wednesday) — There was a row on board last night. One of the officers having been too attentive to a lady had to skedaddle suddenly into the woods, in order to escape the fury of her protector. He has not thought it advisable to reappear. My trusty companion for several days, the poor young Missourian, was taken ill today, and he told me he had a *"right smart little fever* on him." I doctored him with some of the physic which Mr. Maloney had given me, and he got better in the evening.

* One of the passengers on board this steamer was Captain Barney, of the Confederate States Navy, who has since, I believe, succeeded Captain Maffit in the command of the *Florida.*

[73]

We had pickets out in the woods last night. Two of my fellow travelers on that duty fell in with a Negro, and pretending they were Yankees, asked him to join them. He consented, and even volunteered to steal his master's horses. He then received a tremendous thrashing, administered by the two soldiers with their ramrods.

At 9 P. M., to the surprise of all, the captain suddenly made up his mind to descend the river at all hazards. He thought, I suppose, that anything was better than the uncertainty of the last twenty-four hours.

The further we went, the more beautiful was the scenery.

At 4 P. M. we were assured by a citizen on the bank that the gunboats really had retreated; and at 5:30 our doubts were set at rest. To our great satisfaction, we saw the Confederate flag flying from Fort Beauregard, high above the little town of Harrisonburg. After we had landed, I presented my letter of introduction from General Hebert to Colonel Logan, who commands the fort. He introduced me to a German officer, the engineer.

They gave me an account of the attack and repulse of the four Federal gunboats under Commodore Woodford, and supposed to have been the *Pittsburg* (ironclad), the *General Price*, the *Arizona*, and another.

Fort Beauregard is a much more formidable looking work than I expected to see, and its strength had evidently been much underrated at Monroe.

A hill 190 feet high, which rises just in rear of Harrisonburg, has been scarped and fortified. It is situated at an angle of the river, and faces a long "reach" of two miles.

The gunboats, after demanding an unconditional surrender which was treated with great contempt by Colonel Logan, opened

[74]

fire at 2 P. M. on Sunday. They kept it up till 6:30, throwing about one hundred and fifty 9 and 11 inch shell. The gunboats reopened again for about an hour on Monday afternoon, when they finally withdrew, the *Arizona* being crippled.

The fort fired altogether about forty-five 32-pound shot (smooth bore). The range was about a mile.

The garrison thought that they had loosened several of the *Pittsburg's* iron plates. They felt confident they could have sunk the wooden vessels if they had attempted to force the passage. They were naturally much elated with their success, which certainly had not been anticipated on board my steamer or at Monroe.

I had not time to visit the interior of the fort, but I saw the effect of the shell upon the outside. Those which fell in the sand did not burst. Only three men were wounded in the garrison. They told me the deck of the *Pittsburg* was furnished with a parapet of cotton bales for riflemen.

The river at Harrisonburg is about 160 yards broad, and very deep, with a moderate current. The town, being between the vessels and the fort, had, of course, suffered considerably during the bombardment.

When the works are complete they will be much more formidable.

To our great joy, Colonel Logan decided that our vessel should proceed at once to Trinity, which is fifteen miles nearer Natchez (on the Mississippi) than Harrisonburg. We arrived there at 8 P. M., and found that the gunboats had only just left, after having destroyed all the molasses and rum they could find, and carried away a few Negroes.

Six of us pigged in one very small room. We paid a dollar each for this luxury to an old woman, who was most inhospitable and told us she "didn't want to see no soldiers, as the Yanks would come back and burn her house for harboring Rebels."

I am always taken for a Confederate officer, partly from being in their company, and partly on account of my clothes, which happen to be a gray shooting-suit, almost the same color as most of the soldiers' coats.

14th *May* (Thursday) — The officers and soldiers, about thirty in number, who came down the Ouachita in my company, determined to proceed to Natchez today, and a very hard day's work we had of it.

As the Louisianian bank of the Mississippi is completely overflowed at this time of the year, and the river itself is infested with the enemy's gunboats which have run past Vicksburg and Port Hudson, the passage can only be made by a tedious journey in small boats through the swamps and bayous.

Our party left Trinity at 6 A. M. in one big yawl and three skiffs. In my skiff were eight persons, besides a Negro oarsman named "Tucker." This Negro was a very powerful man, very vain and suspectible of flattery. I won his heart by asking him if he wasn't worth 6000 dollars. We kept him up to the mark throughout the journey by plying him with compliments upon his strength and skill. One officer declared to him that he should try to marry his mistress (a widow) on purpose to own him.

After beating up for about eight miles against one of three streams which unite at, and give its name to, Trinity, we turned off to the right, and got into a large dense swamp. The thicket was so tangled and impenetrable that we experienced the greatest difficulty in forcing our way through it. We were often obliged

[76]

to get into the water up to our middles and shove, whilst most of the party walked along an embankment.

After two hours and a half of this sort of work we had to carry our boats bodily over the embankment into a bayou called Log Bayou, on account of the numerous floating logs which had to be encountered. We then crossed a large and beautiful lake, which led us into another dismal swamp, quite as tangled as the former one. Here we lost our way, and got aground several times; but at length, after great exertions, we forced ourselves through it, and reached Lake Concordia, a fine piece of water, several miles in extent, and we were landed at dusk on the plantation of a Mr. Davis.

These bayous and swamps abound with alligators and snakes of the most venomous description. I saw many of the latter swimming about exposed to a heavy fire of six-shooters; but the alligators were frightened away by the leading boat.

The yawl and one of the skiffs beat us, and their passengers reached Natchez about 9 P. M., but the other skiff, which could not boast a Tucker, was lost in the swamp, and passed the night there in a wretched plight.

The weather was most disagreeable, either a burning sun or a downpour of rain.

The distance we did in the skiff was about twenty-eight miles, which took us eleven hours to perform.

On landing we hired at Mr. Davis's a small cart for Mr. Douglas (the wounded Missourian) and our baggage. The rest of us had to finish the day by a trudge of three miles through deep mud, until at length we reached a place called Vidalia. This is on the Louisianian bank of the Mississippi, just opposite Natchez.

At Vidalia I got the immense luxury of a pretty good bed, *all to myself,* which enabled me to take off my clothes and boots for the first time in ten days.

The landlord told us that three of the enemy's gunboats had passed during the day; and as he said their crews were often in the habit of landing at Vidalia, he cautioned the military to be ready to bolt into the woods at any time during the night.

There were two conscripts on board my skiff today, one an Irishman and the other a Pole. They confessed to me privately their extreme dislike of the military profession; but at the same time they acknowledged the enthusiasm of the masses for the war.

CHAPTER 5

Natchez to Mobile

*I Cross the Father of Waters — Trying to Reach Vicksburg —
Dinner with Seven Virgins Seated All in a Row — The Yankees
Cut the Railroad — "What on Earth Are You Doing in Jackson
Just Now?" — Taken for a Spy — Rescued by an Irishman — How
to Save a House from Yankee Raiders — At Joe Johnston's Head-
quarters — Honored with the Only Fork in General Johnston's
Mess — The General Collects Wood for a Locomotive — An
Engineer Shoots a Passenger — People Are Careful What They
Say When a Bullet May Be the Reply*

15th May (Friday) — I nearly slept round the clock after yesterday's exertions. Mr. Douglas and I crossed the father of rivers and
landed on the Mississippi bank at 9 A. M.

Natchez is a pretty little town, and ought to contain about 6000
inhabitants. It is built on the top of a high bluff overlooking the
Mississippi River, which is about three quarters of a mile broad
at this point.

When I reached Natchez I hired a carriage, and, with a letter
of introduction which I had brought from San Antonio, I drove
to the house of Mr. Haller Nutt, distant from the town about
two miles.

The scenery about Natchez is extremely pretty, and the ground
is hilly, with plenty of fine trees. Mr. Nutt's place reminded me
very much of an English gentleman's country seat, except that the
house itself is rather like a pagoda, but it is beautifully furnished.

[79]

Mr. Nutt was extremely civil, and was most anxious that I should remain at Natchez for a few days. But now that I was thoroughly wound up for traveling, I determined to push on to Vicksburg, as all the late news seemed to show that some great operations must take place there before long.

I had fondly imagined that after reaching Natchez my difficulties would have been over; but I very soon discovered that this was a delusive hope. I found that Natchez was full of the most gloomy rumors. Another Yankee raid seemed to have been made into the interior of Mississippi. More railroad is reported to be destroyed, and great doubts were expressed whether I should be able to get into Vicksburg at all.

However, as I found some other people as determined to proceed as myself, we hired a carriage for $100 to drive to Brookhaven, which is the nearest point on the railroad, and is distant from Natchez 66 miles.

My companions were a fat government contractor from Texas, the wounded Missourian Mr. Douglas, and an ugly woman, wife to a soldier in Vicksburg.

We left Natchez at 12 noon, and were driven by a Negro named Nelson. The carriage and the three horses belong to him, and he drives it for his own profit; but he is, nevertheless a slave, and pays his owner $4.50 a week to be allowed to work on his own account. He was quite as vain as Tucker, and even more amusing. He said he "didn't want to see no Yanks, nor to be no freer than he is"; and he thought the war had already lasted four or five years.

Every traveler we met on the road was eagerly asked the questions, "Are the Yanks in Brookhaven? Is the railroad open?" At first we received satisfactory replies; but at 6 P. M. we met an officer driving towards Natchez at a great pace. He gave us the alarming intelligence that *Jackson* was going to be evacuated. Now, as Jackson is the capital city of this state, a great railroad junction, and on the high road to every civilized place from this, our feelings may be imagined, but we did not believe it possible.

On the other hand we were told that General Joseph Johnston had arrived and assumed the command in Mississippi. He appears to be an officer in whom every one places unbounded confidence.

We slept at a farmhouse. All the males were absent at the war, and it is impossible to exaggerate the unfortunate condition of the women left behind in these farmhouses. They have scarcely any clothes, and nothing but the coarsest bacon to eat, and are in miserable uncertainty as to the fate of their relations, whom they hardly ever communicate with. Their slaves, however, generally remain true to them.

Our hostess, though she was reduced to the greatest distress, was well-mannered, and exceedingly well educated; very far superior to a woman of her station in England.

16th May (Saturday) — We started a little before daylight, our team looking so very mean that we expressed doubts as to their lasting — to Mr. Nelson's great indignation.

We breakfasted at another little farmhouse on some unusually tough bacon, and coffee made of sweet potatoes. The natives, under all their misery, were red-hot in favor of fighting for their independence to the last, and I constantly hear the words, "This is the most unjust war ever waged upon a people by mortal man." [1]

At 11 A. M. we met a great crowd of Negroes, who had been run into the swamps to be out of the way of the Yankees, and they were now returning to Louisiana.

At 2 P. M. a wounded soldier gave us the deplorable information that the enemy really was on the railroad between Jackson and Brookhaven, and that Jackson itself was in his hands. This news staggered us all, and Nelson became alarmed for the safety of his wretched animals; but we all determined to go on at all hazards, and see what turned up.

We halted for dinner at a farmhouse, in which were seven virgins, seated all of a row. They were all good-looking, but shy and bashful to a degree I never before witnessed. All the young women in this country seem to be either uncommonly free-spoken, or else extremely shy. The further we went, the more certain became the news of the fall of Jackson.

We passed the night in the veranda of an old farmer. He told us that Grierson's Yankee raid had captured him about three weeks ago. He thought the Yankees were about 1500 strong. They took all good horses, leaving their worn-out ones behind. They destroyed railroad, government property, and arms, and paroled all men, both old and young, but they committed no barbarities. In this manner they traversed all the state of Mississippi without meeting any resistance. They were fine-looking men from the Northwestern states.

17th May (Sunday) — We started again at 4:30 A. M., and met five wounded men, who had been captured and paroled by Banks, in Louisiana. They confirmed everything about the fall of Jackson, which made me consider myself particularly unfortunate, and destined apparently to be always intercepted by the Northern troops, which had happened to be at Alexandria, at Harrisonburg, and now again at Jackson.

At 8 A. M. we reached the little town of Brookhaven, which was full of travelers, principally Confederate soldiers, anxious to rejoin their regiments. Maxey's brigade left this place by road last night to join General Johnston, who is supposed to be concentrating his forces at a place called Canton, not far from Jackson.

I called on Captain Matthews, the officer who commanded at Brookhaven. After introducing myself to him, he promised to assist me, by every means in his power, to join General Johnston.

I then went to a Methodist chapel; a good many soldiers were there, and a great number of women.

At noon, just as I had begun to get in very low spirits about the prospects of getting on, a locomotive arrived from a station called Haslehurst. It brought us the astonishing report that the Yankees had suddenly abandoned Jackson, after destroying all the government, and a good deal of private property.[2]

This news caused our prospects to look brighter.

18th May (Monday) — On getting up this morning, everything appeared very uncertain, and a thousand contradictory reports and rumors were flying about.

At 8 o'clock I called on Captain Matthews, and told him my earnest desire to get on towards Johnston's army at all risks. He kindly introduced me to the conductor of a locomotive, who offered to take me to within a few miles of Jackson, if he was not cut off by the enemy, which seemed extremely probable. At 9 A. M. I seated myself, in company with about twenty soldiers, on the engine, and we started towards Jackson.

On reaching Crystal Springs, halfway to Jackson, we found General Loring's division crossing the railroad and marching east. It had been defeated, with the loss of most of its artillery, three days before, and was now cut off from General Pemberton.[3]

At 5 P. M. the conductor stopped the engine, and put us out at a spot distant nine miles from Jackson. As I could procure no shelter, food, or conveyance there, I found myself in a terrible fix.

At this juncture a French boy rode up on horseback, and volunteered to carry my saddlebags as far as Jackson, if I could walk and carry the remainder.

Gladly accepting this unexpected offer, I started with him to walk up the railroad, as he assured me the Yankees really had gone. During the journey, he gave me a description of their conduct during the short time they had occupied the city.

On arriving within three miles of Jackson, I found the railroad destroyed by the enemy, who after pulling up the track, had made piles of the sleepers, and then put the rails in layers on the top of these heaps. They had then set fire to the sleepers, which had caused the rails to bend when red-hot. The wooden bridges had also been set on fire, and were still smoking.

When within a mile and a half of Jackson, I met four men, who stopped and questioned me very suspiciously, but they at length allowed me to proceed, saying that these "were curious times."

After another mile I reached a mild trench, which was dignified by the name of the fortifications of Jackson. A small fight had taken place there four days previous, when General Johnston had evacuated the city.

When I got inside this trench I came to the spot on which a large body of the Yankees had recently been encamped. They had set fire to a great quantity of stores and arms, which they had been unable to carry away with them. These were still burning, and were partially destroyed. I observed also great numbers of pikes and pikeheads amongst the debris.[4]

At the entrance to the town the French boy took me to the

house of his relatives, and handed me my saddlebags. These French people told me they had been much ill-treated, notwithstanding their French nationality. They showed me their broken furniture, and they assured me that they had been robbed of everything of any value. I then shouldered my saddlebags, and walked through the smoking and desolate streets towards the Bowmont House hotel.

I had not proceeded far before a man with long gray hair and an enormous revolver rode up to me, and offered to carry my saddlebags. He then asked me who I was. After I told him, he thought a few moment, and then said, "Well, sir, you must excuse me, but if you are a British officer, I can't make out what on earth you are doing at Jackson just now." I could not but confess that this was rather a natural idea, and that my presence in this burning town must have seemed rather odd, more especially as I was obliged to acknowledge that I was there entirely of my own free will, and for my own amusement.

Mr. Smythe, for so this individual was named, then told me that if I was really the person I represented myself, I should be well treated by all; but that if I could not prove myself to be an English officer, an event would happen which it was not difficult to foresee, and the idea caused a disagreeable sensation about the throat.

Mr. Smythe then gave me to understand that I must remain a prisoner for the present. He conducted me to a room in the Bowmont House hotel, and I found myself speedily surrounded by a group of eager and excited citizens, who had been summoned by Smythe to *conduct my examination*.

At first they were inclined to be disagreeable. They examined my clothes, and argued as to whether they were of English manufacture.[5] Some, who had been in London, asked me questions about the streets of the metropolis, and about my regiment. One remarked that I was *"mighty young for a lootenant colonel."*

When I suggested that they should treat me with proper respect until I was proved to be a spy, they replied that their city had been brutally pillaged by the Yankees, and that there were many suspicious characters about.

Everything now looked very threatening, and it became evident to me that nothing would relieve the minds of these men so much as a hanging match. I looked in vain for someone to take my part, and I could not even get any person to examine my papers.

At this critical juncture a new character appeared on the scene. He was a big heavy man who said to me, "My name is Dr. Russell; I'm an Irishman, and I hate the British government and the English nation; but if you are really an officer in the Coldstream Guards there is nothing I won't do for you; you shall come to my house and I will protect you."

I immediately showed Dr. Russell my passport and letters of introduction to General Johnston and other Confederate officers. He pronounced them genuine, promised to stand by me, and wanted to take me away with him at once.

But observing that the countenances of Smythe and his colleagues did not by any means express satisfaction at this arrangement, I announced my determination to stay where I was until I was released by the military authorities, with whom I demanded an immediate audience.

A very handsome cavalry officer called Captain Yerger, shortly afterwards arrived. He released me at once — asked me to his mother's house, and promised that I should join a brigade which was to march for General Johnston's camp on the following morning.

All the citizens seemed to be satisfied by the result of my interview with Captain Yerger, and most of them insisted on shaking hands and "liquoring up," in horrible whiskey. Smythe, however, was an exception to this rule. He evidently thought he had effected a grand capture, and was not at all satisfied at the turn of affairs. I believe to his dying day he will think I am a spy; but it was explained to me that his house had been burnt down by the Yankees two days before, which had made him unusually venomous.

They told me that Dr. Russell had saved his property from pillage by seating himself in his veranda, with a loaded double-barreled gun on his knees. When the pillagers approached, he addressed them in the following manner: "No man can die more than once, and I shall never be more ready to die than I am now. There is nothing to prevent your going into this house, except that I shall kill the first two of you who move with this gun. Now then, gentlemen, walk in." This speech is said to have saved Dr. Russell from further annoyance, and his property from the ruin which overtook his neighbors.

Jackson, the capital of the state of Mississippi, is a place of great importance. Four railroads meet here, and have been destroyed in each direction for a distance of from three to five miles. All the numerous factories have been burnt down by the enemy, who were of course justified in doing so; but during the short space of thirty-six hours, in which General Grant occupied the city, his troops had wantonly pillaged nearly all the private houses. They had gutted all the stores, and destroyed what they could not carry away. All this must have been done under the very eyes of General Grant, whose name was in the book of the Bowmont House hotel.

I saw the ruins of the Roman Catholic church, the priest's house, and the principal hotel, which were still smoking, together with many other buildings which could in no way be identified with the Confederate government. The whole town was a miserable wreck, and presented a deplorable aspect.

Nothing could exceed the intense hatred and fury with which its excited citizens speak of the outrages they have undergone — of their desire for a bloody revenge, and of their hope that the Black Flag might be raised.*

I had previously heard the Jacksonians spoken of as not being particularly zealous in the war. Heaven knows General Grant had now converted them into good and earnest Rebels.

At 8 P. M. I called at Captain Yerger's house, and found him with General Gist and another officer lying flat on their stomachs poring over a map. Captain Yerger then introduced me to the ladies of his family, who were extremely pretty, very amiable, and highly patriotic. The house is charming, and, being outside the town, it had by good luck escaped destruction and pillage.

After supper, the ladies played and sang, and I ended an eventful day in a very agreeable manner. General Gist promised that I should accompany his brigade tomorrow on its march towards General Johnston, and Mrs. Yerger insisted that I should pass the night at her house.

In this part of the country the prospects of the Confederacy appeared to be very gloomy. General Joseph Johnston, who commands the whole Western Department, only arrived from Tennessee last Wednesday, and on the following day he found himself

* Since this date, the unfortunate city of Jackson has been again subjected to pillage by the Federals after the capture of Vicksburg.

obliged to abandon Jackson to an overwhelming Northern army, after making a short fight to enable his baggage to escape.

General Pemberton, who had hitherto held the chief command, is abused by all. He was beaten on Saturday at Baker's Creek, where he lost the greater part of his artillery. He had retired into Vicksburg, and was now completely shut up there by the victorious Grant.[6]

General Maxey's brigade, about 5000 strong, was near Brookhaven, and was marching east when I was there. General Loring's force, cut off from Pemberton, was near Crystal Springs. General Johnston, with about 6000 men, was supposed to be near Canton. General Gist's troops, about 5500 strong, were close by, having arrived from South Carolina and Georgia, just too late to defend Jackson.

The enemy under General Grant, in vastly superior force, was pressing Vicksburg very hard, and had now completely invested that fortress.

The great object of the Confederates must, of course, be to unite their scattered forces under so able a general as Johnston, and then relieve Vicksburg.

19th May (Tuesday) — The landlord of the Bowmont House gave a breakfast at 7 A. M. to General Gist and his staff, to which I also was invited.

Shortly afterwards I was given a seat in a curious little vehicle belonging to Lieutenant Martino, a Spaniard, in the Confederate Army. This vehicle caused considerable merriment amongst the soldiers, who called it a chicken wagon.

We left Jackson with the leading troops about 8 A. M., amidst a great waving of handkerchiefs and showers of flowers, thrown

[89]

by the few remaining ladies who were still left in that dilapidated place.

The corps under General Gist consisted of three weak brigades, the leading one composed of Georgians and South Carolinians; the next were Texans, under General Ector; and the last were Arkansians, under General M'Nair. General Gist had twelve good-looking Napoleon guns with him (twelve-pounders). The horses were fine animals, and were in wonderful good condition, considering that they had been ten days on the railroad coming from South Carolina.

The troops were roughly but efficiently clothed; their boots were in good order, and all were armed with Enfield rifles.

The weather was very hot, and we were halted to bivouac for the night, at a spot about seventeen miles from Jackson, on the road towards Vicksburg.

The straggling of the Georgians was on the grandest scale conceivable. The men fell out by dozens, and seemed to suit their own convenience in that respect, without interference on the part of the officers. But I was told that these regiments had never done any marching before, having hitherto been quartered in forts and transported by railroad.

The country is much covered with woods, and is sandy, with very little water.

I did not consider that the troops were marched judiciously; they were halted too long at a time, and not often enough. The baggage was carried on country carts pressed into the service.

We bivouacked in the woods near a very pretty house belonging to a planter called Colonel Robinson. These immense woods make admirable bivouacs.

General States Rights Gist is a South Carolinian, only thirty-two

[90]

years of age, and although not educated as a soldier, he seems easily
to have adapted himself to the military profession. He looks a determined man, and he takes responsibility very coolly. In the early
part of the day he was very doubtful as to the exact whereabouts of
General Johnston; but about noon a courier arrived, from whom
he received important and satisfactory information, otherwise
General Gist had made up his mind for some "nasty work" before
the junction could be effected. He told me that the present expedition was rather inconvenient to him, as he had only been married three days before he left Charleston. He lent me a magnificent rug, and I slept very comfortably in the open air for the first
time since I was in Texas.

20th May (Wednesday) — At 3 A. M. we were awoke by a great
bombardment going on at Vicksburg, which lasted about three
hours.*

The assembly was beaten at 7 A. M. by an old Negro performing
on a cracked drum, and its sound was hailed by the soldiers with
loud yells.

General Gist, his staff, and I, breakfasted with Mr. Robinson,
whose house is charming, and beautifully furnished, and had not
been visited by the Yankees.

We had a crazy old planter, Mr. ——, with us. He insisted upon
accompanying the column, mounted on a miserable animal which
had been left him by the enemy as not being worth carrying away.
The small remains of this poor old man's sense had been shattered
by the Yankees a few days ago. They cleaned him completely out,
taking his horses, mules, cows, and pigs, and stealing his clothes

* I afterwards learnt that this bombardment preceded one of the unsuccessful assaults.

[91   ]

and anything they wanted, destroying what they could not carry away. But what "riled" him most was that he had been visited by a Federal officer, disguised in the Confederate uniform. Poor old ——, full of Rebel zeal, had, on being invited to do so, mounted *en croupe* behind this officer, and unbosomed himself to him. His fury and rage may be imagined at finding himself shortly afterwards in the very midst of the Federal camp; but the Yankee General M'Pherson ordered him to be released; and it appears that the reason of his being kidnapped was to extract from him a large quantity of gold, which he was supposed to have hidden somewhere.

This Mr. (or Major *) —— took a great fancy to me, and insisted on picking some of the silk of Indian corn, which he requested I would present to Queen Victoria to show her how far advanced the crops were in Mississippi. It was almost painful to hear the manner in which this poor old man gloated over the bodies of the dead Yankees at Jackson, and of his intense desire to see more of them put to death.

The column reached the village or town of Livingston at 11 A. M., where I was introduced to a militia general and his pretty daughter. The latter had been married two days before to a wounded Confederate officer, but the happy couple were just on the point of starting for the Yazoo River, as they were afraid of being disturbed in their felicity by the Yankees.

I now heard everyone speaking of the fall of Vicksburg as very possible, and its jeopardy was laid at the door of General Pemberton, for whom no language could be too strong. He was freely called a coward and a traitor. He has the misfortune to be a Northerner by birth, which was against him in the opinion of all here.

* Nearly every man in this part of the country has a military title.

General Gist and I cantered on in front of the column, and reached General Johnston's bivouac at 6 P. M.

General Johnston received me with much kindness, when I presented my letters of introduction, and stated my object in visiting the Confederate armies.[7]

In appearance, General Joseph E. Johnston (commonly called Joe Johnston) is rather below middle height, spare, soldierlike, and well set up; his features are good, and he has lately taken to wear a grayish beard. He is a Virginian by birth, and appears to be about fifty-seven years old.

He talks in a calm, deliberate, and confident manner. To me he was extremely affable, but he certainly possesses the power of keeping people at a distance when he chooses, and his officers evidently stand in great awe of him. He lives very plainly, and at present his only cooking utensils consisted of an old coffeepot and frying pan — both very inferior articles. There was only one fork (one prong deficient) between himself and staff, and this was handed to me ceremoniously as the "guest."

He has undoubtedly acquired the entire confidence of all the officers and soldiers under him. Many of the officers told me they did not consider him inferior as a general to Lee or anyone else.

He told me that Vicksburg was certainly in a critical situation, and was now closely invested by Grant. He said that he (Johnston) had 11,000 men with him (which includes Gist's), hardly any cavalry, and only sixteen pieces of cannon; but if he could get adequate reinforcements, he stated his intention of endeavoring to relieve Vicksburg.

I also made the acquaintance of the Georgian General Walker, a fierce and very warlike fire-eater, who was furious at having been obliged to evacuate Jackson after having only destroyed four hundred Yankees. He told me, "I know I couldn't hold the place, but I did want to kill a few more of the rascals."

At 9 P. M. I returned with General Gist to his camp, as my baggage was there. On the road we were met by several natives, who complained that soldiers were quartering themselves upon them and eating everything.

The bivouacs are extremely pretty at night, the dense woods being lit up by innumerable campfires.

21st *May* (Thursday) — I rejoined General Johnston at 9 A. M., and was received into his mess. Major Eustis and Lieutenant Washington, officers of his staff, are thorough gentlemen, and did all in their power to make me comfortable. The first is a Louisianian of wealth (formerly). His Negro always speaks French. He is brother to the secretary of Mr. Slidell in Paris, and has learnt to become an excellent staff officer.

I was presented to Captain Henderson, who commanded a corps of about fifty "scouts." These are employed on the hazardous duty of hanging about the enemy's camps, collecting information, and communicating with Pemberton in Vicksburg. They are a finelooking lot of men, wild, and very picturesque in appearance.

At 12 noon a Yankee military surgeon came to camp. He had been left behind by Grant to look after the Yankees wounded at Jackson, and he was now anxious to rejoin his general by flag of truce. General Johnston very prudently refused to allow this, and desired that he should be sent to the North *via* Richmond. By a very sensible arrangement, both sides have agreed to treat doctors as noncombatants, and not to make prisoners of war of them.[8]

The chief surgeon in Johnston's army is a very clever and amusing Kentuckian, named Dr. Yandell. He told me he had been educated in England, and might have had a large practice there.

My friend "Major" —— very kindly took me to dine with a neighboring planter, named Harrold, at whose house I met General Gregg, a Texan, who with his brigade fought the Yankees at Raymond a few days ago.

After dinner, I asked Mr. Harrold to take me over the quarters of his slaves, which he did immediately. The huts were comfortable and very clean. The Negroes seemed fond of their master, but he told me they were suffering dreadfully from the effects of the war — he had so much difficulty in providing them with clothes and shoes. I saw an old woman in one of the huts, who had been suffering from an incurable disease for thirteen years, and was utterly useless. She was evidently well cared for, and was treated with affection and care. At all events, she must have benefited largely by the "peculiar institution."

I have often told these planters that I thought the word "slave" was the most repulsive part of the institution, and I have always observed they invariably shirk using it themselves. They speak of their servant, their boy, or their Negroes, but never of their slaves. They address a Negro as boy or girl, or uncle or aunty.

In the evening I asked General Johnston what prospect he thought there was of early operations, and he told me that at present he was too weak to do any good, and he was unable to give me any definite idea as to when he might be strong enough to attack Grant. I therefore made up my mind to be off in a day or two, unless something turned up. I could not afford to wait for events, I have still so much to see.

General Johnston is a very well-read man, and agreeable to converse with. He told me that he considered Marlborough a greater general than Wellington. All Americans have an intense admiration for Napoleon; they seldom scruple to express their regret that he was beaten at Waterloo.

Remarking upon the extreme prevalence of military titles, General Johnston said, "You must be astonished to find how fond all Americans are of titles, though they are republicans; and as they can't get any other sort, they all take military ones."

Whilst seated round the campfire in the evening, one of the officers remarked to me, "I can assure you, Colonel, that nine men out of ten in the South would sooner become subjects of Queen Victoria than return to the Union." "Nine men out of ten!" said General Johnston — "Ninety-nine out of a hundred; I consider that few people in the world can be more fortunate in their government than the British colonies of North America."

But the effect of these compliments was rather spoilt when someone else said they would prefer to serve under the Emperor of the French or the Emperor of Japan to returning to the dominion of Uncle Abe; and it was still more damaged when another officer alluded in an undertone to the infernal regions as a more agreeable alternative than reunion with the Yankees.[9]

22d May (Friday) — The bombardment at Vicksburg was very heavy and continuous this morning.

I had a long conversation with General Johnston, who told me that the principal evils which a Confederate general had to contend against consisted in the difficulty of making combinations, owing to uncertainty about the time which the troops would take to march a certain distance, on account of their straggling propensities.

But from what I have seen and heard *as yet*, it appears to me that the Confederates possess certain great qualities as soldiers, such as individual bravery and natural aptitude in the use of fire-arms, strong, determined patriotism, and boundless confidence in their favorite generals, and in themselves. They are sober of necessity, as there is literally no liquor to be got. They have sufficient good sense to know that a certain amount of discipline is absolutely necessary; and I believe that instances of insubordination are extremely rare.

They possess the great advantage of being led by men of talent and education as soldiers who thoroughly understand the people they have to lead, as well as those they have to beat. These generals, such as Lee, Johnston, Beauregard, or Longstreet, they would follow anywhere, and obey implicitly. But, on the other hand, many of their officers, looking forward to future political advancement based on their present military rank, will not punish their men, or are afraid of making themselves obnoxious by enforcing rigid discipline.

The men are constantly in the habit of throwing away their knapsacks and blankets on a long march, if not carried for them, and though actuated by the strongest and purest patriotism, often ignore their obligations as soldiers. In the early part of the war they were often, when victorious, nearly as disorganized as the beaten. Many would coolly walk off home, under the impression that they had performed their share. But they are becoming better in these respects as the war goes on.* All this would account for the trifling benefits derived by the Confederates from their numerous victories.

* After having lived with the veterans of Bragg and Lee, I was able to form a still higher estimate of Confederate soldiers. Their obedience and forbearance in success, their discipline under disaster, their patience under suffering, under hardships, or when wounded, and their boundless devotion to their country under all circumstances are beyond all praise.

[97]

General Johnston told me that Grant had displayed more vigor than he had expected, by crossing the river below Vicksburg, seizing Jackson by vastly superior force, and, after cutting off communications, investing the fortress thoroughly, so as to take it if possible before a sufficient force could be got to relieve it. His army is estimated at 75,000 men, and General Johnston has very little opinion of the defenses of Vicksburg on the land side. He said the garrison consisted of about 20,000 men.[10]

News has been received that the Yankees were getting up the Yazoo River; and this morning General Walker's division left at 6 A. M. for Yazoo City.

The General and his staff and myself rode into Canton, six miles, and lodged in the house of a planter who owned 700 slaves.

Dr. Yandell is a wonderful mimic, and amused us much by taking off the marriage ceremony, as performed by General Polk in Tennessee — General Morgan of Kentucky notoriety being the bridegroom.*

One of Henderson's scouts caused much hilarity amongst the General's staff this afternoon. He had brought in a Yankee prisoner, and *apologized* to General Johnston for doing so, saying, "I found him in a Negro quarter, and *he surrendered so quick, I couldn't kill him.*" There can be no doubt that the conduct of the Federals in captured cities tends to create a strong indisposition on the part of the Confederates to take prisoners, particularly amongst these wild Mississippians.

General Johnston told me this evening that altogether he had been wounded ten times. He was the senior officer of the old army, who joined the Confederates, and he commanded the Virginian

---

* When I was introduced to General Polk in Tennessee I recognized him at once by Dr. Yandell's imitation, which was most wonderfully accurate.

army until he was severely wounded at the battle of "Seven Pines."*

23d *May* (Saturday) — General Johnston, Major Eustis, and myself, left Canton at 6 A. M. on a locomotive for Jackson.

On the way we talked a good deal about "Stonewall" Jackson. General Johnston said that although this extraordinary man did not possess any great qualifications as a strategist, and was perhaps unfit for the independent command of a large army, yet he was gifted with wonderful courage and determination, and a perfect faith in Providence that he was destined to destroy his enemy. He was much indebted to General Ewell in the Valley campaigns. "Stonewall" Jackson was also most fortunate in commanding the flower of the Virginian troops, and in being opposed to the most incapable Federal commanders, such as Fremont and Banks.[11]

Before we had proceeded twelve miles we were forced to stop and collect wood from the roadside to feed our engine. The General worked with so much energy as to cause his "Seven Pines" wound to give him pain.

We were put out at a spot where the railroad was destroyed, at about four miles from Jackson. A carriage ought to have been in waiting for us, but by some mistake it had not arrived, so we had to foot it. I was obliged to carry my heavy saddlebags. Major Eustis very kindly took my knapsack, and the General carried the cloaks. In this order we reached Jackson, much exhausted, at 9:30 A. M.

General Loring came and reported himself soon after. He is a stout man with one arm. His division had arrived at Jackson from

* Called "Fair Oaks" by the Yankees.

[99]

Crystal Springs about 6000 strong; Evans's brigade, about 3000, had also arrived from Charleston; and Maxey's brigade was in the act of marching into Jackson. I calculate, therefore, that General Johnston must now have nearly 25,000 men between Jackson and the Yazoo.

I took an affectionate farewell of him and his officers, and he returned to Canton at 3 P. M. I shall be much surprised if he is not heard of before long. That portion of his troops which I saw, though they had been beaten and forced to retreat, were in excellent spirits, full of confidence, and clamoring to be led against *only* double their numbers.

I renewed my acquaintance with Dr. Russell, for whose timely protection I shall always feel myself much indebted. I also sent my love to Smythe by several different people.

At 3:30 P. M. I left Jackson in a government ambulance, in company with Captain Brown, of General Johnston's staff, who was extremely useful to me. I had taken the precaution of furnishing myself with a pass from Colonel Ewell, the adjutant general, which I afterwards discovered was absolutely necessary. I was asked for it continually, and on the railroad every person's passport was rigidly examined.

We drove to the nearest point at which the railroad was in working order, a distance of nearly five miles.

We then got into the cars at 6 P. M. for Meridian. This piece of railroad was in a most dangerous state, and enjoys the reputation of being the very worst of all the bad railroads in the South. It was completely worn out, and could not be repaired. Accidents are of almost daily occurrence, and a nasty one had happened the day before.

After we had proceeded five miles, our engine ran off the track, which caused a stoppage of three hours. All male passengers had to get out to push along the cars.

24th May (Sunday) — We reached Meridian at 7:30 A. M., with sound limbs, and only five hours late.

We left for Mobile at 9 A. M., and arrived there at 7:15 P. M. This part of the line was in very good order.

We were delayed a short time, owing to a "difficulty" which had occurred in the up-train. The difficulty was this. The engineer had shot a passenger, then unhitched his engine, cut the telegraph, and bolted up the line, leaving his train planted on a single track. He had allowed our train to pass by shunting himself, until we had done so without any suspicion. The news of this occurrence caused really hardly any excitement amongst my fellow travelers; but I heard one man remark that "it was mighty mean to leave a train to be run into like that." We avoided this catastrophe by singular good fortune.*

* I cut this out of a Mobile paper two days after:

ATTEMPT TO COMMIT MURDER — We learn that while the uptrain on the Mobile and Ohio Railroad was near Beaver Meadow, one of the employees, named Thomas Fitzgerald, went into one of the passenger cars and shot Lieutenant H. A. Knowles with a pistol, the ball entering his left shoulder, going out at the back of his neck, making a very dangerous wound. Fitzgerald then uncoupled the locomotive from the train and started off. When a few miles above Beaver Meadow he stopped and cut the telegraph wires, and then proceeded up the road. When near Lauderdale station he came in collision with the down-train, smashing the engine, and doing considerable damage to several of the cars. It is thought he there took to the woods; at any rate he has made good his escape so far, as nothing of him has yet been heard. The shooting, as we are informed, was that of revenge. It will be remembered that a few months ago Knowles and a brother of Thomas Fitzgerald, named Jack, had a rencounter at Enterprise about a lady, and during which Knowles killed Jack Fitzgerald; afterwards it is stated that Thomas threatened to revenge the death of his brother; so on Sunday morning Knowles was on the train, as stated, going up to Enterprise to stand his trial. Thomas learning that he was on the train, hunted him up and shot him. Knowles, we learn, is now lying in a very critical condition.

[101]

The universal practice of carrying arms in the South is undoubtedly the cause of occasional loss of life, and is much to be regretted. On the other hand, this custom renders altercations and quarrels of very rare occurrence, for people are naturally careful what they say when a bullet may be the probable reply.

By the intercession of Captain Brown, I was allowed to travel in the ladies' car. It was cleaner and more convenient, barring the squalling of the numerous children, who were terrified into good behavior by threats from their Negro nurses of being given to the Yankees.

I put up at the principal hotel at Mobile, the "Battlehouse." The living appeared to be very good by comparison, and cost $8 a day. In consequence of the fabulous value of boots, they must not be left outside the door of one's room, from danger of annexation by a needy and unscrupulous warrior.

CHAPTER 6

Mobile to Shelbyville

Dinner with General Maury — Amazing Reminiscences of "Stone-wall" Jackson — Through Montgomery, Atlanta, and Chatta-nooga — At General Hardee's Headquarters — The General's Flir-tations — General Polk Invites Me to Stay at Shelbyville — The Fury of Southern Women — I Call on General Bragg — In the South, an Aggrieved Husband Is Free to Shoot — "How Can You Subdue Such a Nation as This!"

25th May (Monday) — I was disappointed in the aspect of Mobile. It is a regular rectangular American city, built on a sandy flat and covering a deal of ground for its population, which is about 25,000.

I called on General Maury, for whom I brought a letter of introduction from General Johnston. He is a very gentlemanlike and intelligent but diminutive Virginian, and had only just assumed the command at Mobile.[1]

He was very civil, and took me in a steamer to see the sea defenses. We were accompanied by General Ledbetter the engineer, and we were six hours visiting the forts.

Mobile is situated at the head of a bay thirty miles long. The blockading squadron, eight to ten in number, is stationed outside the bay. Its entrance is defended by Forts Morgan and Gaines; but as the channel between these two forts is a mile wide, they might probably be passed.

[103]

Within two miles of the city, however, the bay becomes very shallow, and the ship channel is both dangerous and tortuous. It is, moreover, obstructed by double rows of pine piles, and all sorts of ingenious torpedoes, besides being commanded by carefully constructed forts, armed with heavy guns, and built either on islands or on piles.[2]

Their names are Fort Pinto, Fort Spanish River, Apalache, and Blakeley.*

The garrisons of these forts complained of their being unhealthy, and I did not doubt the assertion. Before landing, we boarded two ironclad floating batteries. The Confederate fleet at Mobile is considerable, and reflects great credit upon the energy of the Mobilians, as it has been constructed since the commencement of the war. During the trip, I overheard General Maury soliloquizing over a Yankee flag, and saying, "Well, I never should have believed that I could have lived to see the day in which I should detest that old flag." He is cousin to Lieutenant Maury, who has distinguished himself so much by his writings, on physical geography especially. The family seems to be a very military one. His brother is captain of the Confederate steamer *Georgia.*

After landing, I partook of a hasty dinner with General Maury and Major Cummins. I was then mounted on the General's horse, and was sent to gallop round the land defenses with Brigadier General Slaughter and his staff. By great good fortune this was the evening of General Slaughter's weekly inspection, and all the redoubts were manned by their respective garrisons, consisting half of soldiers and half of armed citizens who had been exempted from the conscription either by their age or nationality, or had

* A description of either its sea or land defenses is necessarily omitted.

purchased substitutes. One of the forts was defended by a burly British guard, commanded by a venerable Captain Wheeler.*

After visiting the fortifications, I had supper at General Slaughter's house, and met there some of the refugees from New Orleans. These are now being huddled neck and crop out of that city for refusing to take the oath of allegiance to the United States. Great numbers of women and children are arriving at Mobile every day. They are in a destitute condition, and they add to the universal feeling of exasperation. The propriety of raising the black flag, and giving no quarter, was again freely discussed at General Slaughter's, and was evidently the popular idea.

I heard many anecdotes of the late "Stonewall" Jackson, who was General Slaughter's comrade in the artillery of the old army. It appears that previous to the war he was almost a monomaniac about his health. When he left the U. S. service, he was under the impression that one of his legs was getting shorter than the other. Afterwards his idea was that he only perspired on one side, and that it was necessary to keep the arm and leg of the other side in constant motion in order to preserve the circulation; but it seems that immediately the war broke out, he never made any further allusion to his health. General Slaughter declared that on the night after the terrific repulse of Burnside's army at Fredericksburg, "Stonewall" Jackson had made the following suggestion: "I am of opinion that we ought to attack the enemy at once; and in order to avoid the confusion and mistakes so common in a night attack, I recommend that we should all strip ourselves perfectly naked." †

Blockade-running goes on very regularly at Mobile. The steamers nearly always succeed, but the schooners are generally captured.

* Its members were British subjects exempted from the conscription, but they had volunteered to fight in defense of the city.
† I always forgot to ask General Lee whether this story was a true one.

Tomorrow I shall start for the Tennessean army, commanded by General Braxton Bragg.

26th May (Tuesday) — When I took Colonel Ewell's pass to the provost-marshal's office this morning to be countersigned that official hesitated about stamping it. Luckily, a man in his office came to my rescue, and volunteered to say that, although he didn't know me himself, he had heard me spoken of by others as "a very respectable gentleman."

I was only just in time to catch the twelve o'clock steamer for the Montgomery railroad. I overheard two Negroes on board discussing affairs in general. They were deploring the war, and expressing their hatred of the Yankees for bringing "sufferment on us as well as our masters." Both of them had evidently a great aversion to being "run off," as they called it. One of them wore his master's sword, of which he was very proud, and he strutted about in a most amusing and consequential manner.

I got into the railroad cars at 2:30 P. M. The pace was not at all bad had we not stopped so often and for such a long time for wood and water. I sat opposite a wounded soldier, who told me he was an Englishman from Chelsea. He said he was returning to his regiment, although his wound in the neck often gave him great pain.

The spirit with which wounded men return to the front, even although their wounds are imperfectly healed, is worthy of all praise, and shows the indomitable determination of the Southern people. In the same car there were several quite young boys of fifteen or sixteen who were badly wounded, and one or two were minus arms and legs, of which deficiencies they were evidently very vain.

The country through which we passed was a dense pine forest, sandy soil, and quite desolate, very uninviting to an invading army. We traveled all night.

27th May (Wednesday) — Arrived at Montgomery, the capital of Alabama, at daylight, and left it by another railroad at 5:30 A. M.

All state capitals appear to resemble one another, and look like bits cut off from great cities. One or two streets have a good deal of pretension about them; and the inevitable "Capitol," with its dome, forms the principal feature.

A sentry stands at the door of each railway car, who examines the papers of every passenger with great strictness. Even after that inspection the same ceremony is performed by an officer of the provost-marshal's department, who accompanies every train.* The officers and soldiers on this duty are very civil and courteous, and after getting over their astonishment at finding that I am a British officer, they do all they can to make me comfortable. They ask all sorts of curious questions about the British Army, and often express a strong wish to see *one of our regiments fight*. They can hardly believe that the Coldstream is really dressed in scarlet. To-day they entered gravely into discussion amongst themselves, as to whether British troops would have taken the position at Fredericksburg. The arguments on both sides were very amusing, and opinion was pretty evenly divided.

We met three trains crammed full of soldiers for Johnston's army. They belonged to Breckenridge's division of Bragg's army, and all seemed in the highest spirits, cheering and yelling like demons.

* This rigid inspection is necessary to arrest spies, and prevent straggling and absence without leave.

In the cars today I fell in with the Federal doctor who was refused leave to pass through General Johnston's lines. He was now
en route for Richmond. He was in full Yankee uniform, but was
treated with civility by all the Confederate soldiers. I had a long
talk with him; he seemed a sensible man, and did not attempt to
deny the universal enthusiasm and determination of the Southerners. He told me that General Grant had been very nearly killed at
the taking of Jackson. He thought the war would probably terminate by a blow-up in the North.*

I had to change cars at West Point and at Atlanta. At the latter
place I was crammed into a desperately crowded train for Chattanooga. This country, Georgia, is much more inhabited and cultivated than Alabama. I traveled again all night.

28th May (Thursday) — I arrived at Chattanooga (Tennessee)
at 4:30 A. M., and fell in with Captain Brown again. His Negro
recognized me, and immediately rushed up to shake hands.

After breakfasting at Chattanooga, I started again at 7:30 by
train for Shelbyville, General Bragg's headquarters. This train was
crammed to repletion with soldiers rejoining their regiments, so I
was constrained to sit in the aisle on the floor of one of the cars. I
thought myself lucky even then, for so great was the number of
military, that all "citizens" were ordered out to make way for the
soldiers; but my gray shooting-jacket and youthful appearance
saved me from the imputation of being a "citizen."

Two hours later, the passport officer, seeing who I was, procured me a similar situation in the ladies' car, where I was a little

* Notwithstanding the exasperation with which every Southerner speaks of
a Yankee, and all the talk about black flag and no quarter, yet I never saw a
Federal prisoner ill-treated or insulted in any way, although I have traveled
hundreds of miles in their company.

better off. After leaving Chattanooga, the railroad winds alongside of the Tennessee River, the banks of which are high and beautifully covered with trees. The river itself is wide, and very pretty; but from my position in the tobacco juice I was unable to do justice to the scenery. I saw stockades at intervals all along the railroad, which were constructed by the Federals, who occupied all this country last year.

On arriving at Wartrace at 4 P. M., I determined to remain there, and ask for hospitality from General Hardee, as I saw no prospect of reaching Shelbyville in decent time. Leaving my baggage with the provost marshal at Wartrace, I walked on to General Hardee's headquarters, which were distant about two miles from the railroad. They were situated in a beautiful country, green, undulating, full of magnificent trees, principally beeches, and the scenery was by far the finest I had seen in America as yet.

When I arrived, I found that General Hardee was in company with General Polk and Bishop Elliott of Georgia, and also with Mr. Vallandigham.[3] The latter (called the Apostle of Liberty) is a good-looking man, apparently not much over forty, and had been turned out of the North three days before. Rosecrans had wished to hand him over to Bragg by flag of truce; but as the latter declined to receive him in that manner, he was, as General Hardee expressed it, "dumped down" in the neutral ground between the lines, and left there.

He then received hospitality from the Confederates in the capacity of a destitute stranger. They do not in any way receive him officially, and it does not suit the policy of either party to be identified with one another. He is now living at a private house in Shelbyville, and had come over for the day, with General Polk, on a visit to Hardee. He told the generals, that if Grant was severely beaten in Mississippi by Johnston, he did not think the war could be continued on its present great scale.

When I presented my letters of introduction, General Hardee received me with the unvarying kindness and hospitality which I had experienced from all other Confederate officers. He is a fine, soldierlike man, broad-shouldered and tall. He looks rather like a French officer, and is a Georgian by birth. He bears the reputation of being a thoroughly good soldier, and he is the author of the drillbook still in use by both armies. Until quite lately, he was commanding officer of the military college at West Point. He distinguished himself at the battles of Corinth and Murfreesboro, and now commands the 2d *corps d'armée* of Bragg's army.

He is a widower, and has the character of being a great admirer of the fair sex. During the Kentucky campaign last year, he was in the habit of availing himself of the privilege of his rank and years, and insisted upon kissing the wives and daughters of all the Kentuckian farmers. And although he is supposed to have converted many of the ladies to the Southern cause, yet in many instances their male relatives remained either neutral or undecided. On one occasion General Hardee had conferred the "accolade" upon a very pretty Kentuckian to their mutual satisfaction, when, to his intense disgust, the proprietor produced two very ugly old females, saying, "Now, then, General, if you kiss any you must kiss them all round," which the discomfited general was forced to do, to the great amusement of his officers, who often allude to this contretemps.

Another rebuff which he received, and about which he is often chaffed by General Polk, was when an old lady told him he ought really to "leave off fighting *at his age*." "Indeed, madam," replied Hardee, "and how old do you take me for?" "Why, about the same age as myself — seventy-five." The chagrin of the stalwart and gallant general, at having twenty years added to his age, may be imagined.

Lieutenant General Leonidas Polk, Bishop of Louisiana, who commands the other *corps d'armée*, is a good-looking, gentleman-like man with all the manners and affability of a "grand seigneur." He is fifty-seven years of age — tall, upright, and looks much more the soldier than the clergyman. He is very rich; and I am told he owns seven hundred Negroes. He is much beloved by the soldiers on account of his great personal courage and agreeable manners. I had already heard no end of anecdotes of him told me by my traveling companions, who always alluded to him with affection and admiration. In his clerical capacity I had always heard him spoken of with the greatest respect.

When I was introduced to him he immediately invited me to come and stay at his headquarters at Shelbyville. He told me that he was educated at West Point, and was at that institution with the President, the two Johnstons, Lee, Magruder, &c., and that, after serving a short time in the artillery, he had entered the church.

Bishop Elliott, of Georgia, is a nice old man of venerable appearance and very courteous manners. He is here at the request of General Polk for the purpose of confirming some officers and soldiers. He speaks English exactly like an English gentleman. So, in fact, does General Polk and all the well-bred Southerners, much more so than the ladies, whose American accent can always be detected. General Polk and Mr. Vallandigham returned to Shelbyville in an ambulance at 6:30 P. M.

General Hardee's headquarters were on the estate of Mrs. ——, a very hospitable lady. The two daughters of the General were staying with her, and also a Mrs. ——, who is a very pretty woman. These ladies are more violent against the Yankees than it is possible for a European to conceive. They beat their male relations hollow in their denunciations and hopes of vengeance. It was quite depressing to hear their innumerable stories of Yankee brutality, and I was much relieved when, at a later period of the evening, they subsided into music. After Bishop Elliott had read prayers, I slept in the same room with General Hardee.

29th May (Friday) — I took a walk before breakfast with Dr. Quintard, a zealous Episcopal chaplain, who began life as a surgeon, which enables him to attend to the bodily as well as the spiritual wants of the Tennessean regiment to which he is chaplain. The enemy is about fifteen miles distant, and all the tops of the intervening hills are occupied as signal stations, which communicate his movements by flags in the daytime, and by beacons at night. A signal corps has been organized for this service. The system is most ingenious, and answers admirably.⁴

We all breakfasted at Mrs. ——'s. The ladies were more excited even than yesterday in their diatribes against the Yankees. They insisted on cutting the accompanying paragraph out of today's newspaper, which they declared was a very fair exposition of the average treatment they received from the enemy.* They reproved

* LOSSES OF WILLIAM F. RICKS — The Yankees did not treat us very badly as they returned from pursuing our men beyond Leighton (at least no more than we expected); they broke down our smokehouse door and took seven hams, went into the kitchen and helped themselves to cooking utensils, tin ware, &c.; searched the house, but took nothing. As they passed up the second time we were very much annoyed by them, but not seriously injured; they took the only two mules we had, a cart, our milch cows, and more meat. It was on their return from this trip that our losses were so grievous. They drove their wagons up in our yard and loaded them with the last of our meat, all of our sugar, coffee, molasses, flour, meal, and potatoes. I went to a lieut.-colonel who

Mrs. —— for having given assistance to the wounded Yankees at Wartrace last year; and a sister of Mrs. ——'s, who is a very strong-minded lady, gave me a most amusing description of an interview

---

seemed very busy giving orders, and asked him what he expected me to do; they had left me no provisions at all, and I had a large family, and my husband was away from home. His reply was short and pointed — "Starve, and be d—d, madam." They then proceeded to the carriage-house, took a fine new buggy that we had never used, the cushions and harness of our carriage, then cut the carriage up and left it. They then sent about sixty of the slyest, smoothest-fingered rogues I have ever seen in the Federal army (all the rogues I ever did see were in that army), into the house to search for whiskey and money, while the officers remained in the back-yard trying to hire the servants to tell them where we had money hid. Their search proving fruitless, they loaded themselves with our clothing, bed-clothing, &c.; broke my dishes; stole my knives and forks; refused the keys and broke open my trunks, closets, and other doors. Then came the worst of all — the burners, or, as they call themselves, the "Destroying Angels." They burned our gin-house and press, with 125 bales of cotton, seven cribs containing 600 bolls of corn, our logs, stables, and six stacks of fodder, a wagon, and four Negro cabins, our lumber-room, fine spinning-machine and 500 dollars' worth of thread, axes, hoes, scythe-blades, and all other plantation implements. Then they came with their torches to burn our house, the last remaining building they had left besides the Negro quarter. That was too much; all my pride, and the resolutions that I had made (and until now kept up) to treat them with cool contempt, and never, let the worst come, humble myself to the thievish cutthroats, forsook me at the awful thought of my home in ruins; I must do something, and that quickly; — hardened, thieving villains, as I knew them to be, I would make one effort for the sake of my home. I looked over the crowd, as they huddled together to give orders about the burning, for one face that showed a trace of feeling, or an eye that beamed with a spark of humanity, but, finding none, I approached the nearest group, and pointing to the children (my sister's), I said, "You will not burn the house, will you? You drove those little ones from one home and took possession of it, and this is the only sheltering place they have." "You may thank your God, madam," said one of the ruffians, "that we have left you and your d—d brats with heads to be sheltered." Just then an officer galloped up — pretended to be very much astonished and terribly beset about the conduct of his men — cursed a good deal, and told a batch of falsehoods about not having given orders to burn anything but corn — made divers threats that were forgotten in utterance, and ordered his "Angels" to fall into line — thereby winding up the troubles of the darkest day I have ever seen.

Mrs. Ricks

Losses before this last raid: six mules, five horses, one wagon (four-horse), fifty-two Negroes.

she had had at Huntsville with the astronomer Mitchell, in his capacity as a Yankee general.[5]

It has often been remarked to me that, when this war is over, the independence of the country will be due, in a great measure, to the women. Men declare that had the women been desponding they could never have gone through with it; but, on the contrary, the women have invariably set an example to the men of patience, devotion, and determination. Naturally proud, and with an innate contempt for the Yankees, the Southern women have been rendered furious and desperate by the proceeding of Butler, Milroy, Turchin, &c. They are all prepared to undergo any hardships and misfortunes rather than submit to the rule of such people; and they use every argument which woman can employ to infuse the same spirit into their male relations.

At noon I took leave for the present of General Hardee, and drove over in his ambulance to Shelbyville, eight miles, in company with Bishop Elliott and Dr. Quintard. The road was abominable, and it was pouring with rain. On arriving at General Polk's, he invited me to take up my quarters with him during my stay with Bragg's army, which offer I accepted with gratitude.[6]

After dinner General Polk told me that he hoped his brethren in England did not very much condemn his present line of conduct. He explained to me the reasons which had induced him temporarily to forsake the cassock and return to his old profession. He stated the extreme reluctance he had felt in taking this step. He said that as soon as the war was over, he should return to his episcopal avocations, in the same way as a man, finding his house on fire, would use every means in his power to extinguish the flames, and would then resume his ordinary pursuits.[7] He commanded the Confederate forces at the battle of Perryville and Belmont, as well as his present *corps d'armée* at the battles of Shiloh (Corinth) and Murfreesboro.

At 6:30 P. M., I called on General Bragg, the Commander in chief. This officer is in appearance the least prepossessing of the Confederate generals. He is very thin. He stoops, and has a sickly, cadaverous, haggard appearance, rather plain features, bushy black eyebrows which unite in a tuft on the top of his nose, and a stubby iron-gray beard; but his eyes are bright and piercing. He has the reputation of being a rigid disciplinarian, and of shooting freely for insubordination. I understand he is rather unpopular on this account, and also by reason of his occasional acerbity of manner.[8]

He was extremely civil to me, and gave me permission to visit the outposts, or any part of his army. He also promised to help me towards joining Morgan in Kentucky, and he expressed his regret that a boil on his hand would prevent him from accompanying me to the outposts. He told me that Rosecrans's position extended about forty miles, Murfreesboro (twenty-five miles distant) being his headquarters. The Confederate cavalry inclosed him in a semicircle extending over a hundred miles of country. He told me that West Tennessee, occupied by the Federals, was devoted to the Confederate cause, whilst East Tennessee, now in possession of the Confederates, contained numbers of people of Unionist proclivities. This very place, Shelbyville, had been described to me by others as a "Union hole."

After my interview with General Bragg, I took a ride along the Murfreesboro road with Colonel Richmond, A. D. C. to General Polk. About two miles from Shelbyville, we passed some lines made to defend the position. The trench itself was a very mild affair, but the higher ground could be occupied by artillery in such a manner as to make the road impassable. The thick woods were being cut down in front of the lines for a distance of eight hundred yards to give range.

During our ride I met Major General Cheetham, a stout, rather rough-looking man, but with the reputation of "a great fighter." It is said that he does all the necessary swearing in the 1st *corps d'armée*, which General Polk's clerical character incapacitates him from performing.

Colonel Richmond gave me the particulars of General Van Dorn's death, which occurred about forty miles from this. His loss does not seem to be much regretted, as it appears he was always ready to neglect his military duties for an assignation. In the South it is not considered necessary to put yourself on an equality with a man in such a case as Van Dorn's by calling him out. His life belongs to the aggrieved husband, and "shooting down" is universally esteemed the correct thing, even if it takes place after a lapse of time, as in the affair between General Van Dorn and Dr. Peters.[9]

News arrived this evening of the capture of Helena by the Confederates, and of the hanging of a Negro regiment with forty Yankee officers. Every one expressed sorrow for the blacks, but applauded the destruction of their officers.*

I slept in General Polk's tent, he occupying a room in the house adjoining. Before going to bed, General Polk told me an affecting story of a poor widow in humble circumstances, whose three sons had fallen in battle one after the other, until she had only one left, a boy of sixteen. So distressing was her case that General Polk went himself to comfort her. She looked steadily at

* This afterwards turned out to be untrue.

him, and replied to his condolences by the sentence, "As soon as I can get a few things together, General, you shall have Harry too." The tears came into General Polk's eyes as he related this episode, which he ended by saying, "*How can you subdue such a nation as this!*"

CHAPTER 7

The Stay at Shelbyville

*One of the Most Extraordinary Characters I Ever Met — In a
Baggage Car with General Bragg — Shooting a Deserter — I Meet
General Joe Wheeler — How to Lead Confederate Soldiers —
Watching General Bragg Get Baptized — General Polk's Close
Call — Jealousy between the Armies — Reconnoitering the Feder-
als — Confederate Cavalry Tactics — The Object of Killing a
Yankee Is to Get His Boots*

30th May (Saturday) — It rained hard all last night, but General Polk's tent proved itself a good one. We have prayers both
morning and evening by Dr. Quintard, together with singing, in
which General Polk joins with much zeal. Colonel Gale, who is
son-in-law and volunteer aid-de-camp to General Polk, has placed
his Negro Aaron and a mare at my disposal during my stay.

General Polk explained to me, from a plan, the battle of Murfreesboro. He claimed that the Confederates had only 30,000
troops, including Breckenridge's division, which was not engaged
on the first day. He put the Confederate loss at 10,000 men, and
that of the Yankees at 19,000.[1]

With regard to the battle of Shiloh,* he said that Beauregard's
order to retire was most unfortunate, as the gunboats were doing
no real harm, and if they (the Confederates) had held on, noth-

* Called Pittsburg Landing and Corinth.

[118   ]

ing could have saved the Federals from capture or destruction. The misfortune of Albert Johnston's death, together with the fact of Beauregard's illness and his not being present at that particular spot, were the causes of this battle not being a more complete victory.[2]

Ever since I landed in America, I had heard of the exploits of an Englishman called Colonel St. Leger Grenfell, who is now Inspector General of cavalry to Bragg's army. This afternoon I made his acquaintance, and I consider him one of the most extraordinary characters I ever met.

Although he is a member of a well-known English family, he seems to have devoted his whole life to the exciting career of a soldier of fortune. He told me that in early life he had served three years in a French lancer regiment, and had risen from a private to be a *sous* lieutenant. He afterwards became a sort of consular agent at Tangier, under old Mr. Drummond Hay. Having acquired a perfect knowledge of Arabic, he entered the service of Abd-el-kader, and under that renowned chief he fought the French for four years and a half. At another time of his life he fitted out a yacht, and carried on a private war with the Riff pirates. He was brigade major in the Turkish contingent during the Crimean War, and had some employment in the Indian mutiny. He has also been engaged in war in Buenos Aires and the South American republics.[3]

At an early period of the present troubles he ran the blockade and joined the Confederates. He was adjutant general and right-hand man to the celebrated John Morgan for eight months. Even in this army, which abounds with foolhardy and desperate characters, he has acquired the admiration of all ranks by his reckless daring and gallantry in the field. Both Generals Polk and Bragg spoke to me of him as a most excellent and useful officer, besides

[119   ]

being a man who never lost an opportunity of trying to throw his life away.

He is just the sort of a man to succeed in this army, and among the soldiers his fame for bravery has outweighed his unpopularity as a rigid disciplinarian. He is the terror of all absentees, stragglers, and deserters, and of all commanding officers who are unable to produce for his inspection the number of horses they have been drawing forage for.

He looks about forty-five, but in reality he is fifty-six. He is rather tall, thin, very wiry and active, with a jovial English expression of countenance; but his eyes have a wild, roving look, which is common amongst the Arabs. When he came to me he was dressed in an English staff blue coat, and he had a red cavalry forage cap, which latter, General Polk told me, he always wore in action, so making himself more conspicuous.

He talked to me much about John Morgan, whose marriage he had tried to avert, and of which he spoke with much sorrow. He declared that Morgan was enervated by matrimony, and would never be the same man as he was.[4] He said that in one of the celebrated telegraph tappings in Kentucky, Morgan, the operator, and himself were seated for twelve hours on a clay bank during a violent storm, but the interest was so intense that the time passed like three hours.*[5]

General Polk's son, a young artillery lieutenant, told me this evening that "Stonewall" Jackson was a professor at the military school at Lexington, in which he was a cadet. "Old Jack" was considered a persevering but rather dull master, and was often

---

* This was the occasion when they telegraphed such a quantity of nonsense to the Yankee general, receiving valuable information in return, and such necessary stores by train as Morgan was in need of.

made a butt of by cheeky cadets, whose great ambition was to irritate him, but, however insolent they were, he never took the
slightest notice of their impertinence at the time, although he always had them punished for it afterwards. At the outbreak of the
war, he was called upon by the cadets to make a speech, and these
were his words: "Soldiers make short speeches: *be slow to draw
the sword in civil strife, but when you draw it, throw away the
scabbard.*" Young Polk says that the enthusiasm created by this
speech of Old Jack's was beyond description.

31st May (Sunday) — The Bishop of Georgia preached today to
a very large congregation in the Presbyterian church. He is a most
eloquent preacher; and he afterwards confirmed about twenty people — amongst others, Colonel Gale (over forty years old), and
young Polk. After church, I called again on General Bragg, who
talked to me a long time about the battle of Murfreesboro (in
which he commanded). He said that he retained possession of
the ground he had won for three days and a half, and only retired on account of the exhaustion of his troops, after carrying off
over 6000 prisoners, much cannon, and other trophies. He allowed
that Rosecrans had displayed much firmness, and was "the only
man in the Yankee army who was not badly beaten." He showed
me, on a plan, the exact position of the two armies and also the
field of operations of the renowned guerrillas, Morgan and
Forrest.

Colonel Grenfell called again, and I arranged to visit the outposts with him on Tuesday. He spoke to me in high terms of
Bragg, Polk, Hardee, and Cleburne; but he described some of the
others as "political" generals, and others as good fighters, but il-
literate and somewhat addicted to liquor. He deplored the effects

of politics upon military affairs as very injurious in the Confederate
Army, though not so bad as it is in the Northern.

At 2 P. M. I traveled in the cars to Wartrace, in company with
General Bragg and the Bishop of Georgia. We were put into a
baggage car, and the General and the Bishop were the only persons provided with seats. Although the distance from Shelbyville
to Wartrace is only eight miles, we were one hour and ten minutes in effecting the *trajet*, in such a miserable and dangerous
state were the rails.

On arriving at Wartrace we were entertained by Major General
Cleburne. This officer gave me his history. He is the son of a doctor at or near Ballincolig. At the age of seventeen he ran away from
home and enlisted in Her Majesty's 41st regiment of foot, in which
he served three years as private and corporal. He then brought his
discharge, and emigrated to Arkansas, 'where he studied law, and
eschewing politics, he got a good practice as a lawyer. At the outbreak of the war he was elected captain of his company, then
colonel of his regiment, and has since, by his distinguished services
in all the Western campaigns, been appointed to the command of a
division (10,000 men) — the highest military rank which has
been attained by a foreigner in the Confederate service.

He told me that he ascribed his advancement mainly to the
useful lessons which he had learnt in the ranks of the British Army,
and he pointed with a laugh to his general's white facings, which
he said his 41st experience enabled him to keep cleaner than any
other Confederate general.* He is now thirty-five years of age; but
his hair having turned gray, he looks older. Generals Bragg and

* The 41st regiment wears white facings; so do the generals in the Confederate Army. M. de Polignac has recently been appointed a brigadier; he and
Cleburne are the only two generals amongst the Confederates who are foreigners.

Hardee both spoke to me of him in terms of the highest praise, and said that he had risen entirely by his own personal merit.[6]

At 5 P. M. I was present at a great open-air preaching at General Wood's camp. Bishop Elliott preached most admirably to a congregation composed of nearly 3000 soldiers, who listened to him with the most profound attention. Generals Bragg, Polk, Hardee, Withers, Cleburne, and endless brigadiers, were also present. It is impossible to exaggerate the respect paid by all ranks of this army to Bishop Elliott; and although most of the officers are Episcopalians, the majority of the soldiers are Methodists, Baptists, &c. Bishop Elliott afterwards explained to me that the reason most of the people had become dissenters was because there had been no bishops in America during the "British dominion." And all the clergy, having been appointed from England, had almost without exception stuck by the King in the Revolution, and had had their livings forfeited.

I dined and slept at General Hardee's, but spent the evening at Mrs. ——'s, where I heard renewed philippics directed by the ladies against the Yankees.

I find that it is a great mistake to suppose that the press is gagged in the South, as I constantly see the most violent attacks upon the President — upon the different generals and their measures. Today I heard the officers complaining bitterly of the *Chattanooga Rebel*, for publishing an account of Breckenridge's departure from this army to reinforce Johnston in Mississippi, and thus giving early intelligence to the enemy.

1st June (Monday) — We all went to a review of General Liddell's brigade at Bellbuckle, a distance of six miles. There were three carriages full of ladies, and I rode an excellent horse, the gift of General John Morgan to General Hardee. The weather and

[123   ]

the scenery were delightful. General Hardee asked me particularly whether Mr. Mason had been kindly received in England. I replied that I thought he had, by private individuals. I have often found the Southerners rather touchy on this point.

General Liddell's brigade was composed of Arkansas troops — five very weak regiments which had suffered severely in the different battles, and they cannot be easily recruited on account of the blockade of the Mississippi. The men were good-sized, healthy, and well clothed, though without any attempt at uniformity in color or cut; but nearly all were dressed either in gray or brown coats and felt hats.

I was told that even if a regiment was clothed in proper uniform by the government, it would become parti-colored again in a week, as the soldiers preferred wearing the coarse homespun jackets and trousers made by their mothers and sisters at home. The generals very wisely allow them to please themselves in this respect, and insist only upon their arms and accoutrements being kept in proper order. Most of the officers were dressed in uniform which is neat and serviceable — a bluish-gray frock coat of a color similar to Austrian yagers. The infantry wear blue facings, the artillery red, the doctors black, the staff white, and the cavalry yellow; so it is impossible to mistake the branch of the service to which an officer belongs — nor is it possible to mistake his rank. A second lieutenant, first lieutenant, and captain, wear respectively one, two, and three bars on the collar. A major, lieutenant colonel, and colonel, wear one, two, and three stars on the collar.

Before the marching past of the brigade, many of the soldiers had taken off their coats and marched past the general in their shirt sleeves, on account of the warmth. Most of them were armed with Enfield rifles captured from the enemy. Many, however, had lost or thrown away their bayonets, which they don't appear to value properly, as they assert that they have never met any Yankees who would wait for that weapon. I expressed a desire to see them form square, but it appeared they were "not drilled to such a maneuver" (except square two deep). They said the country did not admit of cavalry charges, even if the Yankee cavalry had stomach to attempt it.

Each regiment carried a "battle flag," blue, with a white border, on which were inscribed the names "Belmont," "Shiloh," "Perryville," "Richmond, Kentucky," and "Murfreesboro." They drilled tolerably well, and an advance in line was remarkably good; but General Liddell had invented several dodges of his own, for which he was reproved by General Hardee.

The review being over, the troops were harangued by Bishop Elliott in an excellent address, partly religious, partly patriotic. He was followed by a Congressman of vulgar appearance, named Hanley, from Arkansas, who delivered himself of a long and uninteresting political oration, and ended by announcing himself as a candidate for re-election. This speech seemed to me (and to others) particularly ill-timed, out of place, and ridiculous, addressed as it was to soldiers in front of the enemy. But this was one of the results of universal suffrage. The soldiers afterwards wanted General Hardee to say something, but he declined. I imagine that the discipline in this army is the strictest in the Confederacy, and that the men are much better marchers than those I saw in Mississippi.

A soldier was shot in Wartrace this afternoon. We heard the volley just as we left in the cars for Shelbyville. His crime was desertion to the enemy; and as the prisoner's brigade was at Tullahoma (twenty miles off), he was executed without ceremony by

[125]

the provost guard.[7] Spies are hung every now and then; but General Bragg told me it was almost impossible for either side to stop the practice.

Bishop Elliott, Dr. Quintard, and myself got back to General Polk's quarters at 5 P. M., where I was introduced to a Colonel Styles, who was formerly United States minister at Vienna.

In the evening I made the acquaintance of General Wheeler, Van Dorn's successor in command of the cavalry of this army, which is over 24,000 strong. He is a very little man, only twenty-six years of age, and was dressed in a coat much too big for him. He made his reputation by protecting the retreat of the army through Kentucky last year. He was a graduate of West Point, and seems a remarkably zealous officer, besides being very modest and unassuming in his manners.

General Polk told me that, notwithstanding the departure of Breckenridge, this army is now much stronger than it was at the time of the battle of Murfreesboro. I think that probably 45,000 infantry and artillery could be brought together immediately for a battle.

2d June (Tuesday) — Colonel Grenfell and I rode to the outposts, starting on the road to Murfreesboro at 6 A. M. It rained hard nearly all day. He explained to me the method of fighting adopted by the Western cavalry, which he said was admirably adapted for this country; but he denied that they could under any circumstances stand a fair charge of regular cavalry in the open. Their system is to dismount and leave their horses in some secure place. One man is placed in charge of his own and three other horses, whilst the remainder act as infantry skirmishers in the dense woods and broken country, making a tremendous row, and deceiving the enemy as to their numbers, and as to their character as infantry or cavalry.

In this manner Morgan, assisted by two small guns, called bulldogs, attacked the Yankees with success in towns, forts, stockades, and steamboats. By the same system, Wheeler and Wharton kept a large pursuing army in check for twenty-seven days, retreating and fighting every day, and deluding the enemy with the idea that they were being resisted by a strong force composed of all three branches of the service.

Colonel Grenfell told me that the only way in which an officer could acquire influence over the Confederate soldiers was by his personal conduct under fire. They hold a man in great esteem who in action sets them an example of contempt for danger; but they think nothing of an officer who is not in the habit of *leading* them. In fact such a man could not possibly retain his position. Colonel Grenfell's expression was, "every atom of authority has to be purchased by a drop of your blood."

He told me he was in desperate hot water with the civil authorities of the state, who accuse him of illegally impressing and appropriating horses, and also of conniving at the escape of a Negro from his lawful owner, and he said that the military authorities were afraid or unable to give him proper protection.

For the first nine miles our road was quite straight and hilly, with a thick wood on either side. We then reached a pass in the hills called Guy's Gap, which, from the position of the hills, is very strong, and could be held by a small force. The range of hills extends as far as Wartrace, but I understand the position could be turned on the left. About two miles beyond Guy's Gap were the headquarters of General Martin, the officer who commands the brigade of cavalry stationed in the neighborhood.

[127   ]

General Martin showed me the letter sent by the Yankees a few days ago by flag of truce with Mr. Vallandigham. This letter was curiously worded, and ended, as far as I can remember, with this expression: "Mr. Vallandigham is therefore handed over to the respectful attention of the Confederate authorities." General Martin told me that skirmishing and bushwhacking went on nearly every day, and that ten days ago the enemy's cavalry, by a bold dash, had captured a fieldpiece close to his own quarters. It was, however, retaken, and its captors were killed.

One of General Martin's staff officers conducted us to the bivouac of Colonel Webb (three miles further along the road), who commanded the regiment on outpost duty there — 51st Alabama Cavalry. This Colonel Webb was a lawyer by profession, and seemed a capital fellow. He insisted on riding with us to the vedettes in spite of the rain, and he also desired his regiment to turn out for us by the time we returned.

The extreme outposts were about two miles beyond Colonel Webb's post, and about sixteen miles from Shelbyville. The neutral ground extended for about three miles. We rode along it as far as it was safe to do so, and just came within sight of the Yankee vedettes. The Confederate vedettes were at an interval of from 300 to 400 yards of each other. Colonel Webb's regiment was in charge of two miles of the front; and, in a similar manner, the chain of vedettes was extended by other corps right and left for more than eighty miles. Scouts are continually sent forward by both sides to collect information.

Rival scouts and pickets invariably fire on one another whenever they meet; and Colonel Webb good-naturedly offered, if I was particularly anxious to see their customs and habits, to send forward a few men and have a little fight. I thanked him much for his kind offer, but begged he wouldn't trouble himself so far on my account. He showed me the house where Vallandigham had been "dumped down" between the outposts when they refused to receive him by flag of truce.

The woods on both sides of the road showed many signs of the conflicts which are of daily occurrence. Most of the houses by the roadside had been destroyed; but one plucky old lady had steadfastly refused to turn out, although her house was constantly an object of contention, and showed many marks of bullets and shell.

Ninety-seven men were employed every day in Colonel Webb's regiment to patrol the front. The remainder of the 51st Alabama were mounted and drawn up to receive Colonel Grenfell on our return from the outposts. They were uniformly armed with long rifles and revolvers, but without sabers, and they were a fine body of young men. Their horses were in much better condition than might have been expected, considering the scanty food and hard duty they had had to put up with for the last five months, without shelter of any kind, except the trees. Colonel Grenfell told me they were a very fair specimen of the immense number of cavalry with Bragg's army.

I got back to Shelbyville at 4:30 P. M., just in time to be present at an interesting ceremony peculiar to America. This was a baptism at the Episcopal Church. The ceremony was performed in an impressive manner by Bishop Elliott, and the person baptized was no less than the commander in chief of the army. The bishop took the general's hand in his own (the latter kneeling in front of the font), and said, "Braxton, if thou hast not already been baptized, I baptize thee," &c. Immediately afterwards he confirmed General Bragg, who then shook hands with General Polk, the officers of their respective staffs, and myself, who were the only spectators.

[129]

The soldiers on sentry at General Polk's quarters this afternoon were deficient both of shoes and stockings. These were the first barefooted soldiers I had as yet seen in the Confederacy.

I had intended to leave Shelbyville tomorrow with Bishop Elliott; but as I was informed that a reconnaissance in force was arranged for tomorrow, I accepted General Polk's kind offer of further hospitality for a couple of days more. Four of Polk's brigades with artillery move to the front tomorrow, and General Hardee is also to push forward from Wartrace. The object of this movement is to ascertain the enemy's strength at Murfreesboro, as rumor asserts that Rosecrans is strengthening Grant in Mississippi, which General Bragg is not disposed to allow with impunity. The weather is now almost chilly.

3d June (Wednesday) — Bishop Elliott left for Savannah at 6 A. M. in a downpour of rain, which continued nearly all day. Grenfell came to see me this morning in a towering rage. He had been arrested in his bed by the civil power on a charge of horse-stealing, and conniving at the escape of a Negro from his master. General Bragg himself had stood bail for him, but Grenfell was naturally furious at the indignity. But even according to his own account, he seems to have acted indiscreetly in the affair of the Negro, and he will have to appear before the civil court next October.

General Polk and his officers were all much vexed at the occurrence, which, however, is an extraordinary and convincing proof that the military had not superseded the civil power in the Southern States; for here was an important officer arrested, in spite of the commander in chief, when in the execution of his office before the enemy. By standing bail, General Bragg gave a most positive proof that he exonerated Grenfell from any malpractices.*

In the evening, after dark, General Polk drew my attention to the manner in which the signal beacons were worked. One light was stationary on the ground, whilst another was moved backwards and forwards over it. They gave us intelligence that General Hardee had pushed the enemy to within five miles of Murfreesboro, after heavy skirmishing all day.

I got out of General Polk the story of his celebrated adventure with the —— Indiana (Northern) regiment, which resulted in the almost total destruction of that corps. I had often during my

---

* I cut this out of a Charleston paper some days after I had parted from Colonel Grenfell: Colonel Grenfell was only obeying General Bragg's orders on depriving the soldier of his horse, and temporarily of his money: —
COLONEL ST. LEGER GRENFELL — The Western army correspondent of the *Mobile Register* writes as follows: — The famous Colonel St. Leger Grenfell, who served with Morgan last summer, and since that time has been Assistant Inspector-general of General Bragg, was arrested a few days since by the civil authorities. The sheriff and his officers called upon the bold Englishman before he had arisen in the morning, and after the latter had performed his toilet duties he buckled on his belt and trusty pistols. The officer of the law remonstrated, and the Englisher damned, and a struggle of half an hour ensued, in which the stout Britisher made a powerful resistance, but, by overpowering force, was at last placed *hors de combat* and disarmed.† The charges were, that he retained in his possession the slave of a Confederate citizen, and refused to deliver him or her up; that meeting a soldier coming to the army leading a horse, he accused him of being a deserter, dismounted him, took his horses and equipments and *money*, stating that deserters were not worthy to have either horses or money, and sent the owner thereof off where he would not be heard of again. The result of the affair was, that Colonel Grenfell, whether guilty or not guilty, delivered up the Negro, horses, and money to the civil authorities. If the charges against him are proven true, then there is no doubt that the course of General Bragg will be to dismiss him from his Staff; but if, on the contrary, malicious slanders are defaming this ally, he is Hercules enough and brave enough to punish them. His bravery and gallantry were conspicuous throughout the Kentucky campaign, and it is hoped that this late tarnish on his fame will be removed; or if it be not, that he will.
† *This is all nonsense — the myrmidons of the law took very good care to pounce upon Colonel Grenfell when he was in bed and asleep.*

travels heard officers and soldiers talking of this extraordinary feat of the "Bishop's." The modest yet graphic manner in which General Polk related this wonderful instance of coolness and bravery was extremely interesting, and I now repeat it, as nearly as I can, in his own words.

"Well, sir, it was at the battle of Perryville, late in the evening — in fact, it was almost dark when Liddell's brigade came into action. Shortly after its arrival I observed a body of men, whom I believed to be Confederates, standing at an angle to this brigade, and firing obliquely at the newly arrived troops. I said, 'Dear me, this is very sad, and must be stopped'; so I turned round, but could find none of my young men, who were absent on different messages; so I determined to ride myself and settle the matter. Having cantered up to the colonel of the regiment which was firing, I asked him in angry tones what he meant by shooting his own friends, and I desired him to cease doing so at once. He answered with surprise, 'I don't think there can be any mistake about it; I am sure they are the enemy.' 'Enemy!' I said; 'why, I have only just left them myself. Cease firing, sir; what is your name, sir?' '*My name is Colonel ——, of the —— Indiana; and pray, sir, who are you?*'

"Then for the first time I saw, to my astonishment, that he was a Yankee, and that I was in rear of a regiment of Yankees. Well, I saw that there was no hope but to brazen it out. My dark blouse and the increasing obscurity befriended me, so I approached quite close to him and shook my fist in his face, saying, 'I'll soon show you who I am, sir; cease firing, sir, at once.' I then turned my horse and cantered slowly down the line, shouting in an authoritative manner to the Yankees to cease firing. At the same time I experienced a disagreeable sensation, like screwing up my back, and calculating how many bullets would be between my shoulders every moment. I was afraid to increase my pace until I got to a small copse, when I put the spurs in and galloped back to my men. I immediately went up to the nearest colonel, and said to him, 'Colonel, I have reconnoitered those fellows pretty closely — and I find there is no mistake who they are; you may get up and go at them.' And I assure you, sir, that the slaughter of that Indiana regiment was the greatest I have ever seen in the war." *

It is evident to me that a certain degree of jealous feeling exists between the Tennessean and Virginian armies. This one claims to have had harder fighting than the Virginian army, and to have been opposed to the best troops and best generals of the North.

The Southerners generally appear to estimate highest the north-western Federal troops, which compose in a great degree the armies of Grant and Rosecrans. They come from the states of Ohio, Iowa, Indiana, &c. The Irish Federals are also respected for their fighting qualities; whilst the genuine Yankees and Germans (Dutch) are not much esteemed.[8]

I have been agreeably disappointed in the climate of Tennessee, which appears quite temperate to what I had expected.

4th June (Thursday) — Colonel Richmond rode with me to the outposts, in order to be present at the reconnaissance which was being conducted under the command of General Cheetham. We reached the field of operations at 2 P. M., and found that Martin's cavalry (dismounted) had advanced upon the enemy about three miles, and, after some brisk skirmishing, had driven in his outposts. The enemy showed about 2000 infantry, strongly posted,

---

* If these lines should ever meet the eyes of General Polk, I hope he will forgive me if I have made any error in recording his adventure.

his guns commanding the turnpike road. The Confederate infantry was concealed in the woods, about a mile in rear of the dismounted cavalry.

This being the position of affairs, Colonel Richmond and I rode along the road so far as it was safe to do so. We then dismounted and sneaked on in the wood alongside the road until we got to within 800 yards of the Yankees, whom we then reconnoitered leisurely with our glasses. We could only count about seventy infantry soldiers, with one fieldpiece in the wood at an angle of the road, and we saw several staff officers galloping about with orders.

Whilst we were thus engaged, some heavy firing and loud cheering suddenly commenced in the woods on our left. Fearing to be outflanked, we remounted and rode back to an open space, about 600 yards to the rear, where we found General Martin giving orders for the withdrawal of the cavalry horses in the front, and the retreat of the skirmishers.

It was very curious to see three hundred horses suddenly emerge from the wood just in front of us, where they had been hidden — one man to every four horses, riding one and leading the other three, which were tied together by the heads. In this order I saw them cross a cotton field at a smart trot, and take up a more secure position. Two or three men cantered about in the rear, flanking up the lead horses. They were shortly afterwards followed by the men of the regiment, retreating in skirmishing order under Colonel Webb, and they lined a fence parallel to us. The same thing went on on our right.

As the firing on our left still continued, my friends were in great hopes that Yankees might be inveigled on to follow the retreating skirmishers until they fell in with the two infantry brigades, which were lying in ambush for them. It was arranged, in that case, that some mounted Confederates should then get in their rear, and so capture a good number; but this simple and ingenious device was frustrated by the sulkiness of the enemy, who now stubbornly refused to advance any further.

The way in which the horses were managed was very pretty, and seemed to answer admirably for this sort of skirmishing. They were never far from the men, who could mount and be off to another part of the field with rapidity, or retire to take up another position, or act as cavalry as the case might require. Both the superior officers and the men behaved with the most complete coolness; and, whilst we were waiting in hopes of a Yankee advance, I heard the soldiers remarking that they "didn't like being done out of their good boots" — one of the principal objects in killing a Yankee being apparently to get hold of his valuable boots.

A tremendous row went on in the woods during this bushwhacking, and the trees got knocked about in all directions by shell; but I imagine that the actual slaughter in these skirmishes is very small, unless they get fairly at one another in the open cultivated spaces between the woods. I did not see or hear of anybody being killed today, although there were a few wounded and some horses killed. Colonel Richmond and Colonel Webb were much disappointed that the inactivity of the enemy prevented my seeing the skirmish assume large proportions, and General Cheatham said to me, "We should be very happy to see you, Colonel, when we are in our regular way of doing business."

After waiting in vain until 5 P. M., and seing no signs of anything more taking place, Colonel Richmond and I cantered back to Shelbyville. We were accompanied by a detachment of General Polk's bodyguard, which was composed of young men of good position in New Orleans. Most of them spoke in the French language, and nearly all had slaves in the field with them, although they ranked only as private soldiers, and had to perform the onerous duties of orderlies (or couriers, as they are called). On our way back we heard heavy firing on our left, from the direction in which General Withers was conducting his share of the reconnaissance with two other infantry brigades.

After dark, General Polk got a message from Cheatham, to say that the enemy had after all advanced in heavy force about 6:15 P. M., and obliged him to retire to Guy's Gap. We also heard that General Cleburne, who had advanced from Wartrace, had had his horse shot under him. The object of the reconnaissance seemed, therefore, to have been attained, for apparently the enemy was still in strong force at Murfreesboro, and manifested no intention of yielding it without a struggle.

I took leave of General Polk before I turned in. His kindness and hospitality have exceeded anything I could have expected. I shall always feel grateful to him on this account, and I shall never think of him without admiration for his character as a sincere patriot, a gallant soldier, and a perfect gentleman.

His aids-de-camp, Colonels Richmond and Yeatman, are also excellent types of the higher class of Southerner. Highly educated, wealthy, and prosperous before the war, they have abandoned all for their country. They, and all other Southern gentlemen of the same rank, are proud of their descent from Englishmen. They glory in speaking English as we do, and that their manners and feelings resemble those of the upper classes in the old country. No staff officers could perform their duties with more zeal and efficiency than these gentlemen, although they were not educated as soldiers.

Sam Houston. *"Sam Houston lived for several years amongst the Cherokee Indians, who used to call him 'the Raven' or the 'Big Drunk'"* (p. 59).

Gen. Joseph E. Johnston. *"He lives very plainly, and at present his only cooking utensils consisted of an old coffeepot and frying pan. There was only one fork (one prong deficient) between himself and staff, and this was handed to me ceremoniously as the 'guest'"* (p. 93).

Gen. T.J. "Stonewall" Jackson. *"It appears that previous to the war he [Jackson] was almost a monomaniac about his health. When he left the U.S. service, he was under the impression that one of his legs was getting shorter than the other"* (p. 105).

U.S. MILITARY BRIDGE OVER THE TENNESSEE AT CHATTANOOGA.

Federal engineers bridge the Tennessee River at Chattanooga. *"After leaving Chattanooga, the railroad winds alongside of the Tennessee River, the banks of which are high and beautifully covered with trees"* (p. 109).

Lt. Gen. Joseph Wheeler. *"In the evening I made the aquaintance of General Wheeler. He is a very little man, only twenty-six years of age, and was dressed in a coat much too big for him"* (p. 126).

Slave pen of Price, Birch & Co., Alexandria. *". . . A great deal of business is evidently done in buying and selling Negroes, for the papers are full of advertisements of slave auctions"* (pp. 142–143).

Fort Sumter interior. *"Fort Sumter now shows but little signs of the battering it underwent from the ironclads eight weeks ago"* (p. 144).

Judah P. Benjamin, Confederate Secretary of State. *"Mr. Benjamin told me that his property had lately been confiscated in New Orleans, and that his two sisters had been turned in to the streets there with only one trunk, which they had been forced to carry themselves"* (p. 166).

President Jefferson Davis. *"Mr. Jefferson Davis struck me as looking older than I expected. He is only fifty-six, but his face is emaciated and much wrinkled"* (p. 167).

Gen. John B. Hood. "*All are ragged and dirty, but full of good humor and confidence in themselves and in their general, Hood*" (p. 191).

Gen. George F. Pickett. "*General Pickett commands one of the divisions in Longstreet's corp. He wears his hair in long ringlets, and is altogether rather a desperate-looking character*" (p. 197).

Gettysburg Battlefield. *"The distance between the Confederate guns and the Yankee position—i.e., between the woods crowning the opposite ridges—was at least a mile—quite open, gently undulating, and exposed to artillery the whole distance"* (p. 210).

Gen. James Longstreet. *". . . Few of them knew General Longstreet, except by reputation. Numbers of them asked me whether the general in front was Longstreet; and when I answered in the affirmative, many would run on a hundred yards in order to take a good look at him"* (p. 202).

Gettysburg, PA. *"We could see the enemy retreating up one of the opposite ridges, pursued by the Confederates with loud yells"* (p. 203).

Barlow's Knoll after the first day of Gettysburg, July 1, 1863. *"At 3 p.m. we began to meet the wounded men coming to the rear, and the number of these soon increased most rapidly, some hobbling alone, others on stretchers carried by the ambulance corps, and others in the ambulance wagons"* (p. 202).

Trossel's House, Gettysburg Battlefield. *"I rode to the field with Colonel Manning, and went over that portion of the ground which, after a fierce contest, had been won. . . . The dead were being buried, but great numbers were still lying about"* (p. 209).

Jeb Stuart. *"He is commonly called Jeb Stuart, on account of his initials. He is a good and gallant soldier, though he sometimes incurs ridicule by his harmless affectation and peculiarities. The other day he rode through a Virginian town, his horse covered with garlands of roses"* (pp. 228–229).

CHAPTER 8

On to Charleston

Traveling with a Woman Soldier — At the Augusta Arsenal and Powder Plant — Arrival at Charleston — Inspecting Fort Sumter — Blockade Running — Missing a Dinner for Lack of Evening Clothes — The Proper Way to Capture Charleston — A Slave Auction Is Not Very Agreeable to an Englishman — Exciting New Submarine Inventions — I Call on General Beauregard — The Real Reason Why Beauregard's Hair Has Turned Gray — Leaving Charleston — The Disadvantage of the Ladies' Car Is the Constant Liability of Being Turned Out of One's Place for a Female

5th June (Friday) — I left Shelbyville at 6 A. M., after having been shaken hands with affectionately by Aaron, and arrived at Chattanooga at 4 P. M. As I was thus far under the protection of Lieutenant Donnelson, of General Polk's staff, I made this journey under more agreeable auspices than the last time. The scenery was really quite beautiful.

East Tennessee is said to contain many people who are more favorable to the North than to the South, and its inhabitants are now being conscripted by the Confederates; but they sometimes object to this operation, and, taking to the hills and woods, commence bushwhacking there.

I left Chattanooga for Atlanta at 4:30 P. M. The train was much crowded with wounded and sick soldiers returning on leave to their homes. A goodish-looking woman was pointed out to me in the cars as having served as a private soldier in the battles of Perry-ville and Murfreesboro. Several men in my car had served with her in a Louisianian regiment, and they said she had been turned out a short time since for her bad and immoral conduct. They told me that her sex was notorious to all the regiment, but no notice had been taken of it so long as she conducted herself prop-erly. They also said that she was not the only representative of the female sex in the ranks. When I saw her she wore a soldier's hat and coat, but had resumed her petticoats.[1]

6th June (Saturday) — Arrived at Atlanta at 3 A. M., and took three hours' sleep at the Trouthouse hotel. After breakfasting, I started again for Augusta at 7 A. M. (174 miles); but the train had not proceeded ten miles before it was brought up by an obstruc-tion, in the shape of a broken-down freight train, one of whose cars was completely smashed. This delayed us for about an hour, but we made up for it afterwards, and arrived at Augusta at 5:15 P. M.

The country through Georgia is undulating, well cultivated, and moderately covered with trees; and this part of the Confederacy has as yet suffered but little from the war. At some of the stations, provisions for the soldiers were brought into the cars by ladies, and distributed gratis. When I refused on the ground of not being a soldier, these ladies looked at me with great suspicion, mingled with contempt, and as their looks evidently expressed the words, "Then why are you not a soldier?" I was obliged to explain to them who I was, and show them General Bragg's pass, which as-tonished them not a little. I was told that Georgia was the only state in which soldiers were still so liberally treated — they have become so very common everywhere else.

On reaching Augusta, I put up at the Planters'-house hotel,

which seemed very luxurious to me after so many hours of the cars. But the Augusta climate is evidently much hotter than Tennessee.

7th June (Sunday) — Augusta is a city of 20,000 inhabitants; but its streets being extremely wide, and its houses low, it covers a vast space. No place that I have seen in the Southern States shows so little traces of the war, and it formed a delightful contrast to the war-worn, poverty-stricken, dried-up towns I had lately visited. I went to the Episcopal Church, and might almost have fancied myself in England. The ceremonies were exactly the same, and the church was full of well-dressed people.

At 2 P. M. I dined at the house of Mr. Carmichael, son-in-law to Bishop Elliott, who told me there were 2000 volunteers in Augusta, regularly drilled and prepared to resist raids. These men were exempted from the conscription, either on account of their age, nationality, or other cause — or had purchased substitutes.

At 3 P. M. Mr. Carmichael sent me in his buggy to call on Colonel Rains, the superintendent of the government works here. My principal object in stopping at Augusta was to visit the powder manufactory and arsenal; but, to my disappointment, I discovered that the present wants of the state did not render it necessary to keep these establishments open on Sundays.

I had a long and most interesting conversation with Colonel Rains, who is a very clever, highly educated, and agreeable officer. He was brought up at West Point, and after a short service in the United States Army, he became professor of chemistry at the Military College. He was afterwards much engaged in the manufacture of machinery in the Northern States. At the commencement of this war, with his usual perspicacity, President Davis selected Colonel Rains as the most competent person to build and to work the government factories at Augusta, giving him carte blanche to act as he thought best; and the result has proved the wisdom of the President's choice.[2]

Colonel Rains told me that at the beginning of the troubles, scarcely a grain of gunpowder was manufactured in the whole of the Southern States. The Augusta powder mills and arsenal were then commenced, and *no less than 7000 lbs. of powder are now made every day* in the powder manufactory. The cost to the government of making the powder is only four cents a pound. The saltpeter (nine tenths of which runs the blockade from England) cost formerly seventy-five cents, but has latterly been more expensive. In the construction of the powder mills, Colonel Rains told me he had been much indebted to a pamphlet by Major Bradley of Waltham Abbey.

At the cannon foundry, one Napoleon 12-pounder is turned out every two days; but it is hoped very soon that one of these guns may be finished daily. The guns are made of a metal recently invented by the Austrians, and recommended to the Confederate government by Mr. Mason. They are tested by a charge of ten pounds of powder, and by loading them to the muzzle with bolts. Two hundred excellent mechanics are exempted from the conscription, to be employed at the mills.

The wonderful speed with which these works have been constructed, their great success, and their immense national value are convincing proofs of the determined energy of the Southern character, now that it has been roused; and also of the zeal and skill of Colonel Rains. He told me that Augusta had been selected as a site for these works on account of its remoteness from the probable seats of war, of its central position, and of its great facilities of transport; for this city can boast of a navigable river and a canal, besides being situated on a central railroad.

Colonel Rains said, that although the Southerners had certainly been hard up for gunpowder at the early part of the war, they were still harder up for percussion caps. An immense number (I forget how many) of these are now made daily in the government factory at Atlanta.

I left Augusta at 7 P. M. by train for Charleston. My car was much crowded with Yankee prisoners.

8th June (Monday) — I arrived at Charleston at 5 A. M., and drove at once in an omnibus to the Charleston hotel. At nine o'clock I called at General Beauregard's office, but to my disappointment, I found that he was absent on a tour of inspection in Florida. He is, however, expected to return in two or three days.

I then called on General Ripley, who commands the garrison and forts of Charleston. He is a jovial character, very fond of the good things of this life; but it is said that he never allows this propensity to interfere with his military duties, in the performance of which he displays both zeal and talent. He has the reputation of being an excellent artillery officer, and although by birth a Northerner, he is a red-hot and indefatigable Rebel. I believe he wrote a book about the Mexican War, and after leaving the old army, he was a good deal in England, connected with the small-arms factory at Enfield, and other enterprises of the same sort. Nearly all the credit of the efficiency of the Charleston fortifications is due to him. And notwithstanding his Northern birth and occasional rollicking habits, he is generally popular.

I then called on Mr. Robertson, a merchant, for whom I had brought a letter of introduction from England. This old gentleman took me on a drive in his buggy at 6 P. M. It appears that at this time of year the country outside the city is quite pestilential, for when we reached the open, Mr. Robertson pointed to a detached house and said, "Now, I wouldn't sleep in that house for one night if you gave money to me for doing so."

I had intended to have visited Mr. Blake, an English gentleman for whom I had a letter, on his Combahee plantation, but Mr. Robertson implored me to abandon this idea. Mr. Robertson was full of the disasters which had resulted from a recent Yankee raid of the Combahee river. It appears that a vast amount of property had been destroyed and slaves carried off. This morning I saw a poor old planter in Mr. Robertson's office, who had been suddenly and totally ruined by this raid. The raiders consisted principally of Northern armed Negroes, and as they met nobody to resist them, they were able to effect their depredations with total impunity. It seems that a good deal of the land about Charleston belongs either to Blakes or Heywards. Mr. Blake lost thirty Negroes in the last raid, but he has lost since the beginning of the war about 150.

Mr. Robertson afterwards took me to see Mrs. ——, who is Mr. Walter Blake's daughter. To me, who had roughed it for ten weeks to such an extent, Charleston appeared most comfortable and luxurious. But its inhabitants must, to say the least, be suffering great inconvenience. The lighting and paving of the city had gone bad completely. Most of the shops were shut up. Those that were open contained but very few goods, and those were at famine prices. I tried to buy a black scarf, but I couldn't find such an article in all Charleston.

An immense amount of speculation in blockade running was going on, and a great deal of business is evidently done in buying and selling Negroes, for the papers are full of advertisements of slave auctions.

That portion of the city destroyed by the great fire presents the appearance of a vast wilderness in the very center of the town, no attempt having been made towards rebuilding it; this desert space looks like the Pompeians ruins, and extends, Mrs. Robertson says, for a mile in length by half a mile in width. Nearly all the distance between the Mills House hotel and Charleston hotel is in this desolate state. The fire began quite by accident, but the violent wind which suddenly arose rendered all attempts to stop the flames abortive.

The deserted state of the wharves is melancholy — the huge placards announcing lines of steamers to New York, New Orleans, and to different parts of the world, still remain, and give one an idea of what a busy scene they used to be. The people, however, all seem happy, contented, and determined. Both the great hotels are crowded; and well dressed, handsome ladies are plentiful. The fare is good, and the charge at the Charleston hotel is eight dollars a day.

9th June (Tuesday) — A Captain Feilden came to call upon me at 9 A. M. He is an Englishman, and formerly served in the 42d Highlanders. He is now in the Confederate Army, and is on the staff of General Beauregard's army. I remember his brother quite well at Sandhurst. Captain Feilden accompanied me to General Ripley's office, and at 12 o'clock the latter officer took us in his boat to inspect Fort Sumter. Our party consisted of an invalid General Davis, a Congressman named Nutt, Captain Feilden, the general, and myself.

We reached Fort Sumter after a pull of about three quarters of an hour.* This now celebrated fort is a pentagonal work built of red brick. It has two tiers of casemates, besides a heavy barbette battery. Its walls are twelve feet thick at the piers, and six feet thick at the embrasures. It rises sheer out of the water, and is apparently situated in the center of the bay, but on its side towards James Island the water is extremely shallow.

It mounts sixty-eight guns, of a motley but efficient description. Ten-inch columbiads predominate, and are perhaps the most useful. They weigh 14,000 lb. (125 cwt.), throw a solid shot weighing 128 lb., and are made to traverse with the greatest ease by means of Yates's system of cogwheels. There are also eight-inch columbiads, rifled forty-two pounders, and Brook guns to throw flat-headed projectiles (General Ripley told me that these Brook guns, about which so much is said, differ but little from the Blakely cannon). Also, there are Parrot guns and Dahlgrens; in fact, a general assortment of every species of ordnance except Whitworths and Armstrongs. But the best gun in the fort is a fine new eleven-inch gun, which had just been fished up from the wreck of the Keokuk; the sister gun from the same wreck is at ——.

The garrison consists of 350 enlisted soldiers under Colonel Rhett. They are called Confederate States regulars, and certainly they saluted in a more soldierlike way than the ordinary volunteers. A great proportion of them are foreigners.

Fort Sumter now shows but little signs of the battering it underwent from the ironclads eight weeks ago.[3] The two faces exposed to fire have been patched up so that large pieces of masonry have a newer appearance than the mass of the building. The guns

* As Fort Sumter must be in a very different state now to what it was when I saw it, I think there can be no harm in describing the fort as it then stood. — Nov., 1863.

[144]

have been removed from the casemates on the eastern face, and the lower tier of casemates has been filled up with earth to give extra strength, and prevent the balls from coming right through into the interior of the work, which happened at the last attack. There is consequently a deep hole in the parade inside Fort Sumter, from which the earth had been taken to fill up these casemates.

The angles of Sumter are being strengthened outside by stone buttresses. Some of the cheeks of the upper embrasures have been faced with blocks of iron three feet long, eight inches thick, and twelve inches wide. I saw the effect of a heavy shot on one of these blocks which had been knocked right away, and had fallen in two pieces on the rocks below, but it had certainly saved the embrasure from further injury that time. I saw some solid fifteen-inch shot which had been fired by the enemy: they weigh 425 lb. I was told that several fifteen-inch shell had stuck in the walls and burst there, tearing away great flakes of masonry, and making holes two feet deep at the extreme.

None of the ironclads would approach nearer than nine hundred yards, and the *Keokuk*, which was the only one that came thus close, got out of order in five minutes, and was completely disabled in a quarter of an hour. She sank on the following morning. Solid ten-inch shot and seven-inch flat-heads were used upon her. Ripley said he would give a great deal for some more eleven-inch guns, but he can't get them except by such chances as the *Keokuk*.

The fight only lasted two hours and twenty-five minutes. Fort Sumter bore nearly the whole weight of the attack, assisted in a slight degree by Moultrie. Only one man was killed, which was caused by the fall of the flagstaff. The Confederates were unable to believe until some time afterwards the real amount of the damage they had inflicted. Nor did they discover until next day that the affair was a serious attack, and not a reconnaissance. General Ripley spoke with the greatest confidence of being able to repulse any other attack of the same sort.

Colonel Rhett, the commandant, entertained us with luncheon in one of the casemates. He is a handsome and agreeable man, besides being a zealous officer. He told me that one of the most efficient of his subordinates was Captain Mitchell, son of the so-called Irish patriot, who is editor of one of the Richmond newspapers.

From the summit of Fort Sumter a good general view is obtained of the harbor, and of the fortifications commanding the approach to Charleston. Castle Pinckney and Fort Sumter are two old masonry works built on islands — Pinckney being much closer to the city than Sumter. Between them is Fort Ripley, which mounts —— heavy guns. Moultrieville, with its numerous forts, called Battery Bee, Fort Moultrie, Fort Beauregard, &c. is on Sullivan's Island, one mile distant from Fort Sumter. There are excellent arrangements of ——, and other contrivances, to foul the screw of a vessel between Sumter and Moultrie. On the other side of Fort Sumter is Fort Johnson, on James Island, Fort Cummins Point, and Fort Wagner, on Morris Island. In fact, both sides of the harbor for several miles appear to bristle with forts mounting heavy guns.

The bar, beyond which we counted thirteen blockaders, is nine miles from the city. Sumter is three and a half miles from the city. Two or three thousand Yankees are now supposed to be on Folly Island, which is next beyond Morris Island, and in a day or two they are to be shelled from the Confederate batteries on Morris

Island. The new Confederate flag, which bears a strong resemblance to the British white ensign, was flying from most of the forts.

In returning we passed several blockade runners, amongst others the steamer *Kate*, with the new double screw.[4] These vessels are painted the same color as the water. As many as three or four often go in and out with impunity during one night; but they never attempt it except in cloudy weather. They are very seldom captured, and charge an enormous price for passengers and freight. It is doubtful whether the traffic of the private blockade runners doesn't do more harm than good to the country by depreciating its currency, and they are generally looked upon as regular gambling speculations. I have met many persons who are of opinion that the trade ought to be stopped, except for government stores and articles necessary for the public welfare.

After we had landed, Captain Feilden took me on board one of the new ironclads which are being built, and which are supposed to be a great improvement upon the *Chicora* and *Palmetto State*. These are already afloat, and did good service last February by issuing suddenly forth, and driving away the whole blockading squadron for one day. Last night these two active little vessels were out to look after some blockaders which were supposed to have ventured inside the bar.

At 5 P. M. I dined with General and Mrs. Ripley. The dinner was a very sumptuous one for a "blockade" dinner, as General Ripley called it. The other guests were General Jordan, Chief of the Staff to Beauregard; General Davis, Mr. Nutt, and Colonel Rhett, of Fort Sumter. The latter told me that if the ironclads had come any closer than they did, he should have dosed them with flat-headed bolts out of the smooth-bore guns, which, he thinks, could travel accurately enough for 500 or 600 yards. Mrs. H—— asked me to an evening party, but the extreme badness of my clothes compelled me to decline the invitation.

10th June (Wednesday) — I dined with Mr. and Mrs. H—— this afternoon, and after dinner they drove me to the Battery, which is the popular promenade. A great many well-dressed people and a few carriages were there, but the H——s say it is nothing to what it was. Most of the horses and carriages have been sent out of Charleston since the last attack. Mrs. H—— told me all the ladies began to move out of Charleston on the morning after the repulse of the *Monitors*, the impression being that the serious attack was about to begin. I talked to her about the smart costumes of the Negro women on Sundays. She said the only difference between them and their mistresses is that a mulatto woman is not allowed to wear a veil.

11th June (Thursday) — General Ripley took me in his boat to Morris Island. We passed Fort Sumter on our left, and got aground for five minutes in its immediate neighborhood; then bearing off towards the right, we passed Fort Cummings Point, and (after entering a narrow creek) Fort Wagner on our left. The latter is a powerful, well-constructed fieldwork, mounting nine heavy guns, and it completely cuts across Morris Island at the end nearest to Fort Sumter. General Ripley pointed at Fort Wagner with some pride.

We landed near the house of the colonel who commanded the troops in Morris Island,* and borrowed his horses to ride to the

---

* This must have been about the spot from whence Fort Sumter was afterwards bombarded. I cannot help thinking that the Confederates made a great

further extremity of the island. We passed the wreck of the *Keo-kuk*, whose turret was just visible above the water, at a distance from the shore of about 1500 yards.

On this beach I also inspected the remains of the so-called *Yankee Devil*, a curious construction, which on the day of the attack had been pushed into the harbor by one of the *Monitors*. This vessel, with her appendage, happened to be the first to receive the fire of Fort Sumter, and after a quarter of an hour *Monitor* and *Devil* got foul of one another, when both came to grief, and the latter floated harmlessly ashore. It seems to have been composed of double twenty-inch beams, forming a sort of platform or stage fifty feet long by twenty broad, from which depended chains with grappling irons to rake up hostile torpedoes. The machine was also provided with a gigantic torpedo of its own, which was to blow up piles or other obstacles.

Morris Island is a miserable, low, sandy desert, and at its further extremity there is a range of low sand hills, which form admirable natural parapets. About ten guns and mortars were placed behind them, and two companies of regular artillery were stationed at this point under the command of Captain Mitchell (the "patriot's" son), to whom I was introduced. He seemed a quiet, unassuming man, and was spoken of by General Ripley as an excellent officer. He told me he expected to be able to open fire in a day or two upon the Yankees in Folly Island and Little Folly. He expressed a hope that a few shell might drive them out from Little Folly, which is only distant 600 yards from his guns. The enemy's large batteries are on Folly Island, 3400 yards off, but within range of

mistake in not fortifying the further end of Morris Island and keeping a larger garrison there, for when the Federals landed, they met with no fortification until they reached Fort Wagner.

Captain Mitchell's rifled artillery, one of which was a twelve-pounder Whitworth.

A blockade runner, named the *Ruby*, deceived by some lights on Folly Island, ran ashore at one o'clock this morning in the narrow inlet between Morris Island and Little Folly. The Yankees immediately opened fire on her, and her crew, despairing of getting her off, set her on fire — a foolish measure, as she was right under Captain Mitchell's guns — and whenever a group of Yankees approached the wreck, a shell was placed in their midst, which effectually checked their curiosity. The *Ruby* was therefore burning in peace. Her crew had escaped, all except one man, who was drowned in trying to save a valuable trunk.

After having conversed some time with Captain Mitchell and his brother officers, we took leave of them; and General Ripley, pursuing his tour of inspection, took me up some of the numerous creeks which intersect the low marshy land of James Island. In one of these I saw the shattered remains of the sham *Keokuk*, which was a wooden imitation of its equally short-lived original, and had been used as a floating target by the different forts.

In passing Fort Sumter, I observed that the eastern face, from which the guns (except those *en barbette*) had been removed, was being further strengthened by a facing of twelve feet of sand, supported by logs of wood. There can be no doubt that Sumter could be destroyed, if a vessel could be found impervious enough to lie pretty close in and batter it for five hours; but with its heavy armament and plunging fire, this catastrophe was not deemed probable.

General Ripley told me that, in his opinion, the proper manner to attack Charleston was to land on Morris Island, take Forts Wagner and Cummings Point, and then turn their guns on Fort Sumter.[5]

He does not think much of the 15-inch guns. The enemy does not dare use more than 35 lbs. of powder to propel 425 lbs. of iron; the velocity consequently is very trifling. He knows and admires the British 68-pounder, weighing 95 cwt., but he does not think it heavy enough effectually to destroy ironclads. He considers the 11-inch gun, throwing a shot of 170 lbs., as the most efficient for that purpose.

In returning from Morris Island, we passed two steamers, which had successfully run the blockade last night, besides the luckless *Ruby*, which had also passed the blockading squadron before she came to grief. The names of the other two are the *Anaconda* and *Racoon*, both fine-looking vessels.

I dined at Mr. Robertson's, at the corner of Rutledge Street, and met Captain Tucker of the navy there. He is a very good fellow, and a perfect gentleman. He commands the *Chicora* gunboat, and it was he who, with his own and another gunboat (*Palmetto State*), crossed the bar last February, and raised the blockade for a few hours. He told me that several Yankee blockaders surrendered, but could not be taken possession of, and the others bolted at such a pace as to render pursuit hopeless, for these little gunboats are very slow. They made the attack at daylight, and though much fired at were never struck. They seem to have taken the Yankees by surprise, and to have created great alarm; but at that time the blockading squadron consisted entirely of improvised men-of-war. Since this exploit, the frigate *Ironsides*, and the sloop of war *Powhatan* have been added to its strength.

It poured with rain during the evening, and we had a violent thunderstorm. General Beauregard returned to Charleston this afternoon.

*　　*　　*

12th June (Friday) — I called at an exchange office this morning, and asked the value of gold; they offered me six to one for it.

I went to a slave auction at 11; but they had been so quick about it that the whole affair was over before I arrived, although I was only ten minutes late. The Negroes — about fifteen men, three women, and three children — were seated on benches, looking perfectly contented and indifferent. I saw the buyers opening the mouths and showing the teeth of their new purchases to their friends in a very businesslike manner. This was certainly not a very agreeable spectacle to an Englishman, and I know that many Southerners participate in the same feeling; for I have often been told by people that they had never seen a Negro sold by auction, and never wished to do so.

It is impossible to mention names in connection with such a subject, but I am perfectly aware that many influential men in the South feel humiliated and annoyed with several of the incidents connected with slavery. And I think that if the Confederate States were *left alone*, the system would be much modified and amended, although complete emancipation cannot be expected; for the Southerners believe it to be as impracticable to cultivate cotton on a large scale in the South, without forced black labor, as the British have found it to produce sugar in Jamaica. They declare that the example the English have set them of sudden emancipation in that island is by no means encouraging. They say that that magnificent colony, formerly so wealthy and prosperous, is now nearly valueless — the land going out of cultivation — the whites ruined — the blacks idle, slothful, and supposed to be in a great measure relapsing into their primitive barbarism.

At twelve o'clock I called by appointment on Captain Tucker,

on board the *Chicora*.* The accommodation below is good, considering the nature and peculiar shape of the vessel; but in hot
weather the quarters are very close and unhealthy. For this reason
she is moored alongside a wharf, on which her crew live. Captain
Tucker expressed great confidence in his vessel during calm
weather, and when not exposed to a plunging fire. He said he
should not hesitate to attack even the present blockading squadron, if it were not for certain reasons which he explained to me.

Captain Tucker expects great results from certain newly invented submarine inventions, which he thinks are sure to succeed.[6]
He told me that in the April attack these two gunboats were
placed in the rear of Fort Sumter, and if, as was anticipated, the
Monitors had managed to force their way past Sumter, they
would have been received from different directions by the powerful
battery *Bee* on Sullivan's Island, by this island, Forts Pinckney and
Ripley, by the two gunboats, and by Fort Johnson on James
Island — a nest of hornets from which perhaps they would never
have returned.

At 1 P. M. I called on General Beauregard, who is a man of
middle height, about forty-seven years of age. He would be very
youthful in appearance were it not for the color of his hair, which
is much grayer than his earlier photographs represent. Some persons account for the sudden manner in which his hair turned
gray by allusions to his cares and anxieties during the last two
years. The real and less romantic reason is to be found in the
rigidity of the Yankee blockade, which interrupts the arrival of
articles of toilet. He has a long straight nose, handsome brown
eyes, and a dark mustache without whiskers, and his manners are

* I have omitted a description of this little gunboat, as she is still doing
good service in Charleston harbor — November, 1863.

extremely polite. He is a New Orleans Creole, and French is his native language.[7]

He was extremely civil to me, and arranged that I should see some of the land fortifications tomorrow. He spoke to me of the inevitable necessity, sooner or later, of a war between the Northern States and Great Britain; and he remarked that if England would join the South at once, the Southern armies, relieved of the present blockade and enormous Yankee pressure, would be able to march right into the Northern States, and, by occupying their principal cities, would give the Yankees so much employment that they would be unable to spare many men for Canada.

He acknowledged that in Mississippi, General Grant had displayed uncommon vigor, and met with considerable success, considering that he was a man of no great military capacity. He said that Johnston was certainly acting slowly and with much caution; but then he had not the veteran troops of Bragg or Lee.

He told me that he (Beauregard) had organized both the Virginian and Tennessean armies. Both are composed of the same materials, both have seen much service, though, on the whole, the first had been the most severely tried. He said that in the Confederate organization a brigade is composed of four regiments, a division ought to number 10,000 men, and a *corps d'armée* 40,000. But I know that neither Polk nor Hardee have got anything like that number.*

At 5:30 P. M. the firing on Morris Island became distinctly audible. Captain Mitchell had evidently commenced his operations against Little Folly.

While I was walking on the battery this evening, a gentleman

---

* A division does nearly always number 10,000 men, but then there are generals in Longstreet's *corps d'armée*.

came up to me and recalled himself to me as Mr. Meyers, of the Sumter, whom I had known at Gibraltar a year ago. This was one of the two persons who were arrested at Tangier by the Acting United States Consul in such an outrageous manner. He told me that he had been kept in irons during his whole voyage in the merchant vessel to the United States; and in spite of the total illegality of his capture on neutral ground, he was imprisoned for four months in Fort Warren, and not released until regularly exchanged as a prisoner of war. Mr. Meyers was now most anxious to rejoin Captain Semmes, or some other rover.

I understand that when the attack took place in April, the garrison of Fort Sumter received the *Monitors* with great courtesy as they steamed up. The three flagstaffs were dressed with flags, the band from the top of the fort played the national airs, and a salute of twenty-one guns was fired, after which the entertainment provided was of a more solid description.

13*th June* (Saturday) — Colonel Rice, aid-de-camp to General Beauregard, rode with me to Secessionville this morning. I was mounted on the horse which the general rode at Manassas and Shiloh. We reached James Island by crossing the long wooden bridge which spans the river Ashley. The land of James Island is low and marshy, and is both by repute and in appearance most unhealthy. Three years ago no white men would have dreamed of occupying it at this time of year; but now that the necessity has arisen, the troops, curiously enough, do not appear to suffer.

Secessionville, the most advanced and most important of the James Island fortifications, is distant by road eight miles from Charleston bridge, with which it is connected by a chain of forts. It was surprised by the enemy just a year ago (June, 1862), and was the scene of a desperate conflict, which resulted in the repulse of the Federals with a loss of nearly 800 men. The Confederates lost 150 men on this occasion, which as yet has been the only serious loss of life at Charleston during the war. Colonel Lamar, who commanded the garrison with great gallantry, was one of the few victims to yellow fever last year.

The Yankees attacked the fort three times with much bravery and determination, and actually reached the superior slope of the parapet before they were driven back. They were within an ace of being successful; and although they deserved great credit for their behavior on that occasion, yet it is understood that the officer who organized the attack has either been dismissed from the service or otherwise punished.

Lieutenant Colonel Brown, the commandant, who showed me over the fort and bombproofs, is quite young, full of zeal, and most anxious to be attacked. He has —— artillerymen to man this and the neighboring works, and two regiments of infantry are also encamped within a short distance.

At the time of the attack on Charleston last April, there were 30,000 men to defend it; since that time 20,000 had been sent into Mississippi to reinforce Johnston. I imagine that, as the fortifications are so very extensive, the Charleston garrison ought to consist of at least 30,000 men.

14*th June* (Sunday) — I went to church at St. Michael's, which is one of the oldest churches in America, and is supposed to have been built a hundred and fifty years ago. The Charlestonians are very proud of it, and I saw several monuments of the time of the British dominion.

This morning I made the acquaintance of a Mr. Sennec, an

officer in the Confederate States Navy. With his wife and daughter, he was about to face the terrors and dangers of running the blockade, having got an appointment in Europe. The ladies told me they had already made one start, but after reaching the bar, the night was not considered propitious, so they had returned. Mr. Sennec is thinking of going to Wilmington, and running from thence, as it is more secure than Charleston.

I dined at Mr. Robertson's this evening, and met a very agreeable party there — two young ladies, who were extremely pretty, General Beauregard, Captain Tucker, of the *Chicora*, and Major Norris, the chief of the secret intelligence bureau at Richmond.

I had a long conversation with General Beauregard, who said he considered the question of ironclads *versus* forts as settled, especially when the fire from the latter is plunging. If the other *Monitors* had approached as close as the *Keokuk*, they would probably have shared her fate. He thought that both flat-headed rifled 7-inch bolts and solid 10-inch balls penetrated the ironclads when within 1200 yards. He agreed with General Ripley that the 15-inch gun is rather a failure; it is so unwieldy that it can only be fired very slowly, and the velocity of the ball is so small that it is very difficult to strike a moving object.

He told me that Fort Sumter was to be covered by degrees with the long green moss which in this country hangs down from the trees: he thinks that when this is pressed it will deaden the effect of the shot without being inflammable; and he also said that, even if the walls of Fort Sumter were battered down, the barbette battery would still remain, supported on the piers.

The Federal frigate *Ironsides* took up her position, during the attack, over 3000 lbs. of powder, which was prevented from exploding owing to some misfortune connected with the communicating wire. General Beauregard and Captain Tucker both seemed to expect great things from a newly invented and extradiabolical torpedo ram.

After dinner, Major Norris showed us a copy of a New York illustrated newspaper of the same character as our *Punch*. In it President Davis and General Beauregard were depicted shoeless and in rags, contemplating a pair of boots, which the latter suggested had better be eaten. This caricature excited considerable amusement, especially when its merits were discussed after Mr. Robertson's excellent dinner. General Beauregard told me he had been educated in the North, and used to have many friends there, but that *now* he would sooner submit to the Emperor of China than return to the Union.

Mr. Walter Blake arrived soon after dinner. He had come up from his plantation on the Combahee River on purpose to see me. He described the results of the late Yankee raid up that river. Forty armed Negroes and a few whites in a miserable steamer were able to destroy and burn an incalculable amount of property, and carry off hundreds of Negroes.

Mr. Blake got off very cheap, having only lost twenty-four this time, but he only saved the remainder by his own personal exertions and determination. He had now sent all his young males two hundred miles into the interior for greater safety. He seemed to have a very rough time of it, living all alone in that pestilential climate. A neighboring planter, Mr. Lowndes, had lost 290 Negroes, and a Mr. Kirkland was totally ruined.

At 7 P. M. Mr. Blake and I called at the office of General Ripley, to whom Mr. Blake, notwithstanding that he is an Englishman of nearly sixty years of age, had served as aid-de-camp during some of the former operations against Charleston. General Ripley told us that shelling was still going on vigorously between Morris and Folly Islands, the Yankees being assisted every now and then by one or more of their gunboats. The General explained to us that these light-draft armed vessels — *river-gropers*, as he called them — were indefatigable at pushing up the numerous creeks, burning and devastating everything. He said that when he became acquainted with the habits of one of these "critturs," he arranged an ambuscade for her, and with the assistance of "his fancy Irishman" (Captain Mitchell), he captured her. This was the case with the steamer *Stono*, but having been caught in this manner by the army, it was lost by the navy shortly afterwards off Sullivan's Island.

News has just been received that Commodore Foote is to succeed Dupont in the command of the blockading squadron. Most of these officers appeared to rejoice in this change, as they say Foote is younger, and likely to show more sport than the venerable Dupont.

15th June (Monday) — I called on General Beauregard to say good-by. Before parting, he told me that his official orders, both from the government and from the town council, were, that he was to allow Charleston to be laid in ashes sooner than surrender it. The Confederates were unanimous in their determination that, whatever happened, the capital of South Carolina should never have to submit to the fate of New Orleans. But General Beauregard did not at all anticipate that such an alternative was imminent.

In answer to my thanks for his kindness and courtesy, he said that the more Europeans that came to the South, the more the Southerners were pleased, as *seeing* was the only way to remove many prejudices. He declared everything here was open and above board, and I really believe this is the case. Most certainly the civil law is not overruled by the military, except in cases of the strongest emergency. The press is allowed the most unlimited freedom, and even license. Whenever excesses take place, and the law is violated, this is caused by the violence of the people themselves, who take the law into their own hands. General Beauregard sent his love to Sir James Fergusson, who had visited him during the early part of the war; so also did General Jordan, Chief of the Staff.

Before taking my departure from the hotel, I was much gratified by meeting M'Carthy, who had just returned from Richmond. He had had the good fortune to cross the Mississippi a little later than me, and he had encountered comparatively few obstacles.

I left Charleston by rail at 2 P. M., in company with Mr. Sennec, his wife, and daughter; and Major Norris, who was extremely kind and useful to me. I declined traveling in the ladies' car, although offered that privilege — the advantage of a small amount of extra cleanliness being outweighed by the screaming of the children, and the constant liability of being turned out of one's place for a female.

Major Norris told me many amusing anecdotes connected with the secret intelligence department, and of the numerous ingenious methods for communicating with the Southern partisans on the other side of the Potomac.

We reached Florence at 9 P. M., where we were detained for some time owing to a breakdown of another train. We then fought our way into some desperately crowded cars, and continued our journey throughout the night.

CHAPTER 9

Charleston to Richmond

Blockade Running As a Product of British Energy and Enterprise — Miss Sennec Is Too Pretty to Risk Collision with a Shell — Another Terrific Fight for a Train Seat — Through the Richmond Defenses — A Talk with Judah Benjamin — A Plea for British Recognition — Visiting Jefferson Davis — "Maine Will Probably Try to Join Canada" — Calling on the Secretary of War — More Executions and Reprisals — Many Richmond Papers Seem Scarcely More Respectable than the New York Ones.

16th June (Tuesday) — Arrived at Wilmington at 5 A. M., and crossed the river there in a steamer. This river was quite full of blockade runners. I counted eight large steamers, all handsome leaden-colored vessels, which ply their trade with the greatest regularity. Half these ships were engaged in carrying goods on government account; and I was told that the quantity of boots, clothing, saltpeter, lead, and tin, which they bring into the country, is very great. I cannot suppose that in ordinary times there would be anything like such a trade as this, at a little place like Wilmington, which shows the absurdity of calling the blockade an efficient one.

This blockade running is an extraordinary instance of British energy and enterprise. When I was at Charleston, I asked Mr. Robertson whether any French vessels had run the blockade. In reply he told me it was a very peculiar fact that "one of the partners of Fraser & Co., being a Frenchman, was extremely anxious to engage a French vessel in the trade. Expense was no object; the ship and the cargo were forthcoming. Nothing was wanted but a French captain and a French crew (to make the ship legally French); but although any amount of money was offered as an inducement, they were not to be found, and this obstacle was insurmountable." Not the slightest difficulty is experienced at Liverpool in officering and manning any number of ships for this purpose.

Major Norris went to call upon Mr. Vallandigham, whom he had escorted to Wilmington as a sort of semi-prisoner some days ago. Mr. Vallandigham was in bed. He told Major Norris that he intended to run the blockade this evening for Bermuda, from whence he should find his way to the Clifton Hotel, Canada, where he intended to publish a newspaper, and agitate Ohio across the frontier. Major Norris found him much elated by the news of his having been nominated for the governorship of Ohio; and he declared if he was duly elected, his state could dictate peace.

In traveling through the country to Wilmington, these two used to converse much on politics; and Major Norris once said to him, "Now, from what you have seen and heard in your journey through the South, you must know that a reconstruction of the old Union, under any circumstances, is utterly impossible." Vallandigham replied, "Well, all I can say is, I *hope*, and at all events I know, that my scheme of a suspension of hostilities is the only one which has any prospect of ultimate success." *

At Wilmington I took leave with regret of Mr. Sennec and his

---

* I have often heard Southerners speak of this proposal of Vallandigham's as *most insidious* and dangerous; but the opinion now is that things have gone too far to permit reunion under any circumstances.

family, who were also to run the blockade this evening. Miss Sennec is much too pretty to risk a collision with a fragment of a shell. But here no one seems to think anything of the risk of passing through the Yankee fleet, as the "runners," though often fired at, are very seldom hit or captured, and their captains are becoming more and more knowing every day. I was obliged to go to the provost-marshal's office to get Beauregard's pass renewed there, as North Carolina is out of his district. In doing so I very nearly missed the train.

I left Wilmington at 7 A. M. The weather was very hot and oppressive, and the cars dreadfully crowded all day. The luxuries of Charleston had also spoiled me for the "road." I could no longer appreciate at their proper value the "hog and hominy" meals which I had been so thankful for in Texas; but I found Major Norris a very agreeable and instructive companion. We changed cars again at Weldon, where I had a terrific fight for a seat, but I succeeded. Experience had made me very quick at this sort of business. I always carry my saddlebags and knapsack with me into the car.

17th June (Wednesday) — We reached Petersburg at 3 A. M., and had to get out and traverse this town in carts, after which we had to lie down in the road until some other cars were opened. We left Petersburg at 5 A. M. and arrived at Richmond at 7 A. M., having taken forty-one hours coming from Charleston.

The railroad between Petersburg and Richmond is protected by extensive fieldworks, and the woods have been cut down to give range. An irruption of the enemy in this direction has evidently been contemplated; and we met a brigade of infantry halfway between Petersburg and Richmond on its way to garrison the latter place, as the Yankees are reported to be menacing in that neighborhood.

The scenery near Richmond is very pretty, and rather English-looking. The view of the James River from the railway bridge is quite beautiful, though the water is rather low at present. The weather was extremely hot and oppressive, and, for the first time since I left Havana, I really suffered from the heat.

At 10 A. M. I called on General Cooper, Adjutant General to the Confederate forces, and senior general in the army. He is brother-in-law to Mr. Mason, the Southern Commissioner in London. I then called upon Mr. Benjamin, the Secretary of State, who made an appointment with me to meet him at his house at 7 P. M.

The public offices are handsome stone buildings, and seem to be well arranged for business. I found at least as much difficulty in gaining access to the great men as there would be in European countries; but when once admitted, I was treated with the greatest courtesy. The anterooms were crowded with people patiently waiting for an audience. The streets of Richmond are named and numbered in a most puzzling manner, and the greater part of the houses are not numbered at all. It is the most hilly city I have ever seen in America, and its population is unnaturally swollen since the commencement of the war.

The fact of there being abundance of ice appeared to me an immense luxury, as I had never seen any before in the South; but it seems that the winters are quite severe in Northern Virginia.

I was sorry to hear in the highest quarters the gloomiest forebodings with regard to the fate of Vicksburg. This fortress is in fact *given up*, and all now despair of General Johnston's being able to effect anything towards its relief.

I kept my appointment with Mr. Benjamin at 7 o'clock. He is

a stout dapper little man, evidently of Hebrew extraction, and of undoubted talent. He is a Louisianian, and was senator for that state in the old United States Congress, and I believe he is accounted a very clever lawyer and a brilliant orator. He told me that he had filled the onerous post of Secretary of War during the first seven months of the secession, and I can easily believe that he found it no sinecure.[1]

We conversed for a long time about the origin of secession, which he indignantly denied was brought about, as the Yankees assert, by the interested machinations of individuals. He declared that, for the last ten years, the Southern statesmen had openly stated in Congress what would take place; but the Northerners never would believe they were in earnest, and had often replied by the taunt, "The South was so bound to, and dependent on the North, that *she couldn't be kicked out of the Union.*"

He said that the Southern armies had always been immensely outnumbered in all their battles, and that until recently General Lee could never muster more than 60,000 effective men. He confessed that the Southern forces consisted altogether of about 350,000 to 400,000 men. When I asked him where they all were, he replied that, on account of the enormous tract of country to be defended, and the immense advantages the enemy possessed by his facilities for sea and river transportation, the South was obliged to keep large bodies of men unemployed, and at great distances from each other, awaiting the sudden invasions or raids to which they were continually exposed. Besides which, the Northern troops, which numbered (he supposed) 600,000 men, having had as yet but little defensive warfare, could all be employed for aggressive purposes.

He asserted that England had still, and had always had it in her power to terminate the war by recognition, and by making a commercial treaty with the South. He denied that the Yankees really would dare to go to war with Great Britain for doing so, however much they might swagger about it. He said that recognition would not increase the Yankee hatred of England, for this, whether just or unjust, was already as intense as it could possibly be.

I then alluded to the supposed ease with which they could overrun Canada, and to the temptation which its unprotected towns must offer to the large numbers of Irish and German mercenaries in the Northern armies. He answered, "They probably could not do that as easily as some people suppose, and they know perfectly well that you could deprive them of California (a far more serious loss) with much greater ease." This consideration, together with the certainty of an entire blockade of their ports, the total destruction of their trade, and an invasion on a large scale by the Southern troops, in reality prevents the possibilty of their declaring war upon England at the present time, any more than they did at the period of their great national humiliation in the Mason-Slidell affair.[2]

Mr. Benjamin told me that his property had lately been confiscated in New Orleans, and that his two sisters had been turned, neck and crop, into the streets there with only one trunk, which they had been forced to carry themselves. Every one was afraid to give them shelter, except an Englishwoman, who protected them until they could get out of the city.

Talking of the just admiration which the English newspapers accorded to "Stonewall" Jackson, he expressed, however, his astonishment that they should have praised so highly his strategic skill in outmaneuvering Pope at Manassas, and Hooker at Chancellorsville, totally ignoring that in both cases the movements were planned and ordered by General Lee, for whom (Mr. Benjamin said) Jackson had the most "childlike reverence."

Mr. Benjamin complained of Mr. Russell of *The Times* for holding him up to fame as a "gambler" — a story which he understood Mr. Russell had learnt from Mr. Charles Sumner at Washington. But even supposing that this was really the case, Mr. Benjamin was of opinion that such a revelation of his private life was in extremely bad taste, after Mr. Russell had partaken of his (Mr. Benjamin's) hospitality at Montgomery.[8]

He said the Confederates were more amused than annoyed at the term "Rebel," which was so constantly applied to them. But he wished mildly to remark that in order to be a "Rebel," a person must rebel against some one who has a right to govern him; and he thought it would be very difficult to discover such a right as existing in the Northern over the Southern States.

In order to prepare a treaty of peace, he said, "It would only be necessary to write on a blank sheet of paper the words 'self-government.' Let the Yankees accord that, and they might fill up the paper in any manner they chose. We don't want any state that doesn't want us; but we only wish that each state should decide fairly upon its own destiny. All we are struggling for is to be let alone."

At 8 P. M. Mr. Benjamin walked with me to the President's dwelling, which is a private house at the other end of the town. I had tea there, and uncommonly good tea, too — the first I had tasted in the Confederacy. Mrs. Davis was unfortunately unwell and unable to see me.

Mr. Jefferson Davis struck me as looking older than I expected. He is only fifty-six, but his face is emaciated and much wrinkled.

He is nearly six feet high, but is extremely thin and stoops a little. His features are good, especially his eye, which is very bright and full of life and humor. I was afterwards told he had lost the sight of his left eye from a recent illness. He wore a linen coat and gray trousers, and he looked what he evidently is, a well-bred gentleman. Nothing can exceed the charm of his manner, which is simple, easy, and most fascinating.[4]

He conversed with me for a long time, and agreed with Benjamin that the Yankees did not really intend to go to war with England if she recognized the South. He said that, when the inevitable smash came — and separation was an accomplished fact — the state of Maine would probably try to join Canada, as most of the intelligent people in that state have a horror of being "under the thumb of Massachusetts." He added, that Maine was inhabited by a hardy, thrifty, seafaring population, with different ideas to the people in the other New England states.

When I spoke to him of the wretched scenes I had witnessed in his own state (Mississippi), and of the miserable, almost desperate, situation in which I had found so many unfortunate women, who had been left behind by their male relations; and when I alluded in admiration to the quiet, calm, uncomplaining manner in which they bore their sufferings and their grief, he said with much feeling that he always considered *silent despair* the most painful description of misery to witness, in the same way that he thought *mute insanity* was the most awful form of madness.

He spoke to me of Grenfell, who, he said, seemed to be serving the Confederacy in a disinterested and loyal manner. He had heard much of his gallantry and good services, and he was very sorry when I told him of Grenfell's quarrel with the civil power.

He confirmed the truth of my remark, that a Confederate general is either considered an Admirable Crichton by the soldiers, or else abused as everything bad. He added, the misfortune was that it is absolutely necessary, in order to insure success, that a general must obtain and preserve this popularity and influence with his men, who were, however, generally very willing to accord their confidence to any officer deserving of it.

With regard to the black-flag-and-no-quarter agitation, he said people would talk a great deal, and even go into action determined to give no quarter. "But," he added, "I have yet to hear of Confederate soldiers putting men to death who have thrown down their arms and held up their hands."

He told me that Lord Russell confessed that the impartial carrying out of the neutrality laws had pressed hard upon the South; and Mr. Davis asserted that the pressure might have been equalized, and yet retained its impartiality, if Great Britain, instead of closing her ports, had opened them to the prizes of both parties. I answered that perhaps this might be overdoing it a little on the other side.

When I took my leave about 9 o'clock, the President asked me to call upon him again. I don't think it is possible for any one to have an interview with him without going away most favorably impressed by his agreeable, unassuming manners, and by the charm of his conversation. While walking home, Mr. Benjamin told me that Mr. Davis's military instincts still predominate, and that his eager wish was to have joined the army instead of being elected President.

During my travels, many people have remarked to me that Jefferson Davis seems in a peculiar manner adapted for his office. His military education at West Point rendered him intimately acquainted with the higher officers of the army; and his post of Sec-

[169   ]

retary of War under the old government brought officers of all ranks under his immediate personal knowledge and supervision. No man could have formed a more accurate estimate of their respective merits. This is one of the reasons which gave the Confederates such an immense start in the ,way of generals; for having formed his opinion with regard to appointing an officer, Mr. Davis is always most determined to carry out his intention in spite of every obstacle. His services in the Mexican war gave him the prestige of a brave man and a good soldier. His services as a statesman pointed him out as the only man who, by his unflinching determination and administrative talent, was able to control the popular will. People speak of any misfortune happening to him as an irreparable evil too dreadful to contemplate.

Before we reached the Spottswood Hotel, we met ——, to whom Mr. Benjamin introduced me. They discussed the great topic of the day — the recapture of Winchester by General Ewell, the news of which had just arrived, and they both expressed their regret that General Milroy should have escaped. It appears that this Yankee commander, for his alleged crimes, had been put *hors de la loi* by the Confederates in the same manner as General Butler. —— said to me, "We hope he may not be taken alive; but if he is, we will not shrink from the responsibility of putting him to death." [5]

18th June (Thursday) — At 10 A. M. I called by appointment on Mr. Sedden, the Secretary at War. His anteroom was crowded with applicants for an interview, and I had no slight difficulty in getting in.[6] Mr. Sedden is a cadaverous but clever-looking man. He received me with great kindness, and immediately furnished me with letters of introduction for Generals Lee and Longstreet.

My friend Major Norris then took me to the President's office and introduced me to the aids-de-camp of the President — Colonels Wood, Lee, and Johnston. The two latter are sons to General Lee and General Albert Sidney Johnston, who was killed at Shiloh.

Major Norris then took me to the capitol and introduced me to Mr. Thompson the librarian, and to Mr. Meyers, who is now sup· posed to look after British interests since the abrupt departure of Mr. Moore, the consul. I was told that Mr. Moore had always been considered a good friend to the Southern cause, and had got into the mess which caused his removal entirely by his want of tact and discretion.

There is a fine view from the top of the capitol; the librarian told me that last year the fighting before Richmond could easily be seen from thence, and that many ladies used to go up for that purpose. Every one said that notwithstanding the imminence of the danger, the population of Richmond continued their daily avocations, and that no alarm was felt as to the result.

The interior of the capitol is decorated with numerous flags captured from the enemy. They are very gorgeous, all silk and gold, and form a great contrast to the little bunting battle flags of the Confederates. Among them I saw two colors which had belonged to the same regiment, the 37th New York (I think). These were captured in different battles; and on the last that was taken there is actually inscribed as a victory the word *Fair Oaks*, which was the engagement in which the regiment had lost its first color.

Mr. Butler King, a member of Congress, whose acquaintance I had made in the Spottswood Hotel, took me to spend the evening at Mrs. S——'s, a charming widow, for whom I had brought a letter from her only son, aid-de-camp to General Magruder, in Texas.

Mrs. S—— is clever and agreeable. She is a highly patriotic Southerner; but she told me that she had stuck fast to the Union until Lincoln's proclamation calling out 75,000 men to coerce the South, which converted her and such a number of others into strong Secessionists. I spent a very pleasant evening with Mrs. S——, who had been much in England, and had made a large acquaintance there.

Mr. Butler King is a Georgian gentleman, also very agreeable and well informed. It is surprising to hear the extraordinary equanimity with which he and hundreds of fellow sufferers talk of their entire ruin and the total destruction of their property. I know many persons in England suppose that Great Britain has now made enemies of both the North and South; but I do not believe this is the case with respect to the South, whatever certain Richmond papers may say. The South looks to England for everything when this war is over. She wants our merchants to buy her cotton, she wants our ships to carry it. She is willing that England should supply her with all the necessaries which she formerly received from the North. It is common to hear people declare they would rather pay twice the price for English goods than trade any more with Yankeedom.

19th June (Friday) — I embarked at 10 A. M. on board a small steamer to visit Drewry's Bluff on the James River, the scene of the repulse of the ironclads *Monitor* and *Galena*. The stream exactly opposite Richmond is very shallow and rocky, but it becomes navigable about a mile below the city. Drewry's Bluff is about eight miles distant, and before reaching it, we had to pass through two bridges — one of boats, and the other a wooden bridge. I was shown over the fortifications by Captain Chatard, Confederate States Navy, who was in command during the absence of Captain Lee. A flotilla of Confederate gunboats was lying just above the obstructions, and nearly opposite to the bluff. Amongst them was the *Yorktown*, alias *Patrick Henry*, which, under the command of my friend Captain Tucker, figured in the memorable *Merrimac* attack. There was also an ironclad called the *Richmond*, and two or three smaller craft. Beyond Drewry's Bluff, on the opposite side of the river, is Chaffin's Bluff, which mounts —— heavy guns, and forms the extreme right of the Richmond defenses on that side of the river.

At the time of the attack by the two Federal ironclads, assisted by several wooden gunboats, there were only three guns mounted on Drewry's Bluff, which is from 80 to 90 feet high. These had been hastily removed from the *Yorktown* and dragged up there by Captain Tucker on the previous day. They were either smoothbore 32-pounders or 8-inch guns, I forget which.[7]

During the contest the *Monitor*, notwithstanding her recent exploits with the *Merrimac*, kept herself out of much danger, partly concealed behind the bend of the river; but her consort, the ironclad *Galena*, approached boldly to within 500 yards of the bluff. The wooden gunboats remained a considerable distance down the river. After the fight had lasted about four hours the *Galena* withdrew much crippled, and has never, I believe, been known to fame since.

The result of the contest goes to confirm the opinion expressed to me by General Beauregard — that ironclads cannot resist the plunging fire of forts, even though that latter can only boast of the old smooth-bore guns.

A Captain Maury took me on board the *Richmond* ironclad, in which vessel I saw a 7-inch treble-banded Brook gun weighing, they told me, 21,000 lbs., and capable of standing a charge of 25 lbs. of powder. Amongst my fellow passengers from Richmond I had observed a very Hibernian-looking prisoner in charge of one soldier. Captain Maury informed me that this individual was being taken to Chaffin's Bluff, where he is to be shot at 12 noon tomorrow for desertion.

Major Norris and I bathed in James River at 7 P. M. from a rocky and very pretty island in the center of the stream.

I spent another very agreeable evening at Mrs. S——'s, and met General Randolph, Mr. Butler King, and Mr. Conrad there; also Colonel Johnston, aid-de-camp to the President. He told me that they had been forced, in order to stop Burnside's executions in Kentucky, to select two Federal captains, and put them under orders for death.

General Randolph looks in weak health. He had for some time filled the post of Secretary of War; but it is supposed that he and the President did not quite hit it off together. Mr. Conrad as well as Mr. King is a member of Congress, and he explained to me that, at the beginning of the war, each state was most desirous of being put (without the slightest necessity) under military law, which they thought was quite the correct remedy for all evil; but so sick did they soon become of this *régime* that at the last session Congress had refused the President the power of putting any place under military law, which is just as absurd in the other direction.

I hear every one complaining dreadfully of General Johnston's inactivity in Mississippi, and all now despair of saving Vicksburg. They deplore its loss, more on account of the effects its conquest may have in prolonging the war than for any other reason. No one seems to fear that its possession, together with Port Hudson, will really enable the Yankees to navigate the Mississippi. Nor do they fear that the latter will be able to prevent communication with the trans-Mississippi country.

Many of the Richmond papers seem to me scarcely more respectable than the New York ones. Party spirit runs high. Liberty of the press is carried to its fullest extent.

Richmond to Hagerstown

Chasing after Lee and Longstreet — Ruined Fences and Lonely Chimneys — I Am Impudent Enough to Win Supper from Two Good-looking Female Citizens — Marching Through the Shenandoah Valley — Winchester, Shuttlecock of the Confederacy — Northern Vengeance on the Rampage — Irishmen Make Good Rebs — First Spoils from Pennsylvania — Gold Brings Results — Crossing the Potomac — A Sulky Reception in Maryland

20th June (Saturday) — Armed with letters of introduction from the Secretary at War for Generals Lee and Longstreet, I left Richmond at 6 A. M., to join the Virginian army. I was accompanied by a sergeant of the Signal Corps, sent by my kind friend Major Norris, for the purpose of assisting me in getting on. We took the train as far as Culpepper, and arrived there at 5:30 P. M., after having changed cars at Gordonsville. Near this place I observed an enormous pile of excellent rifles rotting in the open air. These had been captured at Chancellorsville; but the Confederates have already such a superabundant stock of rifles that apparently they can afford to let them spoil. The weather was quite cool after the rain of last night. The country through which we passed had been in the enemy's hands last year, and was evacuated by them after the battles before Richmond; but at that time it was not their custom to burn, destroy, and devastate — every thing looked green

[176]

and beautiful, and did not in the least give one the idea of a hot country.

In his late daring raid, the Federal General Stoneman crossed this railroad, and destroyed a small portion of it, burned a few buildings, and penetrated to within three miles of Richmond; but he and his men were in such a hurry that they had not time to do much serious harm.[1]

Culpepper was, until five days ago, the headquarters of Generals Lee and Longstreet; but since Ewell's recapture of Winchester, the whole army had advanced with rapidity, and it was my object to catch it up as quickly as possible. On arriving at Culpepper, my sergeant handed me over to another myrmidon of Major Norris, with orders from that officer to supply me with a horse, and take me himself to join Mr. Lawley, who had passed through for the same purpose as myself three days before.

Sergeant Norris, my new chaperon, is cousin to Major Norris, and is a capital fellow. Before the war he was a gentleman of good means in Maryland, and was accustomed to a life of luxury. He now lives the life of a private soldier with perfect contentment, and is utterly indifferent to civilization and comfort. Although he was unwell when I arrived, and it was pouring with rain, he proposed that we should start at once — 6 p. m. I agreed, and we did so. Our horses both had sore backs, were both unfed, except on grass, and mine was deficient of a shoe. They nevertheless traveled well, and we reached a hamlet called Woodville, fifteen miles distant, at 9:30. We had great difficulty in procuring shelter; but at length we overcame the inhospitality of a native, who gave us a feed of corn for our horses, and a blanket on the floor for ourselves.

*   *   *

[177   ]

21st June (Sunday) — We got the horse shod with some delay, and after refreshing the animals with corn and ourselves with bacon, we effected a start at 8:15 A. M. We experienced considerable difficulty in carrying my small saddlebags and knapsack, on account of the state of our horses' backs. Mine was not very bad, but that of Norris was in a horrid state. We had not traveled more than a few miles when the latter animal cast a shoe, which took us an hour to replace at a village called Sperryville.

The country is really magnificent, but as it has supported two large armies for two years, it is now completely cleaned out. It is almost uncultivated, and no animals are grazing where there used to be hundreds. All fences have been destroyed, and numberless farms burnt, the chimneys alone left standing. It is difficult to depict and impossible to exaggerate the sufferings which this part of Virginia has undergone. But the ravages of war have not been able to destroy the beauties of nature — the verdure is charming, the trees magnificent, the country undulating, and the Blue Ridge mountains form the background.

Being Sunday, we met about thirty Negroes going to church, wonderfully smartly dressed, some (both male and female) riding on horseback, and others in wagons; but Mr. Norris informs me that two years ago we should have numbered them by hundreds. We soon began to catch up the sick and broken-down men of the army, but not in great numbers. Most of them were well shod, though I saw two without shoes.

After crossing a gap in the Blue Ridge range, we reached Front Royal at 5 P. M., and we were now in the well-known Shenandoah Valley — the scene of Jackson's celebrated campaigns. Front Royal is a pretty little place, and was the theater of one of the earliest fights in the war, which was commenced by a Maryland regiment of Confederates, who, as Mr. Norris observed, "jumped on to" a Federal regiment from the same state, and "whipped it badly." Since that time the village has changed hands continually, and was visited by the Federals only a few days previous to Ewell's rapid advance ten days ago.

After immense trouble we procured a feed of corn for the horses, and to Mr. Norris's astonishment, I was impudent enough to get food for ourselves by appealing to the kind feelings of two good-looking female citizens of Front Royal, who, during our supper, entertained us by stories of the manner they annoyed the Northern soldiers by disagreeable allusions to "Stonewall" Jackson.

We started again at 6:30, and crossed two branches of the Shenandoah River, a broad and rapid stream. Both the railway and carriage bridges having been destroyed, we had to ford it, and as the water was deep, we were only just able to accomplish the passage. The soldiers, of whom there were a number with us, took off their trousers, and held their rifles and ammunition above their heads. Soon afterwards our horses became very leg-weary; for although the weather had been cool, the roads were muddy and hard upon them.

At 8:30 we came up with Pender's division encamped on the sides of hills, illuminated with innumerable campfires, which looked very picturesque. After passing through about two miles of bivouacs, we begged for shelter in the hayloft of a Mr. Mason. We turned our horses into a field, and found our hayloft most luxurious after forty-six miles' ride at a foot's pace.

"Stonewall" Jackson is considered a regular demigod in this country.

* * *

[179]

22d June (Monday) — We started without food or corn at 6:30 A. M., and soon became entangled with Pender's division on its line of march, which delayed us a good deal. My poor brute of a horse also took this opportunity of throwing two more shoes, which we found it impossible to replace, all the blacksmiths' shops having been pressed by the troops.

The soldiers of this division are a remarkably fine body of men, and look quite seasoned and ready for any work. Their clothing is serviceable, so also are their boots; but there is the usual utter absence of uniformity as to color and shape of their garments and hats: gray of all shades, and brown clothing, with felt hats, predominate. The Confederate troops are now entirely armed with excellent rifles, mostly Enfields. When they first turned out they were in the habit of wearing numerous revolvers and bowie knives. General Lee is said to have mildly remarked: "Gentlemen, I think you will find an Enfield rifle, a bayonet, and sixty rounds of ammunition, as much as you can conveniently carry in the way of arms." They laughed, and thought they knew better; but the six-shooters and bowie knives gradually disappeared; and now none are to be seen among the infantry.

The artillery horses are in poor condition, and only get 3 lbs. of corn * a day. The artillery is of all kinds — Parrots, Napoleons, rifled and smooth bores, all shapes and sizes. Most of them bear the letters U. S., showing that they have changed masters.

The colors of the regiments differ from the blue battle flags I saw with Bragg's army. They are generally red, with a blue St. Andrew's cross showing the stars. This pattern is said to have been invented by General Joseph Johnston, as not so liable to be mistaken for the Yankee flag. The new Confederate flag has evidently been

* Indian corn.

adopted from this battle flag, as it is called. Most of the colors in this division bear the names Manassas, Fredericksburg, Seven Pines, Harpers Ferry, Chancellorsville, &c.[2]

I saw no stragglers during the time I was with Pender's division; but although the Virginian army certainly does get over a deal of ground, yet they move at a slow, dragging pace, and are evidently not good marchers naturally. As Mr. Norris observed to me, "Before this war we were a lazy set of devils; our Negroes worked for us, and none of us ever dreamt of walking, though we all rode a great deal."

We reached Berryville (eleven miles) at 9 A. M. The headquarters of General Lee were a few hundred yards beyond this place. Just before getting there, I saw a general officer of handsome appearance, who must, I knew from description, be the Commander in Chief; but as he was evidently engaged I did not join him, although I gave my letter of introduction to one of his staff.

Shortly afterwards, I presented myself to Mr. Lawley, with whom I became immediately great friends.* He introduced me to General Chilton, the Adjutant General of the army, to Colonel Cole, the Quartermaster General, to Major Taylor, Captain Venables, and other officers of General Lee's staff. He suggested, as the headquarters were so busy and crowded, that he and I should ride to Winchester at once, and afterwards ask for hospitality from the less busy staff of General Longstreet.

I was also introduced to Captain Schreibert, of the Prussian Army, who is a guest sometimes of General Lee and sometimes of General Stuart of the cavalry. He had been present at one of the

---

* The Honorable F. Lawley, author of the admirable letters from the Southern States, which appeared in *The Times* newspaper.

late severe cavalry skirmishes, which have been of constant occurrence since the sudden advance of this army. This advance has been so admirably timed as to allow of the capture of Winchester, with its Yankee garrison and stores, and at the same time of the seizure of the gaps of the Blue Ridge range. All the officers were speaking with regret of the severe wound received in this skirmish by Major Von Bork, another Prussian, but now in the Confederate States service, and aid-de-camp to Jeb Stuart.

After eating some breakfast, Lawley and I rode ten miles into Winchester. My horse, minus his foreshoes, showed signs of great fatigue, but we struggled into Winchester at 5 P. M. I was fortunate enough to procure shoes for the horse, and, by Lawley's introduction, admirable quarters for both of us at the house of the hospitable Mrs. ——, with whom he had lodged seven months before, and who was charmed to see him. Her two nieces, who are as agreeable as they are good-looking, gave us a miserable picture of the three captivities they have experienced under the Federal commanders, Banks, Shields, and Milroy.

The unfortunate town of Winchester seems to have been made a regular shuttlecock by the contending armies. "Stonewall" Jackson rescued it once, and last Sunday week his successor, General Ewell, drove out Milroy. The name of Milroy is always associated with that of Butler, and his rule in Winchester seems to have been somewhat similar to that of his illustrious rival in New Orleans. Should either of these two individuals fall alive into the hands of the Confederates, I imagine that Jeff Davis himself would be unable to save their lives, even if he were disposed to do so.

Before leaving Richmond, I heard every one expressing regret that Milroy should have escaped, as the recapture of Winchester seemed to be incomplete without him. More than 4000 of his men were taken in the two forts which overlook the town. They were carried by assault by a Louisianian brigade with trifling loss. The joy of the unfortunate inhabitants may easily be conceived at this sudden and unexpected relief from their last captivity, which had lasted six months.

During the whole of this time they could not legally buy an article of provisions without taking the oath of allegiance, which they magnanimously refused to do. They were unable to hear a word of their male relations or friends, who were all in the Southern Army. They were shut up in their houses after 8 P. M., and sometimes deprived of light. Part of our kind entertainer's house was forcibly occupied by a vulgar, ignorant, and low-born Federal officer, *ci-devant* driver of a streetcar; and they were constantly subjected to the most humiliating insults, on pretense of searching the house for arms, documents, &c.

To my surprise, however, these ladies spoke of the enemy with less violence and rancor than almost any other ladies I had met with during my travels through the whole Southern Confederacy. When I told them so, they replied that they who had seen many men shot down in the streets before their own eyes knew what they were talking about, which other and more excited Southern women did not.

Ewell's division is in front and across the Potomac; and before I left headquarters this morning, I saw Longstreet's corps beginning to follow in the same direction.

23d *June* (Tuesday) — Lawley and I went to inspect the site of Mr. Mason's (the Southern Commissioner in London) once pretty house — a melancholy scene. It had been charmingly situated near the outskirts of the town, and by all accounts must have been a delightful little place. When Lawley saw it seven months ago, it was then only a ruin; but since that time Northern vengeance (as directed by General Milroy) has satiated·itself by destroying almost the very foundations of the house of this archtraitor, as they call him. Literally not one stone remains standing upon another; and the *débris* seems to have been carted away, for there is now a big hole where the principal part of the house stood. Troops have evidently been encamped upon the ground, which was strewed with fragments of Yankee clothing, accouterments, &c.

I understand that Winchester used to be a most agreeable little town, and its society extremely pleasant. Many of its houses are now destroyed or converted into hospitals. The rest look miserable and dilapidated. Its female inhabitants (for the able-bodied males are all absent in the army) are familiar with the bloody realities of war. As many as 5000 wounded have been accommodated here at one time. All the ladies are accustomed to the bursting of shells and the sight of fighting, and all are turned into hospital nurses or cooks.

From the utter impossibility of procuring corn, I was forced to take the horses out grazing a mile beyond the town for four hours in the morning and two in the afternoon. As one mustn't lose sight of them for a moment, this occupied me all day, while Lawley wrote in the house. In the evening we went to visit two wounded officers in Mrs. ——'s house, a major and a captain in the Louisianian brigade which stormed the forts last Sunday week. I am afraid the captain will die. Both are shot through the body, but are cheery.

They served under "Stonewall" Jackson until his death, and they venerate his name, though they both agree that he has got an efficient successor in Ewell, his former companion in arms; and they

[184]

confirmed a great deal of what General Johnston had told me as to Jackson having been so much indebted to Ewell for several of his victories. They gave us an animated account of the spirits and feeling of the army. At no period of the war, they say, have the men been so well equipped, so well clothed, so eager for a fight, or so confident of success — a very different state of affairs from that which characterized the Maryland invasion of last year, when half of the army were barefooted stragglers, and many of the remainder unwilling and reluctant to cross the Potomac.[8]

Miss —— told me today that dancing and horse racing are forbidden by the Episcopal Church in this part of Virginia.

24th June (Wednesday) — Lawley being in weak health, we determined to spend another day with our kind friends in Winchester. I took the horses out again for six hours to graze, and made acquaintance with two Irishmen, who gave me some cut grass and salt for the horses. One of these men had served and had been wounded in the Southern Army. I remarked to him that he must have killed lots of his own countrymen; to which he replied, "Oh yes, but faix they must all take it as it comes." I have always observed that Southern Irishmen make excellent "Rebs," and have no sort of scruple in killing as many of their Northern brethren as they possibly can.

I saw today many new Yankee graves, which the deaths among the captives are constantly increasing. Wooden headposts are put at each grave, on which is written, "An Unknown Soldier, U. S. A. Died of wounds received upon the field of battle, June 21, 22, or 23, 1863."

A sentry stopped me today as I was going out of town, and when I showed him my pass from General Chilton, he replied with great firmness, but with perfect courtesy, "I'm extremely sorry, sir; but if you were the Secretary of War, or Jeff Davis himself, you couldn't pass without a passport from the provost marshal."

25th June (Thursday) — We took leave of Mrs. —— and her hospitable family, and started at 10 A. M. to overtake Generals Lee and Longstreet, who were supposed to be crossing the Potomac at Williamsport. Before we had got more than a few miles on our way, we began to meet horses and oxen, the first fruits of Ewell's advance into Pennsylvania.

The weather was cool and showery, and all went swimmingly for the first fourteen miles, when we caught up M'Laws's division, which belongs to Longstreet's corps. As my horse about this time began to show signs of fatigue, and as Lawley's pickaxed most alarmingly, we turned them in to some clover to graze, whilst we watched two brigades pass along the road. They were commanded, I think, by Semmes and Barksdale,* and were composed of Georgians, Mississippians, and South Carolinians. They marched very well, and there was no attempt at straggling; quite a different state of things from Johnston's men in Mississippi. All were well shod and efficiently clothed.

In the rear of each regiment were from twenty to thirty Negro slaves, and a certain number of unarmed men carrying stretchers and wearing in their hats the red badges of the ambulance corps; this is an excellent institution, for it prevents unwounded men falling out on pretense of taking wounded to the rear. The knapsacks of the men still bear the names of the Massachusetts, Vermont, New Jersey, or other regiments to which they originally be-

---

* Barksdale was killed, and Semmes mortally wounded, at the battle of Gettysburg.

longed. There were about twenty wagons to each brigade, most of which were marked U. S., and each of these brigades was about 2800 strong. There are four brigades in M'Laws's division. All the men seem in the highest spirits, and were cheering and yelling most vociferously.

We reached Martinsburg (twenty-two miles) at 6 P. M., by which time my horse nearly broke down, and I was forced to get off and walk. Martinsburg and this part of Virginia are supposed to be more Unionist than Southern. However, many of the women went through the form of cheering M'Laws's division as it passed. I dare say they would perform the same ceremony in honor of the Yankees tomorrow.

Three miles beyond Martinsburg we were forced by the state of our horses to insist upon receiving the unwilling hospitality of a very surly native, who was evidently Unionist in his proclivities. We were obliged to turn our horses into a field to graze during the night. This was most dangerous, for the Confederate soldier, in spite of his many virtues, is, as a rule, the most incorrigible horse stealer in the world.

26th June (Friday) — I got up a little before daylight, and not-withstanding the drenching rain, I secured our horses, which to my intense relief were present. But my horse showed a back rapidly getting worse, and both looked "mean" to a degree. Lawley being ill, he declined starting in the rain, and our host became more and more surly when we stated our intention of remaining with him. However, the sight of *real gold* instead of Confederate paper, or even greenbacks, soothed him wonderfully, and he furnished us with some breakfast. All this time M'Laws's division was pass-ing the door; but so strict was the discipline, that the only man who loafed in was immediately pounced upon and carried away captive.

At 2 P. M., the weather having become a little clearer, we made a start, but under very unpromising circumstances. Lawley was so ill that he could hardly ride. His horse was most unsafe, and had cast a shoe; my animal was in such a miserable state that I had not the inhumanity to ride him; but, by the assistance of his tail, I managed to struggle through the deep mud and wet.

We soon became entangled with M'Laws's division, and reached the Potomac, a distance of nine miles and a half, at 5 P. M. The river is both wide and deep, and in fording it (for which purpose I was obliged to mount), we couldn't keep our legs out of the water. The little town of Williamsport is on the opposite bank of the river, and we were now in Maryland. We had the mortification to learn that Generals Lee and Longstreet had quitted Williamsport this morning at 11 o'clock, and were therefore obliged to toil on to Hagerstown, six miles further. This latter place is evidently by no means Rebel in its sentiments, for all the houses were shut up, and many apparently abandoned. The few natives that were about stared at the troops with sulky indifference.

After passing through Hagerstown, we could obtain no certain information of the whereabouts of the two generals, nor could we get any willing hospitality from anyone. But at 9 P. M., our horses being quite exhausted, we forced ourselves into the house of a Dutchman, who became a little more civil at the sight of gold, although the assurance that we were English travelers, and not Rebels, had produced no effect. I had walked today, in mud and rain, seventeen miles, and I dared not take off my solitary pair of boots, because I knew I should never get them on again.

CHAPTER 11

Campaigning in Pennsylvania

With Longstreet at Last — Chambersburg Hears "Dixie" — Taunts from the Natives — "Take Care, Madam, Hood's Boys Are Great at Storming Breastworks" — Seizing Stores and Supplies — A Startling Visitor in the Full Uniform of the Hungarian Hussars — Local Hostility to the War — General Lee, the Handsomest Man of His Age I Ever Saw — Touching Relations between Lee and Longstreet — Lee's Only Fault — We March toward Gettysburg

27th June (Saturday) — Lawley was so ill this morning that he couldn't possibly ride. I therefore mounted his horse a little before daybreak, and started in search of the generals. After riding eight miles, I came up with General Longstreet, at 6:30 A. M., and was only just in time, as he was on the point of moving. Both he and his staff were most kind, when I introduced myself and stated my difficulties. He arranged that an ambulance should fetch Lawley, and he immediately invited me to join his mess during the campaign. He told me (which I did not know) that we were now in Pennsylvania, the enemy's country — Maryland being only ten miles broad at this point. He declared that bushwhackers exist in the woods, who shoot unsuspecting stragglers, and it would therefore be unsafe that Lawley and I should travel alone.

General Longstreet is an Alabamian — a thick-set, determined-looking man, forty-three years of age. He was an infantry major in the old army, and now commands the 1st *corps d'armée*. He is

[189]

never far from General Lee, who relies very much upon his judgment. By the soldiers he is invariably spoken of as "the best fighter in the whole army." Whilst speaking of entering upon the enemy's soil, he said to me, that although it might be fair, in just retaliation, to *apply the torch*, yet doing so would demoralize the army and ruin its now excellent discipline. Private property is to be therefore rigidly protected.

At 7 A. M. I returned with an orderly (or courier, as they are called) to the farmhouse in which I had left Lawley; and after seeing all arranged satisfactorily about the ambulance, I rode slowly on to rejoin General Longstreet near Chambersburg, which is a Pennsylvanian town, distant twenty-two miles from Hagerstown. I was with M'Laws's division, and observed that the moment they entered Pennsylvania, the troops opened the fences and enlarged the road about twenty yards on each side, which enabled the wagons and themselves to proceed together. This is the only damage I saw done by the Confederates. This part of Pennsylvania is very flourishing, highly cultivated, and, in comparison with the Southern States, thickly peopled. But all the cattle and horses having been seized by Ewell, farm labor had now come to a complete standstill.

In passing through Greencastle we found all the houses and windows shut up, the natives in their Sunday clothes standing at their doors regarding the troops in a very unfriendly manner. I saw no straggling into the houses, nor were any of the inhabitants disturbed or annoyed by the soldiers. Sentries were placed at the doors of many of the best houses, to prevent any officer or soldier from getting in on any pretense.

I entered Chambersburg at 6 P. M. This is a town of some size and importance. All its houses were shut up; but the natives were in the streets, or at the upper windows, looking in a scowling and bewildered manner at the Confederate troops, who were marching gayly past to the tune of "Dixie's Land." The women (many of whom were pretty and well dressed) were particularly sour and disagreeable in their remarks. I heard one of them say, "Look at Pharaoh's army going to the Red Sea." [1]

Others were pointing and laughing at Hood's ragged Jacks, who were passing at the time. This division, well known for its fighting qualities, is composed of Texans, Alabamians, and Arkansians, and they certainly are a queer lot to look at. They carry less than any other troops; many of them have only got an old piece of carpet or rug as baggage; many have discarded their shoes in the mud; all are ragged and dirty, but full of good humor and confidence in themselves and in their general, Hood. They answered the numerous taunts of the Chambersburg ladies with cheers and laughter.

One female had seen fit to adorn her ample bosom with a huge Yankee flag, and she stood at the door of her house, her countenance expressing the greatest contempt for the barefooted Rebs; several companies passed her without taking any notice; but at length a Texan gravely remarked, "Take care, madam, for Hood's boys are great at storming breastworks when the Yankee colors is on them." After this speech the patriotic lady beat a precipitate retreat.

Sentries were placed at the doors of all the principal houses, and the town was cleared of all but the military passing through or on duty. Some of the troops marched straight through the town, and bivouacked on the Carlisle road. Others turned off to the right, and occupied the Gettysburg turnpike. I found Generals Lee and Longstreet encamped on the latter road, three-quarters of a mile from the town.

[191]

General Longstreet and his staff at once received me into their mess, and I was introduced to Major Fairfax, Major Latrobe, and Captain Rogers of his personal staff; also to Major Moses, the Chief Commissary, whose tent I am to share. He is the most jovial, amusing, clever son of Israel I ever had the good fortune to meet. The other officers of Longstreet's headquarter's staff are Colonel Sorrell, Lieutenant Colonel Manning (ordnance officer), Major Walton, Captain Goree, and Major Clark, all excellent good fellows, and most hospitable.*

Lawley is to live with three doctors on the headquarters staff. Their names are Cullen, Barkdale, and Maury; they form a jolly trio, and live much more luxuriously than their generals.

Major Moses tells me that his orders are to open the stores in Chambersburg by force, and seize all that is wanted for the army in a regular and official manner, giving in return its value in Confederate money on a receipt. The storekeepers have doubtless sent away their most valuable goods on the approach of the Confederate Army. Much also has been already seized by Ewell, who passed through nearly a week ago. But Moses was much elated at having already discovered a large supply of excellent felt hats, hidden away in a cellar, which he "annexed" at once.

I was told this evening the numbers which have crossed the Potomac, and also the number of pieces of artillery. There is a large train of ammunition; for if the army advances any deeper into the enemy's country, General Lee cannot expect to keep his communications open to the rear; and as the staff officers say, "In

* Having lived at the headquarters of all the principal Confederate generals, I am able to affirm that the relation between their staffs and themselves, and the way the duty is carried on, is very similar to what it is in the British Army. All the generals — Johnston, Bragg, Polk, Hardee, Longstreet, and Lee — are thorough soldiers, and their staffs are composed of gentlemen of position and education, who have now been trained into excellent and zealous staff officers.

every battle we fight we must capture as much ammunition as we use." This necessity, however, does not seem to disturb them, as it has hitherto been their regular style of doing business.

Ewell, after the capture of Winchester, had advanced rapidly into Pennsylvania, and has already sent back great quantities of horses, mules, wagons, beefs, and other necessaries. He is now at or beyond Carlisle, laying the country under contribution, and making Pennsylvania support the war, instead of poor, used-up, and worn-out Virginia. The corps of Generals A. P. Hill and Long-street are now near this place, all full of confidence and in high spirits.

28th June (Sunday) — No officer or soldier under the rank of a general is allowed into Chambersburg without a special order from General Lee, which he is very chary of giving; and I hear of officers of rank being refused this pass.

Moses proceeded into town at 11 A. M., with an official requisition for three days' rations for the whole army in this neighborhood. These rations he is to seize by force, if not voluntarily supplied.

I was introduced to General Hood this morning. He is a tall, thin, wiry-looking man, with a grave face and a light-colored beard, thirty-three years old, and is accounted one of the best and most promising officers in the army. By his Texan and Alabamian troops he is adored. He formerly commanded the Texan brigade, but has now been promoted to the command of a division. His troops are accused of being a wild set, and difficult to manage; and it is the great object of the chiefs to check their innate plundering propensities by every means in their power.

I went into Chambersburg at noon, and found Lawley ensconced in the Franklin Hotel. Both he and I had much difficulty in getting into that establishment — the doors being locked, and only opened with the greatest caution. Lawley had had a most painful journey in the ambulance yesterday, and was much exhausted. No one in the hotel would take the slightest notice of him, and all scowled at me in a most disagreeable manner. Half-a-dozen Pennsylvanian viragos surrounded and assailed me with their united tongues to a deafening degree.

Nor would they believe me when I told them I was an English spectator and a noncombatant. They said I must be either a Rebel or a Yankee — by which expression I learned for the first time that the term Yankee is as much used as a reproach in Pennsylvania as in the South. The sight of gold, which I exchanged for their greenbacks, brought about a change, and by degrees they became quite affable. They seemed very ignorant, and confused Texans with Mexicans.

After leaving Lawley pretty comfortable, I walked about the town and witnessed the pressing operations of Moses and his myrmidons. Neither the Mayor nor the corporation were to be found anywhere, nor were the keys of the principal stores forthcoming until Moses began to apply the axe. The citizens were lolling about the streets in a listless manner, and showing no great signs of discontent. They had left to their women the task of resisting the commissaries — a duty which they were fully competent to perform. No soldiers but those on duty were visible in the streets.

In the evening I called again to see Lawley, and found in his room an Austrian officer, in the full uniform of the Hungarian hussars.[2] He had got a year's leave of absence, and has just succeeded in crossing the Potomac, though not without much trouble and difficulty. When he stated his intention of wearing his uniform, I explained to him the invariable custom of the Confederate soldiers, of never allowing the smallest peculiarity of dress or appearance to pass without a torrent of jokes, which, however good-humored, ended in becoming rather monotonous.

I returned to camp at 6 P. M. Major Moses did not get back till very late, much depressed at the ill success of his mission. He had searched all day most indefatigably, and had endured much contumely from the Union ladies, who called him "a thievish little Rebel scoundrel," and other opprobrious epithets. But this did not annoy him so much as the manner in which everything he wanted had been sent away or hidden in private houses, which he was not allowed by General Lee's order to search. He had only managed to secure a quantity of molasses, sugar, and whiskey. Poor Moses was thoroughly exhausted; but he endured the chaff of his brother officers with much good humor, and they made him continually repeat the different names he had been called. He said that at first the women refused his Confederate "trash" with great scorn, but they ended in being very particular about the odd cents.

29th June (Monday) — We are still at Chambersburg. Lee has issued a remarkably good order on nonretaliation, which is generally well received; but I have heard of complaints from fire-eaters, who want vengeance for their wrongs; and when one considers the numbers of officers and soldiers with this army who have been totally ruined by the devastations of Northern troops, one cannot be much surprised at this feeling.

I went into Chambersburg again, and witnessed the singular good behavior of the troops towards the citizens. I heard soldiers saying to one another that they did not like being in a town in which they were very naturally detested. To anyone who has seen *as I have* the ravages of the Northern troops in Southern towns, this forbearance seems most commendable and surprising. Yet these Pennsylvanian Dutch * don't seem the least thankful, and really appear to be unaware that their own troops have been for two years treating Southern towns with ten times more harshness. They are the most unpatriotic people I ever saw, and openly state that they don't care which side wins, provided they are left alone. They abuse Lincoln tremendously.

Of course, in such a large army as this there must be many instances of bad characters, who are always ready to plunder and pillage whenever they can do so without being caught. The stragglers, also, who remain behind when the army has left, will doubtless do much harm. It is impossible to prevent this; but everything that can be done is done to protect private property and noncombatants, and I can say, from my own observation, with wonderful success. I hear instances, however, in which soldiers, meeting well-dressed citizens, have made a "long arm" and changed hats, much to the disgust of the latter, who are still more annoyed when an exchange of boots is also proposed. Their superfine broadcloth is never in any danger.

General Longstreet is generally a particularly taciturn man; but this evening he and I had a long talk about Texas, where he had been quartered a long time. He remembered many people whom I had met quite well, and was much amused by the description of my travels through that country.

I complimented him upon the manner in which the Confederate sentries do their duty, and said that they were quite as strict as, and ten times more polite than, regular soldiers. He replied, laughing, that a sentry, after refusing you leave to enter a camp, might

---

* This part of Pennsylvania is much peopled with the descendants of Germans, who speak an unintelligible language.

very likely, if properly asked, show you another way in, by which you might avoid meeting a sentry at all.

I saw General Pendleton and General Pickett today. Pendleton is Chief of Artillery to the army, and was a West Pointer; but in more peaceable times he fills the post of Episcopal clergyman in Lexington, Virginia. Unlike General Polk, he unites the military and clerical professions together, and continues to preach whenever he gets a chance. On these occasions he wears a surplice over his uniform.

General Pickett commands one of the divisions in Longstreet's corps.* He wears his hair in long ringlets, and is altogether rather a desperate-looking character. He is the officer who, as Captain Pickett of the U. S. Army, figured in the difficulty between the British and United States in the San Juan Island affair, under General Harney, four or five years ago.

30th June (Tuesday) — This morning, before marching from Chambersburg, General Longstreet introduced me to the Commander in Chief. General Lee is, almost without exception, the handsomest man of his age I ever saw. He is fifty-six years old, tall, broad-shouldered, very well made, well set up — a thorough soldier in appearance; and his manners are most courteous and full of dignity. He is a perfect gentleman in every respect. I imagine no man has so few enemies, or is so universally esteemed. Throughout the South, all agree in pronouncing him to be as near perfection as a man can be. He has none of the small vices, such as smoking, drinking, chewing, or swearing, and his bitterest enemy never accused him of any of the greater ones.[8]

* M'Laws, Hood, and Pickett are the three divisional commanders or major generals in Longstreet's *corps d'armée*.

He generally wears a well-worn long gray jacket, a high black felt hat, and blue trousers tucked into his Wellington boots. I never saw him carry arms;* and the only mark of his military rank are the three stars on his collar. He rides a handsome horse, which is extremely well groomed. He himself is very neat in his dress and person, and in the most arduous marches he always looks smart and clean.†

In the old army he was always considered one of its best officers; and at the outbreak of these troubles, he was lieutenant colonel of the 2d cavalry. He was a rich man, but his fine estate was one of the first to fall into the enemy's hands. I believe he has never slept in a house since he had commanded the Virginian army, and he invariably declines all offers of hospitality, for fear the person offering it may afterwards get into trouble for having sheltered the Rebel General.

The relations between him and Longstreet are quite touching — they are almost always together. Longstreet's corps complain of this sometimes, as they say that they seldom get a chance of detached service, which falls to the lot of Ewell. It is impossible to please Longstreet more than by praising Lee.† I believe these two generals to be as little ambitious and as thoroughly unselfish as any men in the world. Both long for a successful termination of the war, in order that they may retire into obscurity.

"Stonewall" Jackson (until his death the third in command of their army) was just such another simple-minded servant of his country. It is understood that General Lee is a religious man, though not so demonstrative in that respect as Jackson; and, un-

* I never saw either Lee or Longstreet carry arms. A. P. Hill generally wears a sword.
† I observed this during the three days' fighting at Gettysburg, and in the retreat afterwards, when everyone else looked, and was, extremely dirty.

like his late brother in arms, he is a member of the Church of England. His only faults, so far as I can learn, arise from his excessive amiability.

Some Texan soldiers were sent this morning into Chambersburg to destroy a number of barrels of excellent whiskey, which could not be carried away. This was a pretty good trial for their discipline, and they did think it rather hard lines that the only time they had been allowed into the enemy's town was for the purpose of destroying their beloved whiskey. However, they did their duty like good soldiers.

We marched six miles on the road towards Gettysburg, and encamped at a village called (I think) Greenwood. I rode Lawley's old horse, he and the Austrian using the doctor's ambulance. In the evening General Longstreet told me that he had just received intelligence that Hooker had been disrated, and that Meade was appointed in his place. Of course he knew both of them in the old army, and he says that Meade is an honorable and respectable man, though not, perhaps, so bold as Hooker.[5]

I had a long talk with many officers about the approaching battle, which evidently cannot now be delayed long, and will take place on this road instead of in the direction of Harrisburg, as we had supposed. Ewell, who has laid York as well as Carlisle under contribution, has been ordered to reunite. Everyone, of course, speaks with confidence.

I remarked that it would be a good thing for them if on this occasion they had cavalry to follow up the broken infantry in the event of their succeeding in beating them. But to my surprise they all spoke of their cavalry as not efficient for that purpose. In fact, Stuart's men, though excellent at making raids, capturing wagons and stores, and cutting off communications, seem to have no idea of charging infantry under any circumstances. Unlike the cavalry with Bragg's army, they wear swords, but seem to have little idea of using them — they hanker after their carbines and revolvers. They constantly ride with their swords between their left leg and the saddle, which has a very funny appearance; but their horses are generally good, and they ride well. The infantry and artillery of this army don't seem to respect the cavalry very much, and often jeer at them. I was forced to abandon my horse here, as he was now lame in three legs, besides having a very sore back.

CHAPTER 12

Gettysburg

Marching with the Stonewall Brigade — Firing Becomes Distinctly Audible — Yankees on the Run — "The Position into Which the Enemy Was Driven Is Evidently a Strong One" — Longstreet's Forebodings at Day's End — Up before Dawn on July 2d — Longstreet Whittles at a Conference — Another Attack — The Rebel Yell — General Lee Watches Alone — Polkas Mixed with Gunfire — Limited Gains at Nightfall — Plans for July 3d — Pickett to Bear the Brunt — A Furious Cannonade — Longstreet Wishes He Were Somewhere Else — The General Gets a Silver Flask — Lee Rallies the Troops — "This Has Been a Sad Day for Us, Colonel" — Desperate Moments — Lines Reorganized — "'Uncle Robert' Will Get Us in to Washington Yet!" — Taking Stock the Day After — The Decision to Retreat

1st July (Wednesday) — We did not leave our camp till noon, as nearly all General Hill's corps had to pass our quarters on its march towards Gettysburg. One division of Ewell's also had to join in a little beyond Greenwood, and Longstreet's corps had to bring up the rear.

During the morning I made the acquaintance of Colonel Walton, who used to command the well-known Washington Artillery, but he is now chief of artillery to Longstreet's *corps d'armée*. He is a big man, *ci-devant* auctioneer in New Orleans, and I understand he pines to return to his hammer.

Soon after starting we got into a pass in the South Mountain, a continuation, I believe, of the Blue Ridge range, which is broken by the Potomac at Harpers Ferry. The scenery through the pass is very fine. The first troops, alongside of whom we rode, belonged to Johnson's division of Ewell's corps. Among them I saw, for the first time, the celebrated "Stonewall" Brigade, formerly commanded by Jackson. In appearance the men differ little from other Confederate soldiers, except, perhaps, that the brigade contains more elderly men and fewer boys. All (except, I think, one regiment) are Virginians.

As they have nearly always been on detached duty, few of them knew General Longstreet, except by reputation. Numbers of them asked me whether the general in front was Longstreet; and when I answered in the affirmative, many would run on a hundred yards in order to take a good look at him. This I take to be an immense compliment from any soldier on a long march.

At 2 P. M. firing became distinctly audible in our front, but although it increased as we progressed, it did not seem to be very heavy.[1]

A spy who was with us insisted upon there being "a pretty tidy bunch of *blue-bellies* in or near Gettysburg," and he declared that he was in their society three days ago.

After passing Johnson's division, we came up to a Florida brigade, which is now in Hill's corps; but as it had formerly served under Longstreet, the men knew him well. Some of them (after the General had passed) called out to their comrades, "Look out for work now, boys, for here's the old bulldog again."

At 3 P. M. we began to meet wounded men coming to the rear, and the number of these soon increased most rapidly, some hobbling alone, others on stretchers carried by the ambulance corps, and others in the ambulance wagons. Many of the latter were stripped nearly naked, and displayed very bad wounds. This spectacle, so revolting to a person unaccustomed to such sights, produced no impression whatever upon the advancing troops, who certainly go under fire with the most perfect nonchalance. They show no enthusiasm or excitement, but the most complete indifference. This is the effect of two years' almost uninterrupted fighting.

We now began to meet Yankee prisoners coming to the rear in considerable numbers. Many of them were wounded, but they seemed already to be on excellent terms with their captors, with whom they had commenced swapping canteens, tobacco, &c. Among them was a Pennsylvanian colonel, a miserable object from a wound in his face. In answer to a question, I heard one of them remark, with a laugh, "We're pretty nigh whipped already." We next came to a Confederate soldier carrying a Yankee color, belonging, I think, to a Pennsylvania regiment, which he told us he had just captured.

At 4:30 P. M. we came in sight of Gettysburg, and joined General Lee and General Hill, who were on the top of one of the ridges which form the peculiar feature of the country round Gettysburg. We could see the enemy retreating up one of the opposite ridges, pursued by the Confederates with loud yells. The position into which the enemy had been driven was evidently a strong one. His right appeared to rest on a cemetery, on the top of a high ridge to the right of Gettysburg, as we looked at it.

General Hill now came up and told me he had been very unwell all day, and in fact he looks very delicate. He said he had had two of his divisions engaged, and had driven the enemy four miles into his present position, capturing a great many prisoners, some cannon, and some colors. He said, however, that the Yankees had fought with a determination unusual to them. He pointed out a railway cutting, in which they had made a good stand; also, a field in the center of which he had seen a man plant the regimental color, round which the regiment had fought for some time with much obstinacy, and when at last it was obliged to retreat, the color-bearer retired last of all, turning round every now and then to shake his fist, at the advancing Rebels. General Hill said he felt quite sorry when he saw this gallant Yankee meet his doom.[2]

General Ewell had come up at 3:30, on the enemy's right (with part of his corps), and completed his discomfiture. General Reynolds, one of the best Yankee generals, was reported killed. Whilst we were talking, a message arrived from General Ewell, requesting Hill to press the enemy in the front, whilst he performed the same operation on his right. The pressure was accordingly applied in a mild degree, but the enemy were too strongly posted, and it was too late in the evening for a regular attack.

The town of Gettysburg was now occupied by Ewell, and was full of Yankee dead and wounded. I climbed up a tree in the most commanding place I could find, and could form a pretty good general idea of the enemy's position, although the tops of the ridges being covered with pine woods, it was very difficult to see anything of the troops concealed in them.

The firing ceased about dark, at which time I rode back with General Longstreet and his staff to his headquarters at Cashtown, a little village eight miles from Gettysburg. At that time troops were pouring along the road, and were being marched towards the position they are to occupy tomorrow.

In the fight today nearly 6000 prisoners had been taken, and 10 guns. About 20,000 men must have been on the field on the Confederate side. The enemy had two *corps d'armée* engaged. All the prisoners belong, I think, to the 1st and 11th corps. This day's work is called a "brisk little scurry," and all anticipate a "big battle" tomorrow.

I observed that the artillerymen in charge of the horses dig themselves little holes like graves, throwing up the earth at the upper end. They ensconce themselves in these holes when under fire.

At supper this evening, General Longstreet spoke of the enemy's position as being "very formidable." He also said that they would doubtless intrench themselves strongly during the night.* The staff officers spoke of the battle as a certainty, and the universal feeling in the army was one of profound contempt for an enemy whom they have beaten so constantly, and under so many disadvantages.

2d July (Thursday) — We all got up at 3:30 A. M., and breakfasted a little before daylight. Lawley insisted on riding, notwithstanding his illness. Captain —— and I were in a dilemma for horses; but I was accommodated by Major Clark (of this staff), whilst the stout Austrian was mounted by Major Walton. The Austrian, in spite of the early hour, had shaved his cheeks and *ciréd* his mustaches as beautifully as if he was on parade at Vienna.[8]

Colonel Sorrell, the Austrian, and I arrived at 5 A. M. at the same commanding position we were on yesterday, and I climbed up a tree in company with Captain Schreibert of the Prussian Army. Just below us were seated Generals Lee, Hill, Longstreet, and Hood, in consultation — the two latter assisting their deliberations

* I have the best reason for supposing that the fight came off prematurely, and that neither Lee nor Longstreet intended that it should have begun that day. I also think that their plans were deranged by the events of the first.

by the truly American custom of *whittling* sticks. General Heth was also present; he was wounded in the head yesterday, and although not allowed to command his brigade, he insists upon coming to the field.⁴

At 7 A. M. I rode over part of the ground with General Longstreet, and saw him disposing of M'Laws's division for today's fight. The enemy occupied a series of high ridges, the tops of which were covered with trees, but the intervening valleys between their ridges and ours were mostly open, and partly under cultivation. The cemetery was on their right, and their left appeared to rest upon a high rocky hill. The enemy's forces, which were now supposed to comprise nearly the whole Potomac army, were concentrated into a space apparently not more than a couple of miles in length.

The Confederates inclosed them in a sort of semicircle, and the extreme extent of our position must have been from five to six miles at least. Ewell was on our left, his headquarters in a church (with a high cupola) at Gettysburg; Hill in the center; and Longstreet on the right. Our ridges were also covered with pine woods at the tops, and generally on the rear slopes.

The artillery of both sides confronted each other at the edges of these belts of trees, the troops being completely hidden. The enemy was evidently intrenched, but the Southerners had not broken ground at all. A dead silence reigned till 4:45 P. M., and no one would have imagined that such masses of men and such a powerful artillery were about to commence the work of destruction at that hour.

Only two divisions of Longstreet were present today — M'Laws's and Hood's — Pickett being still in the rear. As the whole morning was evidently to be occupied in disposing the troops for the attack,

I rode to the extreme right with Colonel Manning and Major Walton, where we ate quantities of cherries and got a feed of corn for our horses. We also bathed in a small stream, but not without some trepidation on my part, for we were almost beyond the lines, and were exposed to the enemy's cavalry.

At 1 P. M. I met a quantity of Yankee prisoners who had been picked up straggling. They told me they belonged to Sickles's corps (3d, I think), and had arrived from Emmetsburg during the night. About this time skirmishing began along part of the line, but not heavily.

At 2 P. M. General Longstreet advised me, if I wished to have a good view of the battle, to return to my tree of yesterday. I did so, and remained there with Lawley and Captain Schreibert during the rest of the afternoon. But until 4:45 P. M. all was profoundly still, and we began to doubt whether a fight was coming off today at all.

At that time, however, Longstreet suddenly commenced a heavy cannonade on the right. Ewell immediately took it up on the left. The enemy replied with at least equal fury, and in a few moments the firing along the whole line was as heavy as it is possible to conceive. A dense smoke arose for six miles. There was little wind to drive it away, and the air seemed full of shells — each of which appeared to have a different style of going, and to make a different noise from the others. The ordnance on both sides is of a very varied description.

Every now and then a caisson would blow up — if a Federal one, a Confederate yell would immediately follow. The Southern troops, when charging, or to express their delight, always yell in a manner peculiar to themselves. The Yankee cheer is much more like ours; but the Confederate officers declare that the Rebel yell

[207]

has a particular merit, and always produces a salutary and useful effect upon their adversaries. A corps is sometimes spoken of as a "good yelling regiment." [5]

As soon as the firing began, General Lee joined Hill just below our tree, and he remained there nearly all the time, looking through his fieldglass — sometimes talking to Hill and sometimes to Colonel Long of his staff. But generally he sat quite alone on the stump of a tree. What I remarked especially was, that during the whole time the firing continued, he only sent one message, and only received one report. It is evidently his system to arrange the plan thoroughly with the three corps commanders, and then leave to them the duty of modifying and carrying it out to the best of their abilities.

When the cannonade was at its height, a Confederate band of music, between the cemetery and ourselves, began to play polkas and waltzes, which sounded very curious, accompanied by the hissing and bursting of the shells.[6]

At 5:45 all became comparatively quiet on our left and in the cemetery; but volleys of musketry on the right told us that Longstreet's infantry were advancing, and the onward progress of the smoke showed that he was progressing favorably. About 6:30 there seemed to be a check, and even a slight retrograde movement. Soon after 7, General Lee got a report by signal from Longstreet to say "We are doing well."

A little before dark the firing dropped off in every direction, and soon ceased altogether. We then received intelligence that Longstreet had carried everything before him for some time, capturing several batteries, and driving the enemy from his positions; but when Hill's Florida brigade and some other troops gave way, he was forced to abandon a small portion of the ground he had won,

together with all the captured guns, except three. His troops, however, bivouacked during the night on ground occupied by the
enemy this morning.

Everyone deplores that Longstreet *will* expose himself in such a
reckless manner. Today he led a Georgian regiment in a charge
against a battery, hat in hand, and in front of everybody.[7] General
Barksdale was killed and Semmes mortally wounded; but the most
serious loss was that of General Hood, who was badly wounded in
the arm early in the day. I heard that his Texans are in despair.
Lawley and I rode back to the General's camp, which had been
moved to within a mile of the scene of action. Longstreet, however, with most of his staff, bivouacked on the field.

Major Fairfax arrived at about 10 p. m. in a very bad humor. He
had under his charge about 1000 to 1500 Yankee prisoners who
had been taken today; among them a general, whom I heard one of
his men accusing of having been "so G—d d—d drunk that he had
turned his guns upon his own men." But, on the other hand, the
accuser was such a thundering blackguard, and proposed taking
such a variety of oaths in order to escape from the U. S. Army, that
he is not worthy of much credit. A large train of horses and mules,
&c., arrived today, sent in by General Stuart, and captured, it is
understood, by his cavalry, which had penetrated to within 6 miles
of Washington.

3d July (Friday) — At 6 a. m. I rode to the field with Colonel
Manning, and went over that portion of the ground which, after
a fierce contest, had been won from the enemy yesterday evening.
The dead were being buried, but great numbers were still lying
about; also many mortally wounded, for whom nothing could be
done. Amongst the latter were a number of Yankees dressed in bad

imitations of the Zouave costume.[8] They opened their glazed eyes, as I rode past, in a painfully imploring manner.

We joined Generals Lee and Longstreet's staff. They were reconnoitering and making preparations for renewing the attack. As we formed a pretty large party, we often drew upon ourselves the attention of the hostile sharpshooters, and were two or three times favored with a shell. One of these shells set a brick building on fire which was situated between the lines. This building was filled with wounded, principally Yankees, who, I am afraid, must have perished miserably in the flames. Colonel Sorrell had been slightly wounded yesterday, but still did duty. Major Walton's horse was killed, but there were no other casualties amongst my particular friends.

The plan of yesterday's attack seems to have been very simple — first a heavy cannonade all along the line, followed by an advance of Longstreet's two divisions and part of Hill's corps. In consequence of the enemy's having been driven back some distance, Longstreet's corps (part of it) was in a much more forward situation than yesterday. But the range of heights to be gained was still most formidable, and evidently strongly intrenched.

The distance between the Confederate guns and the Yankee position — *i. e.*, between the woods crowning the opposite ridges — was at least a mile — quite open, gently undulating, and exposed to artillery the whole distance. This was the ground which had to be crossed in today's attack. Pickett's division, which had just come up, was to bear the brunt in Longstreet's attack, together with Heth and Pettigrew in Hill's corps. Pickett's division was a weak one (under 5000), owing to the absence of two brigades.

At noon all Longstreet's dispositions were made. His troops for attack were deployed into line, and lying down in the woods; his batteries were ready to open. The general then dismounted and went to sleep for a short time. The Austrian officer and I now rode off to get, if possible, into some commanding position from whence we could see the whole thing without being exposed to the tremendous fire which was about to commence. After riding about for half an hour without being able to discover so desirable a situation, we determined to make for the cupola, near Gettysburg, Ewell's headquarters. Just before we reached the entrance to the town, the cannonade opened with a fury which surpassed even that of yesterday.

Soon after passing through the toll gate at the entrance of Gettysburg, we found that we had got into a heavy cross fire; shells both Federal and Confederate passing over our heads with great frequency. At length two shrapnel shells burst quite close to us, and a ball from one of them hit the officer who was conducting us. We then turned round and changed our views with regard to the cupola — the fire of one side being bad enough, but preferable to that of both sides. A small boy of twelve years was riding with us at the time. This urchin took a diabolical interest in the bursting of the shells, and screamed with delight when he saw them take effect. I never saw this boy again, or found out who he was.[9]

The road at Gettysburg was lined with Yankee dead, and as they had been killed on the 1st, the poor fellows had already begun to be very offensive. We then returned to the hill I was on yesterday. But finding that, to see the actual fighting, it was absolutely necessary to go into the thick of the thing, I determined to make my way to General Longstreet. It was then about 2:30.

[211   ]

After passing General Lee and his staff, I rode on through the woods in the direction in which I had left Longstreet.

I soon began to meet many wounded men returning from the front. Many of them asked in piteous tones the way to a doctor or an ambulance. The further I got, the greater became the number of the wounded. At last I came to a perfect stream of them flocking through the woods in numbers as great as the crowd in Oxford Street in the middle of the day. Some were walking alone on crutches composed of two rifles, others were supported by men less badly wounded than themselves, and others were carried on stretchers by the ambulance corps; but in no case did I see a sound man helping the wounded to the rear, unless he carried the red badge of the ambulance corps. They were still under a heavy fire; the shells were continually bringing down great limbs of trees, and carrying further destruction amongst this melancholy procession.

I saw all this in much less time than it takes to write it, and although astonished to meet such vast numbers of wounded, I had not seen *enough* to give me any idea of the real extent of the mischief.

When I got close up to General Longstreet, I saw one of his regiments advancing through the woods in good order; so, thinking I was just in time to see the attack, I remarked to the General that "I wouldn't have missed this for anything." Longstreet was seated at the top of a snake fence at the edge of the wood, and looking perfectly calm and imperturbed. He replied, laughing, "The devil you wouldn't! I would like to have missed it very much; we've attacked and been repulsed: look there!" [10]

For the first time I then had a view of the open space between the two positions, and saw it covered with Confederates slowly

and sulkily returning towards us in small broken parties, under a
heavy fire of artillery. But the fire where we were was not so bad
as further to the rear: for although the air seemed alive with shell,
yet the greater number burst behind us.

The General told me that Pickett's division had succeeded in
carrying the enemy's position and capturing his guns, but after
remaining there twenty minutes, it had been forced to retire, on
the retreat of Heth and Pettigrew on its left. No person could
have been more calm or self-possessed than General Longstreet
under these trying circumstances, aggravated as they now were
by the movements of the enemy, who began to show a strong disposition to advance. I could now thoroughly appreciate the term
bulldog, which I had heard applied to him by the soldiers. Difficulties seem to make no other impression upon him than to make
him a little more savage.

Major Walton was the only officer with him when I came up —
all the rest had been put into the charge. In a few minutes Major
Latrobe arrived on foot, carrying his saddle, having just had his
horse killed. Colonel Sorrell was also in the same predicament,
and Captain Goree's horse was wounded in the mouth.

The General was making the best arrangements in his power to
resist the threatened advance, by advancing some artillery, rallying the stragglers, &c. I remember seeing a General (Pettigrew,
I think it was)* come up to him, and report that "he was unable
to bring his men up again." Longstreet turned upon him and replied with some sarcasm: "Very well; never mind, then, General;
just let them remain where they are: the enemy's going to advance, and will spare you the trouble."

He asked for something to drink. I gave him some rum out of

* This officer was afterwards killed at the passage of the Potomac.

my silver flask, which I begged he would keep in remembrance of the occasion; he smiled, and, to my great satisfaction, accepted the memorial. He then went off to give some orders to M'Laws's division. Soon afterwards I joined General Lee, who had in the meanwhile come to that part of the field on becoming aware of the disaster.

If Longstreet's conduct was admirable, that of General Lee was perfectly sublime. He was engaged in rallying and in encouraging the broken troops, and was riding about a little in front of the wood, quite alone — the whole of his staff being engaged in a similar manner further to the rear. His face, which is always placid and cheerful, did not show signs of the slightest disappointment, care, or annoyance; and he was addressing to every soldier he met a few words of encouragement, such as, "All this will come right in the end; we'll talk it over afterwards; but, in the meantime, all good men must rally. We want all good and true men just now," &c.

He spoke to all the wounded men that passed him, and the slightly wounded he exhorted "to bind up [their] hurts and take up a musket" in this emergency. Very few failed to answer his appeal, and I saw many badly wounded men take off their hats and cheer him. He said to me, "This has been a sad day for us, Colonel — a sad day; but we can't expect always to gain victories." He was also kind enough to advise me to get into some more sheltered position, as the shells were bursting round us with considerable frequency.

Notwithstanding the misfortune which had so suddenly befallen him, General Lee seemed to observe everything, however trivial. When a mounted officer began licking his horse for shying at the bursting of a shell, he called out, "Don't whip him,

[214]

Captain; don't whip him. I've got just such another foolish horse myself, and whipping does no good."

I happened to see a man lying flat on his face in a small ditch, and I remarked that I didn't think he seemed dead; this drew General's Lee attention to the man, who commenced groaning dismally. Finding appeals to his patriotism of no avail, General Lee had him ignominiously set on his legs by some neighboring gunners.

I saw General Willcox (an officer who wears a short round jacket and a battered straw hat) come up to him, and explain, almost crying, the state of his brigade. General Lee immediately shook hands with him and said cheerfully, "Never mind, General, *all this has been* MY *fault* — it is *I* that have lost this fight, and you must help me out of it in the best way you can."

In this manner I saw General Lee encourage and reanimate his somewhat dispirited troops, and magnanimously take upon his own shoulders the whole weight of the repulse. It was impossible to look at him or to listen to him without feeling the strongest admiration, and I never saw any man fail him except the man in the ditch.[11]

It is difficult to exaggerate the critical state of affairs as they appeared about this time. If the enemy or their general had shown any enterprise, there is no saying what might have happened. General Lee and his officers were evidently fully impressed with a sense of the situation; yet there was much less noise, fuss, or confusion of orders than at an ordinary field day. The men, as they were rallied in the wood, were brought up in detachments, and lay down quietly and coolly in the positions assigned to them.

We heard that Generals Garnett and Armistead were killed, and General Kemper mortally wounded; also, that Pickett's division had only one field officer unhurt. Nearly all this slaughter took place in an open space about one mile square, and within one hour.

At 6 P. M. we heard a long and continuous Yankee cheer, which we at first imagined was an indication of an advance; but it turned out to be their reception of a general officer, whom we saw riding down the line, followed by about thirty horsemen. Soon afterwards I rode to the extreme front, where there were four pieces of rifled cannon almost without any infantry support. To the nonwithdrawal of these guns is to be attributed the otherwise surprising inactivity of the enemy.

I was immediately surrounded by a sergeant and about half-a-dozen gunners, who seemed in excellent spirits and full of confidence, in spite of their exposed situation. The sergeant expressed his ardent hope that the Yankees might have spirit enough to advance and receive the dose he had in readiness for them. They spoke in admiration of the advance of Pickett's division, and of the manner in which Pickett himself had led it. When they observed General Lee they said, "We've not lost confidence in the old man: this day's work won't do him no harm. 'Uncle Robert' will get us into Washington yet; you bet he will!" &c.

Whilst we were talking, the enemy's skirmishers began to advance slowly, and several ominous sounds in quick succession told us that we were attracting their attention, and that it was necessary to break up the conclave. I therefore turned round and took leave of these cheery and plucky gunners.

At 7 P. M., General Lee received a report that Johnson's division of Ewell's corps had been successful on the left, and had gained important advantages there. Firing entirely ceased in our front about this time; but we now heard some brisk musketry on our right, which I afterwards learned proceeded from Hood's Texans, who had managed to surround some enterprising Yankee cavalry, and were slaughtering them with great satisfaction. Only eighteen out of four hundred are said to have escaped.

At 7:30, all idea of a Yankee attack being over, I rode back to Moses's tent, and found that worthy commissary in very low spirits, all sorts of exaggerated rumors having reached him. On my way I met a great many wounded men, most anxious to inquire after Longstreet, who was reported killed; when I assured them he was quite well, they seemed to forget their own pain in the evident pleasure they felt in the safety of their chief. No words that I can use will adequately express the extraordinary patience and fortitude with which the wounded Confederates bore their sufferings.

I got something to eat with the doctors at 10 P. M., the first for fifteen hours.

I gave up my horse today to his owner, as from death and exhaustion the staff are almost without horses.

4th July (Saturday) — I was awoke at daylight by Moses complaining that his valuable trunk, containing much public money, had been stolen from our tent whilst we slept. After a search it was found in a wood hard by, broken open and minus the money. Dr. Barksdale had been robbed in the same manner exactly. This is evidently the work of those rascally stragglers, who shirk going under fire, plunder the natives, and will hereafter swagger as the heroes of Gettysburg.

Lawley, the Austrian, and I walked up to the front about eight o'clock, and on our way we met General Longstreet, who was in a high state of amusement and good humor. A flag of truce had just come over from the enemy, and its bearer announced among other things that "General Longstreet was wounded, and a prisoner, but would be taken care of." General Longstreet sent back word that he was extremely grateful, but that, being neither wounded nor a prisoner, he was quite able to take care of himself.[12] The iron endurance of General Longstreet is most extraordinary. He seems to require neither food nor sleep. Most of his staff now fall fast asleep directly they get off their horses, they are so exhausted from the last three days' work.

Whilst Lawley went to headquarters on business, I sat down and had a long talk with General Pendleton (the parson), chief of artillery. He told me the exact number of guns in action yesterday. He said that the universal opinion is in favor of the 12-pounder Napoleon guns as the best and simplest sort of ordnance for field purposes.* Nearly all the artillery with this army has either been captured from the enemy or cast from old 6-pounders taken at the early part of the war.

At 10 A. M. Lawley returned from headquarters, bringing the news that the army is to commence moving in the direction of Virginia this evening. This step is imperative from want of ammunition. But it was hoped that the enemy might attack during the day, especially as this is the Fourth of July, and it was calculated that there was still ammunition for one day's fighting. The ordnance train had already commenced moving back towards Cashtown, and Ewell's immense train of plunder had been proceeding towards Hagerstown by the Fairfield road ever since an early hour this morning.

---

* The Napoleon 12-pounders are smooth-bore brass guns, with chambers, very light, and with long range. They were invented or recommended by Louis Napoleon years ago. A large number are being cast at Augusta and elsewhere.

Johnson's division had evacuated during the night the position it had gained yesterday. It appears that for a time it was actually in possession of the cemetery, but had been forced to retire from thence from want of support by Pender's division, which had been retarded by that officer's wound. The whole of our left was therefore thrown back considerably.

At 1 P. M. the rain began to descend in torrents, and we took refuge in the hovel of an ignorant Pennsylvanian boor. The cottage was full of soldiers, none of whom had the slightest idea of the contemplated retreat, and all were talking of Washington and Baltimore with the greatest confidence.

At 2 P. M. we walked to General Longstreet's camp, which had been removed to a place three miles distant, on the Fairfield road. General Longstreet talked to me for a long time about the battle. He said the mistake they had made was in not concentrating the army more, and in failing to make the attack yesterday with 30,000 men instead of 15,000.[18]

The advance had been in three lines, and the troops of Hill's corps who gave way were young soldiers, who had never been under fire before. He thought the enemy would have attacked had the guns been withdrawn. Had they done so at that particular moment immediately after the repulse, it would have been awkward; but in that case he had given orders for the advance of Hood's division and M'Laws's on the right. I think, after all, that General Meade was right not to advance — his men would never have stood the tremendous fire of artillery they would have been exposed to.

Rather over 7000 Yankees were captured during the three days; 3500 took the parole; the remainder were now being marched to Richmond, escorted by the remains of Pickett's division. It is impossible to avoid seeing that the cause of this check to the Confederates lies in the utter contempt felt for the enemy by all ranks.

Wagons, horses, mules, and cattle captured in Pennsylvania, the solid advantages of this campaign, have been passing slowly along this road (Fairfield) all day. Those taken by Ewell are particularly admired. So interminable was this train that it soon became evident that we should not be able to start till late at night. As soon as it became dark we all lay round a big fire, and I heard reports coming in from the different generals that the enemy was *retiring*, and had been doing so all day long. M'Laws reported nothing in his front but cavalry vedettes.

But this, of course, could make no difference to General Lee's plan: ammunition he must have — he had failed to capture it from the enemy (according to precedent); and as his communications with Virginia were intercepted, he was compelled to fall back towards Winchester, and draw his supplies from thence. General Milroy had kindly left an ample stock at that town when he made his precipitate exit some weeks ago. The army was also incumbered with an enormous wagon train, the spoils of Pennsylvania, which it is highly desirable to get safely over the Potomac.

Shortly after 9 P. M. the rain began to descend in torrents. Lawley and I luckily got into the doctors' covered buggy, and began to get slowly under way a little after midnight.

CHAPTER 13

Back into Maryland

The Night Was Very Bad — False Alarms — Ewell Arrives to Confer — General McLaws Eats General Longstreet's Supper — Planning to Return to England — A Slave Captures His Liberator — Hagerstown Again — Panic in the Dark — These Cavalry Fights Are Miserable Affairs — Meeting Jeb Stuart — Longstreet Advises How to Cross the Lines — Farewell to Lee — Warnings on Getting into Yankee Clutches — A Great Deal Depends upon Falling into the Hands of a Gentleman

5th July (Sunday) — The night was very bad — thunder and lightning, torrents of rain — the road knee-deep in mud and water, and often blocked up with wagons "come to grief." I pitied the wretched plight of the unfortunate soldiers who were to follow us. Our progress was naturally very slow indeed, and we took eight hours to go as many miles.[1]

At 8 A. M. we halted a little beyond the village of Fairfield, near the entrance to a mountain pass. No sooner had we done so and lit a fire, than an alarm was spread that Yankee cavalry were upon us. Several shots flew over our heads, but we never could discover from whence they came.

News also arrived of the capture of the whole of Ewell's beautiful wagons.* These reports created a regular stampede amongst

* It afterwards turned out that all escaped but thirty-eight.[2]

[**221**]

the wagoners, and Longstreet's drivers started off as fast as they could go. Our medical trio, however, firmly declined to budge, and came to this wise conclusion, partly urged by the pangs of hunger, and partly from the consideration that, if the Yankee cavalry did come, the crowded state of the road in our rear would prevent our escape. Soon afterwards, some Confederate cavalry were pushed to the front, who cleared the pass after a slight skirmish.

At noon, Generals Lee and Longstreet arrived, and halted close to us. Soon afterwards Ewell came up. This is the first time I ever saw him. He is rather a remarkable-looking old soldier, with a bald head, a prominent nose, and rather a haggard, sickly face. Having so lately lost his leg above the knee, he is still a complete cripple, and falls off his horse occasionally. Directly he dismounts he has to be put on crutches. He was "Stonewall" Jackson's co-adjutor during the celebrated Valley campaigns, and he used to be a great swearer — in fact, he is said to have been the only person who was unable to restrain that propensity before Jackson; but since his late (rather romantic) marriage, he has (to use the American expression) "joined the Church." When I saw him he was in a great state of disgust in consequence of the supposed loss of his wagons, and refused to be comforted by General Lee.

I joined Longstreet again, and, mounted on Lawley's venerable horse, started at 3 P. M. to ride through the pass. At 4 P. M. we stopped at a place where the roads fork, one leading to Emmetsburg, and the other to Hagerstown. Major Moses and I entered a farmhouse, in which we found several women, two wounded Yankees, and one dead one, the result of this morning's skirmish. One of the sufferers was frightfully wounded in the head; the other was hit in the knee. The latter told me he was an Irishman, and had served in the Bengal Europeans during the Indian Mutiny. He now belonged to a Michigan cavalry regiment, and had already imbibed American ideas of Ireland's wrongs, and all that sort of trash. He told me that his officers were very bad, and that the idea in the army was that M'Clellan had assumed the chief command.

The women in this house were great Abolitionists. When Major Fairfax rode up, he inquired of one of them whether the corpse was that of a Confederate or Yankee (the body was in the veranda, covered with a white sheet). The woman made a gesture with her foot, and replied, "If it was a Rebel, do you think it would be here long?" Fairfax then said, "Is it a woman who speaks in such a manner of a dead body which can do no one any harm?" She thereupon colored up, and said she wasn't in earnest.

At 6 o'clock we rode on again (by the Hagerstown road), and came up with General Longstreet at 7:30. The road was full of soldiers marching in a particular lively manner — the wet and mud seemed to have produced no effect whatever on their spirits, which were as boisterous as ever. They had got hold of colored prints of Mr. Lincoln, which they were passing about from company to company with many remarks upon the personal beauty of Uncle Abe. The same old chaff was going on of "Come out of that hat — I know you're in it — I sees your legs a-dangling down," &c.

When we halted for the night, skirmishing was going on in front and rear — Stuart in front and Ewell in rear. Our bivouac being near a large tavern, General Longstreet had ordered some supper there for himself and his staff; but when we went to devour it, we discovered General M'Laws and his officers rapidly finishing it. We, however, soon got more, the Pennsylvanian proprietors

[223]

being particularly anxious to propitiate the General, in hopes that he would spare their livestock, which had been condemned to death by the ruthless Moses.

During supper, women came rushing in at intervals, saying — "Oh, good heavens, now they're killing our fat hogs. Which is the General? Which is the Great Officer? Our milch cows are now going." To all which expressions Longstreet replied, shaking his head in a melancholy manner — "Yes, madam, it's very sad — very sad; and this sort of thing has been going on in Virginia more than two years — very sad." We all slept in the open, and the heavy rain produced no effect upon our slumbers.

I understand it is impossible to cross the lines by flag of truce. I therefore find myself in a dilemma about the expiration of my leave.

6th July (Monday) — Several horses were stolen last night, mine nearly so. It is necessary to be very careful, in order to prevent this misfortune. We started at 6:30, but got on very slowly, so blocked up was the road with wagons, some of which had been captured and burnt by the enemy yesterday. It now turned out that all Ewell's wagons escaped except thirty-eight, although, at one time, they had been all in the enemy's hands.

At 8:30 we halted for a couple of hours, and Generals Lee, Longstreet, Hill, and Willcox had a consultation. I spoke to —— about my difficulties with regard to getting home, and the necessity of doing so, owing to the approaching expiration of my leave. He told me that the army had no intention at present of retreating for good, and advised me to stop with them and see what turned up. He also said that some of the enemy's dispatches had been intercepted, in which the following words occur: — "The noble but unfortunate army of the Potomac has again been obliged to retreat before superior numbers."

I particularly observed the marching today of the 21st Mississippi, which was uncommonly good. This regiment all wear short round jackets, a most unusual circumstance, for they are generally unpopular in the South.

At 12 o'clock we halted again, and all set to work to eat cherries, which was the only food we got between 5 A. M. and 11 P. M.

I saw a most laughable spectacle this afternoon — a Negro dressed in full Yankee uniform, with a rifle at full cock, leading along a barefooted white man, with whom he had evidently changed clothes. General Longstreet stopped the pair, and asked the black man what it meant. He replied, "The two soldiers in charge of this here Yank have got drunk, so for fear he should escape I have took care of him, and brought him through that little town." The consequential manner of the Negro, and the supreme contempt with which he spoke to his prisoner, were most amusing.

This little episode of a Southern slave leading a white Yankee soldier through a Northern village, *alone and of his own accord*, would not have been gratifying to an abolitionist. Nor would the sympathizers both in England and in the North feel encouraged if they could hear the language of detestation and contempt with which the numerous Negroes with the Southern armies speak of their liberators.*

* From what I have seen of the Southern Negroes, I am of opinion that the Confederates could, if they chose, convert a great number into soldiers; and from the affection which undoubtedly exists as a general rule between the slaves and their masters, I think that they would prove more efficient than black troops under any other circumstances. But I do not imagine that such an experiment will be tried, except as a very last resort. . . .

[225]

I saw General Hood in his carriage. He looked rather bad, and has been suffering a good deal. The doctors seem to doubt whether they will be able to save his arm. I also saw General Hampton, of the cavalry, who has been shot in the hip, and has two saber-cuts on the head, but he was in very good spirits.

A short time before we reached Hagerstown there was some firing in front, together with an alarm that the Yankee cavalry was upon us. The ambulances were sent back; but some of the wounded jumped out, and, producing the rifles which they had not parted with, they prepared to fight. After a good deal of desultory skirmishing, we seated ourselves upon a hill overlooking Hagers-town, and saw the enemy's cavalry driven through the town pur-sued by yelling Confederates.

A good many Yankee prisoners now passed us. One of them who was smoking a cigar, was a lieutenant of cavalry, dressed very smartly, and his hair brushed with the greatest care. He formed rather a contrast to his ragged escort, and to ourselves, who had not washed or shaved for ever so long.

About 7 P. M. we rode through Hagerstown, in the streets of which were several dead horses and a few dead men. After pro-ceeding about a mile beyond the town we halted, and General Longstreet sent four cavalrymen up a lane, with directions to re-port everything they saw. We then dismounted and lay down. About ten minutes later (it being nearly dark) we heard a sudden rush — a panic — and then a regular stampede commenced, in the midst of which I descried our four cavalry heroes crossing a field as fast as they could gallop.

All was now complete confusion; officers mounting their horses, and pursuing those which had got loose, and soldiers climbing over fences for protection against the supposed advancing Yankees.

[226]

In the middle of the din I heard an artillery officer shouting to his "cannoneers" to stand by him, and plant the guns in a proper position for enfilading the lane. I also distinguished Longstreet walking about, hustled by the excited crowd, and remarking, in angry tones, which could scarcely be heard, and to which no attention was paid. "Now, you don't know what it is — you don't know what it is."

Whilst the row and confusion were at their height, the object of all this alarm at length emerged from the dark lane, in the shape of a domestic four-wheel carriage, with a harmless load of females. The stampede had, however, spread, increased in the rear, and caused much harm and delay.

Cavalry skirmishing went on until quite dark, a determined attack having been made by the enemy, who did his best to prevent the trains from crossing the Potomac at Williamsport. It resulted in the success of the Confederates; but every impartial man confesses that these cavalry fights are miserable affairs. Neither party has any idea of serious charging with the saber. They approach one another with considerable boldness, until they get to within about forty yards, and then, at the very moment when a dash is necessary, and the sword alone should be used, they hesitate, halt, and commence a desultory fire with carbines and revolvers.

An Englishman named Winthrop, a captain in the Confederate Army, and formerly an officer in H. M.'s 22d regiment, although not in the cavalry himself, seized the colors of one of the regiments, and rode straight at the Yankees in the most gallant manner, shouting to the men to follow him. He continued to distinguish himself by leading charges until his horse was unfortunately killed. I heard his conduct on this occasion highly spoken of by all. Stuart's cavalry can hardly be called cavalry in the European sense of the word; but, on the other hand, the country in which they are accustomed to operate is not adapted for cavalry.

—— was forced at last to give up wearing even his Austrian forage cap; for the last two days soldiers on the line of march had been visiting his ambulance in great numbers, under the impression (encouraged by the driver) that he was a Yankee general. The idea now was that the army would remain some days in or near its present position until the arrival of the ammunition from Winchester.

7th July (Tuesday) — Lawley, the Austrian, and I drove into Hagerstown this morning, and General Longstreet moved into a new position on the Williamsport road, which he was to occupy for the present. We got an excellent room in the Washington Hotel on producing greenbacks.

Public opinion in Hagerstown seems to be pretty evenly divided between North and South, and probably accommodates itself to circumstances. For instance, yesterday the women waved their handkerchiefs when the Yankee cavalry were driven through the town, and today they went through the same compliment in honor of 3500 Yankee (Gettysburg) prisoners whom I saw march through en route for Richmond. I overhead the conversation of some Confederate soldiers about these prisoners. One remarked, with respect to the Zouaves, of whom there were a few — "Those red-breeched fellows look as if they could fight, but they don't, though; no, not so well as the bluebellies."

Lawley introduced me to General Stuart in the streets of Hagerstown today. He is commonly called Jeb Stuart, on account of his initials. He is a good-looking, jovial character, exactly like his photographs. He has certainly accomplished wonders, and done

[228   ]

excellent service in his peculiar style of warfare. He is a good and gallant soldier, though he sometimes incurs ridicule by his harmless affectation and peculiarities. The other day he rode through a Virginian town, his horse covered with garlands of roses.

He also departs considerably from the severe simplicity of dress adopted by other Confederate generals; but no one can deny that he is the right man in the right place. On a campaign, he seems to roam over the country according to his own discretion, and always gives a good account of himself, turning up at the right moment; and hitherto he has never got himself into any serious trouble.

I rode to General Longstreet's camp, which is about two miles in the direction of Williamsport, and consulted him about my difficulties with regard to my leave. He was most good-natured about it, and advised me under the circumstances to drive in the direction of Hancock; and in the event of being ill-treated on the way, to insist upon being taken before the nearest U. S. officer of the highest rank, who would probably protect me. I determined to take his advice at once; so I took leave of him and of his officers.

Longstreet is generally a very taciturn and undemonstrative man, but he was quite affectionate in his farewell. His last words were a hearty hope for the speedy termination of the war. All his officers were equally kind in their expressions on my taking leave, though the last sentence uttered by Latrobe was not entirely reassuring — "You may take your oath he'll be caught for a spy." [3]

I then rode to General Lee's camp, and asked him for a pass to get through his lines. We had a long talk together, and he told me of the raid made by the enemy, for the express purpose of arresting his badly wounded son (a Confederate brigadier general), who was lying in the house of a relation in Virginia. They insisted upon carrying him off in a litter, though he had never been

[229   ]

out of bed, and had quite recently been shot through the thigh. This seizure was evidently made for purposes of retaliation. His life has since been threatened, in the event of the South retaliating for Burnside's alleged military murders in Kentucky.

But few officers, however, speak of the Northerners with so much moderation as General Lee. His extreme amiability seems to prevent his speaking strongly against anyone. I really felt quite sorry when I said good-by to so many gentlemen from whom I had received so much disinterested kindness.

I am now about to leave the Southern States, after traveling quite alone throughout their entire length and breadth, including Texas and the trans-Mississippi country, for nearly three months and a half, during which time I have been thrown amongst all classes of the population — the highest and lowest, and the most lawless.

Although many were very sore about the conduct of England, I never received an uncivil word from anybody, but, on the contrary, I have been treated by all with more than kindness.* I have never met a man who was not anxious for a termination of the war; and I have never met a man, woman, or child who contemplated its termination as possible without an entire separation from the *now* detested Yankee. I have never been asked for alms or a gratuity by any man or woman, black or white. Everyone knew who I was, and all spoke to me with the greatest confidence.

I have rarely heard any person complain of the almost total ruin which had befallen so many. All are prepared to undergo still greater sacrifices — they contemplate and prepare to receive greater

* The only occasion on which I was roughly handled was when I had the misfortune to enter the city of Jackson, Mississippi, just as the Federals evacuated it. I do not complain of that affair, which, under the circumstances, was not to be wondered at.

[230]

reverses which it is impossible to avert. They look to a successful termination of the war as certain, although few are sanguine enough to fix a speedy date for it, and nearly all bargain for its lasting at least all Lincoln's presidency.

Although I have always been with the Confederates in the time of their misfortunes, yet I never heard any person use a desponding word as to the result of the struggle. When I was in Texas and Louisiana, Banks seemed to be carrying everything before him, Grant was doing the same in Mississippi, and I certainly did not bring luck to my friends at Gettysburg. I have lived in bivouacs with all the Southern armies, which are as distinct from one another as the British is from the Austrian, and I have never once seen an instance of insubordination.

When I got back to Hagerstown, I endeavored to make arrangements for a horse and buggy to drive through the lines. With immense difficulty I secured the services of a Mr. ——, to take me to Hancock, and as much farther as I chose to go, for a dollar a mile (greenbacks). I engaged also to pay him the value of his horse and buggy, in case they should be confiscated by either side. He was evidently extremely alarmed, and I was obliged to keep him up to the mark by assurances that his horse would inevitably be seized by the Confederates, unless protected by General Lee's pass in my possession.

8th July (Wednesday) — My conductor told me he couldn't go today on account of a funeral, but he promised faithfully to start tomorrow. Everyone was full of forebodings as to my probable fate when I fell into Yankee clutches. In deference to their advice I took off my gray shooting-jacket, in which they said I was sure to be taken for a Rebel, and I put on a black coat. But I scouted all well-meant advice as to endeavoring to disguise myself as an "American citizen," or to conceal the exact truth in any way. I was aware that a great deal depended upon falling into the hands of a gentleman, and I did not believe these were so rare in the Northern Army as the Confederates led me to suppose.

CHAPTER 14

Hagerstown to New York

Passing beyond the Confederate Lines — First Contact with Unionists — Arrested on Suspicion — Handed Over to General Kelly — A Clean Bill of Health — "The Only Federal Officers I Have Come in Contact with Were Gentlemen" — By Stage to Johnstown — To Philadelphia by That Admirable and Ingenious Yankee Notion, the Sleeping Car — The Luxury of New York — Northern Overconfidence — Draft Riots — I Board the S. S. China

9th July (Thursday) — I left Hagerstown at 8 A. M., in my conductor's good buggy, after saying farewell to Lawley, the Austrian, and the numerous Confederate officers who came to see me off, and wish me good luck. We passed the Confederate advanced post at about two miles from Hagerstown, and were allowed to pass on the production of General Lee's authority.

I was now fairly launched beyond the Confederate lines for the first time since I had been in America. Immediately afterwards we began to be asked all sorts of inquisitive questions about the Rebels, which I left to my driver to answer. It became perfectly evident that this narrow strip of Maryland is entirely Unionist.

At about 12 o'clock we reached the top of a high hill, and halted to bait our horse at an inn called Fairview. No sooner had we descended from the buggy than about twenty rampageous Unionists appeared, who told us they had come up to get a good view of the big fight in which the G—d d—d Rebels were to be all captured, or drowned in the Potomac.

My appearance evidently did not please them from the very first. With alarm I observed them talking to one another, and pointing at me. At length a particularly truculent-looking individual with an enormous mustache approached me, and fixing his eyes long and steadfastly upon my trousers, he remarked, in the surliest possible tones, "Them breeches is a d—d bad color." This he said in allusion, not to their dirty state, but to the fact of their being gray, the Rebel color.

I replied to this very disagreeable assertion in as conciliating a way as I possibly could; and in answer to his question as to who I was, I said that I was an English traveler. He then said that his wife was an English lady from Preston. I next expressed my pride of being a countryman of his wife's. He then told me in tones that admitted of no contradiction, that Preston was just forty-five miles east of London; and he afterwards launched into torrents of invectives against the Rebels, who had *run him* out of Virginia; and he stated his intention of killing them in great numbers to gratify his taste.

With some difficulty I prevailed upon him and his rabid brethren to drink, which pacified them slightly for a time; but when the horse was brought out to be harnessed, it became evident I was not to be allowed to proceed without a row. I therefore addressed the crowd, and asked them quietly who among them wished to detain me. I told them at the same time, that I would not answer any questions put by those who were not persons in authority, but that I should be most happy to explain myself to any officer of the United States Army.

At length they allowed me to proceed, on the understanding

that my buggy driver should hand me over to General Kelly, at Hancock. The driver was provided with a letter for the general, in which I afterwards discovered that I was denounced as a spy, and "handed over to the General *to be dealt with as justice to our cause demands.*" We were then allowed to start, the driver being threatened with condign vengeance if he let me escape.

After we had proceeded about six miles we fell in with some Yankee cavalry, by whom we were immediately captured, and the responsibility of my custody was thus removed from my conductor's shoulders. A cavalry soldier was put in charge of us, and we passed through the numerous Yankee outposts under the title of "*Prisoners.*"

The hills near Hancock were white with Yankee tents, and there were, I believe, from 8000 to 10,000 Federals there. I did not think much of the appearance of the Northern troops. They are certainly dressed in proper uniform, but their clothes are badly fitted, and they are often round-shouldered, dirty, and slovenly in appearance; in fact, bad imitations of soldiers. Now, the Confederate has no ambition to imitate the regular soldier at all. He looks the genuine Rebel; but in spite of his bare feet, his ragged clothes, his old rug, and toothbrush stuck like a rose in his buttonhole,* he has a sort of devil-may-care, reckless, self-confident look, which is decidedly taking.

At 5 P. M. we drove up in front of the door of General Kelly's quarters, and to my immense relief I soon discovered that he was a gentleman.¹ I then explained to him the whole truth, concealing nothing. I said I was a British officer on leave of absence, traveling for my own instruction; that I had been all the way to Mexico,

---

* This tooth-brush in the buttonhole is a very common custom, and has a most quaint effect.

and entered the Southern States by the Rio Grande, for the express purpose of not breaking any legally established blockade. I told him I had visited all the Southern armies in Mississippi, Tennessee, Charleston, and Virginia, and seen the late campaign as General Longstreet's guest, but had in no way entered the Confederate service.

I also gave him my word that I had not got in my possession any letters, either public or private, from any person in the South to any person anywhere else. I showed him my British passport and General Lee's pass as a British officer; and I explained that my only object in coming North was to return to England in time for the expiration of my leave; and I ended by expressing a hope that he would make my detention as short as possible.

After considering a short time, he said that he would certainly allow me to go on, but that he could not allow my driver to go back. I felt immensely relieved at the decision, but the countenance of my companion lengthened considerably. It was, however, settled that he should take me on to Cumberland, and General Kelly good-naturedly promised to do what he could for him on his return.

General Kelly then asked me in an off-hand manner whether all General Lee's army was at Hagerstown; but I replied, laughing, "You of course understand, General, that, having got that pass from General Lee, I am bound by every principle of honor not to give you any information which can be of advantage to you." He laughed and promised not to ask me any more questions of that sort. He then sent his aid-de-camp with me to the provost marshal, who immediately gave me a pass for Cumberland.

On my return to the General's, I discovered the perfidious driver (that zealous Southerner a few hours previous) hard at work communicating to General Kelly all he knew, and a great deal more besides; but, from what I heard, I don't think his information was very valuable.

I was treated by General Kelly and all his officers with the greatest good-nature and courtesy, although I had certainly come among them under circumstances suspicious, to say the least. I felt quite sorry that they should be opposed to my Southern friends, and I regretted still more that they should be obliged to serve with or under a Butler, a Milroy, or even a Hooker. I took leave of them at six o'clock; and I can truly say that the only Federal officers I have ever come in contact with were gentlemen.

We had got four miles beyond Hancock, when the tire of one of our wheels came off, and we had to stop for a night at a farmhouse. I had supper with the farmer and his laborers, who had just come in from the fields, and the supper was much superior to that which can be procured at the first hotel at Richmond. All were violent Unionists, and perfectly under the impression that the Rebels were totally demoralized, and about to lay down their arms. Of course I held by tongue, and gave no one reason to suppose that I had ever been in Rebeldom.

10th July (Friday) — The drive from Hancock to Cumberland is a very mountainous forty-four miles — total distance from Hagerstown, sixty-six miles. We met with no further adventure on the road, although the people were very inquisitive, but I never opened my mouth. One woman in particular, who kept a toll bar, thrust her ugly old head out of an upper window, and yelled out, "Air they a-fixin' for another battle out there?" jerking her head in the direction of Hagerstown. The driver replied that, although the bunch of Rebels there was pretty big, yet he could not answer for their fixing arrangements, which he afterwards explained to me meant digging fortifications.

We arrived at Cumberland at 7 P. M. This is a great coal place, and a few weeks ago it was touched up by "Imboden," who burnt a lot of coal barges, which has rendered the people rabid against the Rebs. I started by stage for Johnstown at 8:30 P. M.

11*th July* (Saturday) — I hope I may never for my sins be again condemned to travel for thirty hours in an American stage on a used-up plank road. We changed carriages at Somerset. All my fellow travelers were of course violent Unionists, and invariably spoke of my late friends as Rebels or Rebs. They had all got into their heads that their Potomac army, not having been thoroughly thrashed, as it always has been hitherto, had achieved a tremendous victory; and that its new chief, General Meade, who in reality was driven into a strong position, which he had sense enough to stick to, is a wonderful strategist.

They all hope that the remnants of Lee's army will not be allowed to ESCAPE over the Potomac; whereas, when I left the army two days ago, no man in it had a thought of escaping over the Potomac, and certainly General Meade was not in a position to attempt to prevent the passage, if crossing had become necessary.[2]

I reached Johnstown on the Pennsylvania Railway at 6 P. M., and found that town in a great state of excitement in consequence of the review of two militia companies. These were receiving garlands from the fair ladies of Johnstown in gratitude for their daring conduct in turning out to resist Lee's invasion. Most of the men seemed to be respectable mechanics, not at all adapted for an early interview with the Rebels. The garlands supplied were as big and apparently as substantial as a ship's life buoys, and the recipients looked particularly helpless after they had got them. Heaven help those Pennsylvanian braves if a score of Hood's Texans had caught sight of them!

Left Johnstown by train at 7:30 P. M., and by paying half a dollar, I secured a berth in a sleeping car — a most admirable and ingenious Yankee notion.

12th July (Sunday) — The Pittsburgh and Philadelphia Railway is, I believe, accounted one of the best in America, which did not prevent my spending eight hours last night off the line; but, being asleep at the time, I was unaware of the circumstance. Instead of arriving at Philadelphia at 6 A. M., we did not get there till 3 P. M. Passed Harrisburg at 9 A. M. It was full of Yankee soldiers, and has evidently not recovered from the excitement consequent upon the late invasion, one effect of which has been to prevent the cutting of the crops by the calling out of the militia.

At Philadelphia I saw a train containing one hundred and fifty Confederate prisoners, who were being stared at by a large number of the *beau monde* of Philadelphia. I mingled with the crowd which was chaffing them. Most of the people were good-natured, but I heard one suggestion to the effect that they should be taken to the river, "and every mother's son of them drowned there."

I arrived at New York at 10 P. M., and drove to the Fifth Avenue Hotel.[3]

13th July (Monday) — The luxury and comfort of New York and Philadelphia strike one as extraordinary after having lately come from Charleston and Richmond. The greenbacks seem to be nearly as good as gold. The streets are as full as possible of well-dressed people, and are crowded with able-bodied civilians capable

[239]

of bearing arms, who have evidently no intention of doing so. They apparently *don't feel the war at all* here; and until there is a grand smash with their money, or some other catastrophe to make them feel it, I can easily imagine that they will not be anxious to make peace.

I walked the whole distance of Broadway to the consul's house, and nothing could exceed the apparent prosperity. The street was covered with banners and placards inviting people to enlist in various high-sounding regiments. Bounties of $550 were offered, and huge pictures hung across the street, on which numbers of ragged *Graybacks*,* terror depicted on their features, were being pursued by the Federals.

On returning to the Fifth Avenue, I found all the shopkeepers beginning to close their stores, and I perceived by degrees that there was great alarm about the resistance to the draft which was going on this morning. On reaching the hotel I perceived a whole block of buildings on fire close by. Engines were present, but were not allowed to play by the crowd.

In the hotel itself, universal consternation prevailed, and an attack by the mob had been threatened. I walked about in the neighborhood, and saw a company of soldiers on the march, who were being jeered at and hooted by small boys, and I saw a Negro pursued by the crowd take refuge with the military. He was followed by loud cries of "Down with the b——y nigger! Kill all niggers!" &c.

Never having been in New York before, and being totally ignorant of the state of feeling with regard to Negroes, I inquired of a bystander what the Negroes had done that they should want to

* The Northerners call the Southerners "Graybacks," just as the latter call the former "Bluebellies," on account of the color of their dress.[4]

kill them? He replied civilly enough — "Oh sir, they hate them here; they are the innocent cause of all these troubles." [5]

Shortly afterwards, I saw a troop of citizen cavalry come up. The troopers were very gorgeously attired, but evidently experienced so much difficulty in sitting their horses, that they were more likely to excite laughter than any other emotion.

14th July (Tuesday) — At breakfast this morning two Irish waiters, seeing I was a Britisher, came up to me one after another, and whispered at intervals in hoarse Hibernian accents — "It's disgraceful, sir. I've been drafted, sir. I'm a Briton. I love my country. I love the Union Jack, sir." I suggested an interview with Mr. Archibald, but neither of them seemed to care about going to the *counsel* just yet. These rascals have probably been hard at work for years, voting as free and enlightened American citizens, and abusing England to their hearts' content.

I heard everyone talking of the total demoralization of the Rebels as a certain fact, and all seemed to anticipate their approaching destruction. All this sounded very absurd to me, who had left Lee's army four days previously as full of fight as ever — much stronger in numbers, and ten times more efficient in every military point of view, than it was *when it crossed the Potomac to invade Maryland a year ago.*

In its own opinion, Lee's army has not lost any of its prestige at the battle of Gettysburg, in which it most gallantly stormed strong intrenchments defended by the whole army of the Potomac, which never ventured outside its works, or approached in force within half a mile of the Confederate artillery.

The result of the battle of Gettysburg, together with the fall of Vicksburg and Port Hudson, seems to have turned everybody's head completely, and has deluded them with the idea of the speedy and complete subjugation of the South. I was filled with astonishment to hear the people speaking in this confident manner, when one of their most prosperous states had been so recently laid under contribution as far as Harrisburg; and Washington, their capital itself, having just been saved by a fortunate turn of luck. Four fifths of the Pennsylvanian spoil had safely crossed the Potomac before I left Hagerstown.

The consternation in the streets seemed to be on the increase. Fires were going on in all directions, and the streets were being patrolled by large bodies of police followed by special constables, the latter bearing truncheons, but not looking very happy. I heard a British captain making a deposition before the consul, to the effect that the mob had got on board his vessel, and cruelly beaten his colored crew. As no British man-of-war was present, the French Admiral was appealed to, who at once requested that all British ships with colored crews might be anchored under the guns of his frigate.

The reports of outrages, hangings, and murder were now most alarming, the terror and anxiety were universal. All shops were shut: all carriages and omnibuses had ceased running. No colored man or woman was visible or safe in the streets, or even in his own dwelling. Telegraphs were cut, and railroad tracks torn up. The draft was suspended, and the mob evidently had the upper hand.

The people who can't pay $300 naturally hate being forced to fight in order to liberate the very race who they are most anxious should be slaves. It is their direct interest not only that all slaves should remain slaves, but that the free Northern Negroes who compete with them for labor should be sent to the South also.

* * *

[242]

15th July (Wednesday) — The hotel this morning was occupied by military, or rather by creatures in uniform. One of the sentries stopped me; and on my remonstrating to his officer, the latter blew up to the sentry, and said, "You are only to stop persons in military dress — don't you know what military dress is?" "No," responded this efficient sentry — and I left the pair discussing the definition of a soldier. I had the greatest difficulty in getting a conveyance down to the water. I saw a stone barricade in the distance, and heard firing going on — and I was not at all sorry to find myself on board the *China*.

CHAPTER 15

Postscript

Northern Illusions — How the South Will Draw Men for Its Armies — How Supplies Will Continue to Flow — Northern Indifference — Southern Will to Win — "I Never Can Believe That in the Nineteenth Century the Civilized World Will be Condemned to Witness the Destruction of Such a Gallant Race"

During my voyage home in the *China,* I had an opportunity of discussing with many intelligent Northern gentlemen all that I had seen in my Southern travels. We did so in a very amicable spirit, and I think they rendered justice to my wish to explain to them without exaggeration the state of feeling amongst their enemies. Although these Northerners belonged to quite the upper classes, and were not likely to be led blindly by the absurd nonsense of the sensation press at New York, yet their ignorance of the state of the case in the South was very great.[1]

The recent successes had given them the impression that the last card of the South was played. Charleston was about to fall; Mobile, Savannah, and Wilmington would quickly follow; Lee's army, they thought, was a disheartened, disorganized mob; Bragg's army in a still worse condition, fleeing before Rosecrans, who would carry everything before him. They felt confident that the fall of the Mississippian fortresses would prevent communication from

[244]

one bank to the other, and that the great river would soon be open to peaceful commerce.

All these illusions have since been dispelled, but they probably still cling to the idea of the great exhaustion of the Southern *personnel.*

But this difficulty of recruiting the Southern armies is not so great as is generally supposed. As I have already stated, no Confederate soldier is given his discharge from the army, however badly he may be wounded. Instead, he is employed at such labor in the public service as he may be capable of performing, and his place in the ranks is taken by a sound man hitherto exempted. The slightly wounded are cured as quickly as possible, and are sent back at once to their regiments. *The women take care of this.* The number actually killed, or who die of their wounds, are the only total losses to the state, and these form but a small proportion of the enormous butcher's bills which seem at first so very appalling.

I myself remember, with General Polk's corps, a fine-looking man who had had both his hands blown off at the wrists by unskillful artillery practice in one of the early battles. A currycomb and brush were fitted into his stumps, and he was engaged in grooming artillery horses with considerable skill. This man was called a hostler; and, as the war drags on, the number of these handless hostlers will increase.

By degrees the clerks at the offices, the orderlies, the railway and post-office officials, and the stage drivers will be composed of maimed and mutilated soldiers. The number of exempted persons all over the South is still very large, and they can easily be exchanged for worn veterans.

Besides this fund to draw upon, a calculation is made of the number of boys who arrive each year at the fighting age. These are all "panting for the rifle," but have been latterly wisely forbidden the ranks until they are fit to undergo the hardships of a military life.

By these means, it is the opinion of the Confederates that they can keep their armies recruited up to their present strength for several years; and, if the worst comes to the worst, they can always fall back upon their Negroes as the last resort; but I do not think they contemplate such a necessity as likely to arise for a considerable time.

With respect to the supply of arms, cannon, powder, and military stores, the Confederates are under no alarm whatever. Augusta furnishes more than sufficient gunpowder; Atlanta, copper caps, &c. The Tredegar Works at Richmond, and other foundries, cast more cannon than is wanted; and the Federal generals have always hitherto proved themselves the most indefatigable purveyors of artillery to the Confederate government. Even in those actions which they claim as drawn battles or as victories, such as Corinth, Murfreesboro, and Gettysburg, they have never failed to make over cannon to the Southerners without exacting any in return.

My Northern friends on board the *China* spoke much and earnestly about the determination of the North to crush out the Rebellion at any sacrifice. But they did not show any disposition to *fight themselves* in this cause, although many of them would have made most eligible recruits; and if they had been Southerners, their female relations would have made them enter the army whether their inclinations led them that way or not.

I do not mention this difference of spirit by way of making any odious comparisons between North and South in this respect, because I feel sure that these Northern gentlemen would emulate the example of their enemy if they could foresee any danger of a Southern Butler exercising his infamous sway over Philadelphia, or of a Confederate Milroy ruling with intolerable despotism in Boston, by withholding the necessaries of life from helpless women with one hand, whilst tendering them with the other a hated and absurd oath of allegiance to a detested government.

But the mass of respectable Northerners, though they may be willing to pay, do not very naturally feel themselves called upon to give their blood in a war of aggression, ambition, and conquest. For this war is essentially a war of conquest. If ever a nation did wage such a war, the North is now engaged, with a determination worthy of a more hopeful cause, in endeavoring to conquer the South.

But the more I think of all that I have seen in the Confederate States of the devotion of the whole population, the more I feel inclined to say with General Polk — "How can you subdue such a nation as this!" Even supposing that their extermination were a feasible plan, as some Northerners have suggested, I never can believe that in the nineteenth century the civilized world will be condemned to witness the destruction of such a gallant race.

Editor's Notes

CHAPTER 1

At the Mouth of the Rio Grande

1. Fremantle landed at the last point where it was possible to enter the Confederate States "legitimately." All Southern ports were by now under Northern blockade. But by landing in Mexico and crossing the Texas border, Fremantle was able to start his odyssey without violating his sense of protocol. Other less sensitive foreigners were turning the same loophole to great commercial advantage — hence the seventy ships anchored off the Rio Grande. Seven months later, the North closed off this last Southern link with the outside world, and Fremantle would have had either to bury his scruples or forego his trip. On November 2, the Federals landed a force at the mouth of the Rio Grande and took Brownsville four days later. The area was lost to the Confederates for good.

2. Fremantle's diary is perhaps the best of all sources on what the Confederate soldier actually looked like. He was a far cry from the romantic figure in gray and gold braid that is usually pictured today. Never was there a more motley army — hardly anybody dressed alike and very few even wore gray. Thus, Fremantle finds Duff's cavalry wearing flannel shirts and high black hats; the 3rd Texas Infantry in an assortment of French *képis*, wide-awakes and Mexican hats; Pyron's regiment at Galveston in "every variety of costume"; Walker's Division in Louisiana wearing ragged civilian clothes; Liddell's Arkansas brigade marching by their general in shirt sleeves; Pender's Division in Virginia sporting every shade of gray and brown; Hood's troops at Chambersburg, ragged and dirty,

carrying only old pieces of carpet, in which they rolled up the few odds and ends they used on the march.

The Confederate Army's crazy-quilt appearance, of course, stemmed from the blockade and the insignificant Southern textile industry. There was some effort to develop a standard uniform at the start of the war, and some units, like the Maryland Line and the Washington Artillery, looked as natty as the Federals, but by the time Fremantle arrived practically the only standard equipment in the Southern Army was the toothbrush, which, curiously, the typical Confederate soldier sported in his buttonhole.

3. In a way, the ambulance was the jeep of the Civil War. As yet, it enjoyed no special status as a conveyance for the wounded, and there was no question of ethics in using one as a sort of all-purpose vehicle. People spoke of "good" and "bad" ambulances, and, as usual, the generals had the best.

4. Brigadier General Barnard E. Bee died in the Civil War's first big battle at Bull Run, but he made a greater contribution than many a general who lived through Appomattox. As his soldiers retreated in confusion up the Henry House hill before the advancing Union troops, he rushed up to General Thomas J. Jackson, who was standing with his brigade at the top of the hill, backstopping the Confederate line of defense. "General, they're beating us back!" cried Bee. "Then, sir, we will give them the bayonet," was Jackson's reply. Completely inspired, Bee turned to his retreating troops and shouted, "Look! There is Jackson standing like a stone wall! Rally behind the Virginians!" Bee was shot dead within minutes, but his words gave Jackson an imperishable nickname.

5. The early days of the Civil War found many privates living like generals — and the generals often living like privates. "Gentlemen rankers" of the 1st South Carolina Regiment marched with their personal slaves trotting along in the rear. The 3rd Alabama traveled with one hundred body servants to prepare meals and handle the regiment's housekeeping chores. At this point, it was often considered poor taste for a well-to-do man even to want to be an officer. In sharp contrast, most of the top Confederate leaders

lived in Spartan simplicity. Lee, for instance, usually refused to stay in a house when in the field, insisting instead on an ordinary army tent.

6. The Northern blockade posed some legal ticklers. One was the status of the Rio Grande, which served both the Confederate States and neutral Mexico. About five weeks before Fremantle's arrival, the Union Navy captured the English-owned *Peterhoff*, a ship bound for Matamoros with cargo for both Mexico and the Confederacy. British jingoists (and, of course, all Southerners) were indignant, claiming that the *Peterhoff* was a neutral ship going to a neutral destination. But the British government declined to go to the mat on the issue. Ultimately the U.S. Supreme Court decided that the *Peterhoff* should be freed, the goods bound for Mexico should be released, and the material destined for the Confederacy should be kept as legitimate contraband.

7. Fremantle was visiting Mexico at the start of a French experiment in imperialism, which culminated in setting up the puppet Emperor Maximilian. Two years before, internal disorder and financial chaos in Mexico had reached a point where France, Britain and Spain had decided jointly to intervene to safeguard their nationals' interests. In early 1862 all three countries occupied several ports along the coast. France, however, had far more ambitious objectives than collecting a few debts; Napoleon III was interested in a full-scale colonial venture. By April, the British and Spanish had pulled out, and the French had their fingers in everything. Napoleon III's troops slowly fanned out over the country, with the Mexicans under Juárez fighting back every inch of the way. The French were checked in 1862 at Puebla, but by the time of Fremantle's arrival, they were on the march again.

The Mexican "victory" at Puebla, which Fremantle helped celebrate, was insignificant, and by June the French had captured Mexico City and established their own government. The following year, the puppet Maximilian was installed as Emperor, and the French subjugation of the country continued. But the Confederacy's doom was Maximilian's doom. As soon as the Civil

War was over, Washington demanded that the French withdraw their troops. The idea of facing Grant and Lee's hardened veterans fighting on the same side was too much, and the French quickly acceded. By early 1867, the last French troops had gone; by May, the deserted Maximilian was captured by the resurgent Mexicans; by June, he was executed.

8. The pre-dinner cocktail may seem out of place as a mid-nineteenth century frontier custom, but actually Washington Irving referred to the drink as early as 1809 in *Knickerbocker*.

9. Cocktail parties for Fremantle were more than good fellow-ship; they were good politics. The feeling was growing that the South would never make it without foreign aid, and by now almost any English visitor was hopefully given VIP treatment. Fremantle basked in the favors that flowed. He was serenaded with "God Save the Queen"; he found that everybody toasted the crown; on trains he was allowed to travel in the ladies' car; in hotels he sometimes could even have a bed to himself. Other visiting Englishmen were treated in the same manner.

Hospitality was especially lavish during these spring days of '63. Foreign recognition seemed tantalizingly near, so near that perhaps just one more favorable impression might do the trick. U.S. Ambassador Charles Francis Adams had warned Washington that Britain might recognize the South if there was no big Union victory by February. None had occurred; instead there was another Union disaster by May. Lee triumphed at Chancellorsville, and British Foreign Minister Lord Russell was reported to have asked Palmerston, the Prime Minister, whether the time had not arrived for intervention. Gladstone increased the optimism by a speech at Newcastle praising Jefferson Davis for creating a new nation.

All hopes were dashed at Gettysburg. The British government suddenly heard Washington's protests about the Confederate rams being built in the Laird shipyards. Previously Palmerston had maintained the ships were destined for the Turkish Navy; now the masquerade was tacitly acknowledged, and the British government appeased both Washington and the Laird stockholders by taking over the boats for the Royal Navy. Meanwhile, in France, Napoleon III also recovered his hearing and complied with demands from Washington to stop the construction of some rams that were quietly being built in French shipyards.

Actually, the South was never as close to British recognition as Confederate leaders hoped. The British Liberal Party was in power, and once slavery became the main issue of the war, it could never afford to recognize Southern independence. On the other hand, the Conservative Party, which seemed such a good bet to most Southerners, was certainly nothing to bank on. It contained many Southern sympathizers, but these were never in the saddle, and official party policy was definitely hands-off. The Conservatives were all for strict neutrality (which made them sometimes look pro-South), and all for anything to needle the Liberals in power. But that was as far as it went. As William Devereaux Jones puts it in his penetrating analysis of the Conservative position, "Party policy was not founded on sentiment or bonds of sympathy, but on party tradition and political expediency." (See "The British Conservatives and the American Civil War," *American Historical Review*, April 1953, pp. 527–543.)

10. The life of an English consul in Matamoros at this time could wreck any man's health — particularly since no pay went with the job. The town swarmed with smugglers and adventurers seeking quick profits in trade across the border with the blockaded Confederacy. Local officials were quick to put the bite on these fly-by-nights, and in an era when the flag followed commerce, the consul was constantly besieged with demands for protection. On the other hand, Don Pablo's sudden illness must be considered in light of the way he and Fremantle spent the day before: six and one-half hours of wine-drinking at Mr. Maloney's and a night at the Grand Fandango — all in all, a good foundation for a colossal hangover.

11. Every good Confederate had a pet contempt for Yankee military prowess. It ran this way: the Northern soldier was a

clerk, a drudge, a dreary bluenose, who had no spirit or red blood in his veins; the Southern soldier, on the other hand, was a dashing cavalier, equally adept in the art of war or living graciously. Actually, the tables were sometimes completely turned. Take Chancellorsville. The Confederate line-up included Lee, who never had liquor at his mess, Jackson, who wouldn't touch the stuff, and Stuart, who had promised his father he'd never drink. Opposing this trio was Hooker, with a hard-drinking staff and a headquarters that resembled a brothel.

12. Some Southerners were anything but ardent Confederates. The South, like the North, found many of its citizens cool to the war and some who even favored the other side. Fremantle spotlights the Germans in Texas, but Union sympathizers were numerous in parts of Georgia, in the Appalachians, in western Virginia and in supposedly pro-Southern Maryland. In Tennessee tension reached such a point that Bragg once forbade his men to accept pies from local citizens for fear they were poisoned. Maryland's coolness was especially galling. Lee had marched in to "liberate" the state in 1862, only to find nobody wanted to be liberated. This was quite contrary to the stirring lyrics of "Maryland, My Maryland," which went in part:

> She is not dead, nor deaf, nor dumb —
> Huzza! She spurns the Northern scum!
> She breathes — she burns! She'll come! She'll come!
> Maryland, My Maryland!

The verse was soon parodied by lines which ran:

> We can't stay here to meet the foe.
> We might get shot and killed, you know.
> But when we're safe, we'll brag and blow,
> Maryland, my Maryland.

13. The Confederate capture of the U.S.S. *Harriet Lane* was the climax of perhaps the wildest New Year's Eve Galveston ever had. It all began when the Federal fleet seized Galveston in the fall of '62. This was followed up in December when 260 men of

the 42nd Massachusetts Volunteers were sent to occupy the town. The force was completely inadequate, and they made matters worse by penning themselves up on the town wharf.

The Confederates quickly struck back. General John Magruder had just taken charge in Texas and was full of ideas. He decided on a joint sea-land operation against the Federal troops and ships in the harbor. Late New Year's Eve, a large Southern force crept stealthily over the unguarded causeway that connected Galveston with the mainland. Meanwhile, two Confederate gunboats, the *Neptune* and the *Bayou City*, edged quietly up the coast from Houston. These were commanded by Major Leon Smith, an old California steamboat skipper flatteringly described by Fremantle as a "seafaring man." On board were some 360 cavalry sharpshooters hiding behind cotton bales.

Soon after midnight, the Confederates on shore ushered in the New Year with a sudden blaze of gunfire. But it began to look like a Southern fiasco when they discovered their scaling ladders couldn't reach the wharf where the Massachusetts boys grimly held out. Then, with a crash, the cavalry-manned flotilla joined the fray. While the *Harriet Lane* literally skipped cannon balls across the water at the onrushing gunboats, the *Bayou City* ran alongside the Union ship and the Texas cavalrymen swarmed aboard. The *Harriet Lane* struck her colors, the Union troops ashore surrendered, and a truce was called while Commodore Renshaw of the Federal fleet pondered an ultimatum for the surrender of his other ships.

Renshaw refused and ordered his ships to leave. He may or may not have formally called off the truce, but he was certainly in a hurry. In his haste, he ran his own ship onto a mudflat. He ordered her scuttled. Still overhasty, he set off the charge too soon and blew himself up with his ship. All in all, it was a glorious New Year's celebration, agreed the Confederate fans who had come up from Houston on a special spectator boat chartered for the occasion.

CHAPTER 2

From Brownsville to San Antonio

1. Fremantle was probably "taken" when he managed to exchange his gold for Confederate dollars at a rate of only 4 to 1. He himself notes that a month later (when, if anything, the Confederate dollar should have been strengthened by Chancellorsville) he could get 6 to 1 in Charleston. But that was nothing, compared to what he could have had three months later. A week after Gettysburg the exchange rate went to 10 to 1. By December '64, the rate had deteriorated to 30 to 1. On January 11, 1865, it was 60 to 1; a week later 70 to 1; and after that nobody was interested.

2. Perhaps out of an Englishman's natural respect for the judiciary, Fremantle never identifies the judge who became his assistant mule driver. Longstreet, however, is not so reticent. In his outspoken memoirs, the General refers to Colonel Fremantle's magistrate, and identifies him as Judge Hyde, "whom I had met years before while in army service on the Texas frontier." (James Longstreet, *From Manassas to Appomattox*, 1896, p. 344.)

3. Fremantle was a great booster of Southern womanhood, and judging from his diary, the Confederacy at least had no shortage of belles. At Galveston, he found the ladies "pretty." At Shreveport, he thought that General Kirby Smith's wife was an "extremely pretty" woman. At Jackson, he thought the ladies were "pretty," but some of them were depressingly shy. At Shelbyville, the ladies were "very pretty." At the Robertsons' party in Charleston, the ladies were (as usual) "extremely pretty." At Winchester, he found girls as agreeable as they were "good-looking." Even in Yankee Chambersburg, the women were "pretty," although this time they were also "sour" and "disagreeable."

4. When Fremantle encountered Major General John B. Magruder he was meeting the Confederacy's most elegant general. Coming from an old Virginia family, Magruder attended West

Point, distinguished himself in the Mexican War, and went on to a career of wonderful European junkets. He took to international society immediately. Few U.S. military figures have circulated through more drawing rooms, balanced more teacups, charmed more ladies with more small talk. He was full of foppish mannerisms — and had the clothes to go with them. Usually he wore red-striped pants, a crimson-lined coat and a black cocked hat with a huge plume. Small wonder he was called "Prince John."

Magruder's star quickly rose at the start of the war. He won the first Confederate victory at Big Bethel, where his 1800 troops threw back a larger Union force. He did even better early in the Peninsular campaign. At Yorktown, his 12,000 men bluffed 75,000 Union troops, until Joe Johnston's army could come to his aid. Then his star fell. He was late hitting McClellan at Savage's Station during the Seven Days' Battle. He was badly repulsed at Malvern Hill during the same campaign. Worse still, he was rumored to have been drinking.

Magruder was officially vindicated, but he lost his command and was transferred to Texas. There, he died on the vine, although his flair and dash put him briefly back in the limelight when he twice used Confederate soldiers to beat the Union Navy — once at Galveston, later at the Sabine Pass. When the war ended, Magruder experimented briefly with exile in Mexico, but he soon came back — Mexico was obviously no place for elegant, precious "Prince John" Magruder.

5. Of all the Northern generals, McClellan was the leader most liked by the Confederates. Certainly, this was partly because they were never afraid of him. Also, McClellan respected Southern private property and opposed abolition of slavery. In addition, he reminded people of Napoleon, and the French military tradition enjoyed a great vogue in the South at this time. Most of all, McClellan may have appealed to Southerners because he, alone among the Northern generals, thought of war very much the way the Confederates did. He too wanted to fight not a war but a tournament

— full of protocol, ritual and little niceties. When he launched his Peninsular campaign, McClellan made a great point of sending Mrs. Lee through the lines by carriage to Richmond. It's hard to imagine generals like Pope or Sheridan doing the same.

6. As the most enthusiastic party boy in the Confederate Army, General Magruder went in heavily for charades, parlor games and amateur theatricals. These tastes served him well. Early in 1862, his small command at Yorktown suddenly found itself face to face with McClellan's whole army, which had been brought down the Chesapeake Bay, landed on the Virginia shore, and was advancing on Richmond from the east. The main Confederate Army was miles away, expecting an attack from the north and west. Magruder's job was to hold off 75,000 men with 12,000 men until reinforcements could arrive. He did it by staging a theatrical masterpiece. His officers shouted commands to imaginary units. A few carts rumbled back and forth over the same hidden stretch of road, looking like an endless wagon train. The same soldiers marched by a clearing in sight of the Union force, went back out of sight to the starting point, then marched by again and again. The Union Army stopped and cautiously laid siege: the Confederate reinforcements arrived in time.

He repeated this stunt on an even larger scale when Lee launched his great counterattack that wrecked McClellan's campaign. Lee had put his whole strength on the left of his line, leaving at the right end only Magruder and some 20,000 soldiers to discourage 100,000 Union troops from breaking through to Richmond. This time, Magruder used all the old tricks plus meaningless bugle calls, campfires for nonexistent soldiers, and an endless variety of sound effects. In the face of such opposition, McClellan didn't dare launch a counterattack of his own. He retreated instead to the James River, ending the threat to Richmond. Seen in this light, the talent show Magruder put on for Fremantle must have been very impressive.

7. It's easy to see why Fremantle found it hard to tear himself away from General Magruder's party. Magruder was a great Anglo-

phile and liked nothing better than to impress British officers. On one occasion before the war, when entertaining some British officers at his mess, Magruder had begged and borrowed all the gold plate, cut glass and rich furniture he could find for entertaining the Englishmen. However, he assured them that these luxuries were but the debris of the former splendor of his mess. Later, one of the dazzled Englishmen remarked to the general, "We do not wish to be inquisitive, but we have been so much impressed by this magnificence that we are constrained to believe that American officers are paid handsomely. What is your monthly pay?"

"Damned if I know," sighed Prince John indifferently, and turning to his servant, he asked, "Jim, what is my monthly pay?"

The latter was discreetly silent, perhaps because the problem of remembering $65 a month was hard for him too.

8. Fremantle throws fascinating light on slavery and the way the institution was regarded by both white and Negro during the Civil War. In some respects, the picture seems brighter than might be expected. On several occasions, we see an almost minstrel-show world of Negroes happily parading about in clothes far finer than the white folks wore. We also have the interesting picture of slaves earning good money on the side. For instance, there was John, General Scurry's body servant, who earned high pay as a barber; and there was Nelson, the slave at Natchez, who even paid his owner $4.50 a week to be allowed to run his own livery stable. In addition, there's considerable evidence of Negroes who would rather stay slaves than be free. Some expressed hatred of the Yankees, and others even captured their liberators.

But all the good is swamped by the bad. The very idea of slavery so repelled Fremantle that he never could swallow the pill, despite his inclinations to support the South. It was the same story all over the world, and Fremantle shows that the Confederates themselves realized their propaganda handicap. But somehow, with the irony of a Greek tragedy, they struggled along, sensing that "their peculiar institution" might ruin them, yet never knowing to rid themselves of it.

9. Texas at this time abounded with "filibusters" — adventurers who cashed in on chaos south of the border by organizing expeditions within the United States to participate (at a price) in Latin American revolutions.

CHAPTER 3

From San Antonio to Houston

1. Fremantle arrived just as inflation began to wreck the Confederate economy. The price of a stage ticket wasn't all that was going up. He found coffee had risen to $7 a pound in San Antonio, and when he sold his trunk in that town he received $32 for a very old pair of boots, $42 for five shirts and $25 for an old overcoat. In an agricultural economy it was natural, but today it seems strange that food still ran very low — he reports that he coud get a good meal for a dollar.

All this was just the start of the big toboggan ride. Corn meal was still $17 a bushel when Fremantle made his visit; by January 1865, it had risen to $75 a bushel. In the same period, coal rose from $20.50 to $100 a ton; wood from $30 to $100 a cord; butter from $3.50 to $20 a pound; bacon from $1.50 to $20 a pound. Whiskey ran about $28 to $35 a bottle during Fremantle's visit; the sky was the limit two years later. Near the end, prices soared at a hideous pace. On January 6, 1865, flour was quoted at $500 a barrel; on January 14 a barrel cost $1000; on January 18, $1250; on March 20, $1500. The whole terrifying picture is vividly depicted in statistics carefully kept by J. B. Jones, an unsung clerk in the Confederate War Department, who with morbid exactness recorded for history the collapse of his own standard of living.

2. The South was magnificently equipped if the war could have been won by singing. No soldiers ever liked to sing more than the Confederates. None ever had more bloodthirsty songs to sing. For instance, take "The Texan Marseillaise," a little number that Fre-

mantle undoubtedly heard during his San Antonio song-fest. Its somewhat uncompromising chorus ran:

> Arm! Arm! ye Southern braves!
> Scatter yon Vandal hordes!
> Despots and bandits, fitting food
> For vultures and your swords.

Another favorite ballad carried the boastful title, "You Can Never Win Them Back." One verse is enough to show the mood:

> We may fall before the fire of your legions,
> Paid in gold for murd'rous hire — bought allegiance!
> But for every drop that's shed
> You shall leave a mound of dead;
> And the vultures shall be fed in our regions.

These songs were typical. In the quiet of an evening campfire, Johnny Reb might softly croon "The Girl I Left Behind Me," but when stirred to mass singing, he was in no gentle mood. Even "Dixie" took a beating. Most versions were a far cry from those familiar Uncle Remus-type words about being "born in early on a frosty mornin'." More likely, the Confederates lustily roared out a verse like this:

> Strong as lions, swift as eagles,
> Back to their kennels hound those beagles!
> To arms! To arms! To arms! in Dixie!
> Cut the unequal bonds asunder!
> Let them hence each other plunder!
> To arms! To arms! To arms! in Dixie!
> Advance the flag of Dixie!
> Hurrah! Hurrah!
> For Dixie land we'll take our stand,
> To live or die for Dixie!

3. General Grant said the Confederate draft robbed the cradle and the grave. The law covered all men from 16 to 60; those from 18 to 45 were tagged for regular military duty, and the rest for the home guard. But it wasn't as tough as it sounds. States Rights governors like Vance, of North Carolina, and Brown, of Georgia, in-

sisted that even the most petty state officials be exempt; doctors handed out certificates of disability by the bushel; local judges were happy to grant writs of habeas corpus, demanding release of draftees. At the time of Fremantle's visit, only 700 conscripts a month were available even in Virginia, comparatively a patriotic hotbed. In 1864, the Conscript Bureau drafted only 13,000 out of some 150,000 men examined.

But the biggest weakness of the system was a provision in the law which allowed a drafted man to send a substitute instead of himself. This appalling rule led to endless abuses and chicanery. The price of a substitute rose from $500 in 1862 to $6000 by November '63, and many a seedy character made a handsome profit by selling himself as a substitute, deserting and reselling, and so on. The original draftee escaped service, the substitute made money, but the army suffered incalculable damage. Finally, in December '63, the substitute law was abolished, but the Confederate draft system was so full of holes by this time that it never performed the job it was designed to do. Nor were matters helped by the attitude of the volunteers; as one put it, "The pride of the volunteers was sorely tried by conscripts, the most despised class in the Army . . . they could not bear the thought of having these men for comrades and felt the flag insulted when claimed by one of them as 'his flag.' " (*Southern Historical Society Papers*, November 1876, p. 230.)

4. Most Southerners regarded the war as a crusade against the arbitrary exercise of power by some men over others. They tried to make everything they did conform to this lofty purpose. Accordingly, officers were to be elected rather than appointed, and in this way man's right to guide his own destiny would somehow be preserved. The result was chaos, and by 1863 the Confederacy had reluctantly buried its scruples and returned to the usual way of running an army.

5. By the time of Fremantle's visit, the Southern cotton crop was only 500,000 bales a year, as against a normal 4,000,000 to 5,000,000 bales before the war. This was no war shortage; it was

deliberate policy. The Confederate government was convinced that cotton made the world go round, that the economic survival of every industrial country depended on a steady supply — after all, 20 per cent of the working people of Britain alone were in the cotton-spinning industry. Therefore, why not force foreign intervention by holding up all shipments? Other countries would have to come in, or be ruined. The argument seemed unbeatable, and the embargo was launched.

Hardship and unemployment followed abroad, as predicted . . . but no intervention. It was all a hideous miscalculation, and the South was left without the one source of revenue that might have kept Confederate finances on a sound basis. By 1863, thoughtful Southerners winced to recall that just five years before, Senator James H. Hammond had thundered, "You dare not make war upon cotton! No power on earth dares make war upon it! Cotton is King!"

6. Confederate railroads were often more perilous than the battlefield. They were usually laid out carelessly, and there were virtually no supplies for maintenance or repair. At the very time Fremantle was rattling across Texas, some Southern railroad presidents gathered in Richmond to appraise the problem. They decided they needed 49,500 tons of rails a year to keep the lines in trim — but total mill capacity in the South was only 20,000 tons, and most of this was needed to make guns. The situation, in short, was hopeless.

7. Brigadier General William R. Scurry (ultimately killed at Jenkin's Ferry) was one of the readiest extemporaneous speakers in Texas. Once he went to Shreveport driving an ox cart, and arrived there begrimed with the dirt of the road, to find a public celebration going on, and a number of speakers holding forth. Somebody pushed Scurry forward and called for a speech. He poured forth a torrent of eloquence that held the crowd spellbound until some exuberant spirit yelled at the top of his voice, "Go it, Dirty-shirt!" Scurry went it.

8. Sam Houston was deposed as governor of Texas on March 17,

[263]

1861, when he refused to take the Confederate oath of allegiance; he claimed the Texas vote for secession simply meant people wanted to leave the Union and as far as he was concerned the Texas Republic lived again. If being thrown out was a bitter blow, he didn't show it. In fact, he refused Union Army help to reclaim his governorship on March 29. He was resigned to doing whatever the Texas people wanted, and this remained his attitude until his death in July '63, only ten weeks after meeting Fremantle.

9. The Confederate soldiers liked to dance so much that they solved the partner shortage by dancing with each other. Their favorite was square dancing, which Fremantle calls "an American cotillion," but a close second, curiously enough, was the waltz. This was so popular that the army's bands would often play waltzes instead of marches while the army was tramping across the countryside.

10. Major General Nathaniel Prentiss Banks well earned the nickname "Commissary Banks." During the Valley campaign, this politician-turned soldier lost enormous quantities of desperately needed supplies to Jackson's ragged Rebels. Included in the booty: all Banks's medical stores, which filled one of the largest warehouses in Winchester; 100 head of cattle, 34,000 pounds of bacon, flour, salt, sugar, coffee, bread and cheese (plus countless more taken by the troops themselves); $125,185 worth of quartermaster's stores; 9354 small arms, two cannon and a large amount of ammunition.

In the wake of his defeats in the east, Banks was transferred to the west in late '62. There, he served first as military governor of New Orleans, then as commander of the forces that took Port Hudson (last Confederate stronghold on the Mississippi) and finally as leader of an expedition to restore Texas to the Union. He did all right for a while, but finally was turned back in the Red River campaign during the spring of '64. This was one defeat too many, and he soon was virtually superseded by General E. R. S. Canby, never to play an important military role again.

It's probably going too far to say that Brigadier General Godfrey

Weitzel was responsible for whatever success Banks had in the west. But it is true that Weitzel was immediately beneath Banks during the only period when the latter looked good, and the conclusion does seem logical when the military careers of the two men are compared. Banks was an ex-governor of Massachusetts without previous military experience. Weitzel was one of those flashing, able twenty-seven-year-old brigadiers, fresh from West Point, tops in engineering experience, altogether the kind of young man that an unsuccessful political general would certainly appreciate having around.

CHAPTER 4

From Houston to Natchez

1. Fremantle lived to regret giving away his evening clothes to General Scurry's slave John. Note that one month and five days later in Charleston, he writes, "Mrs. H—— asked me to an evening party, but the extreme badness of my clothes compelled me to decline the invitation."

2. The Confederate soldiers' sense of humor seems to irritate Fremantle, and the suspicion grows that he was upset because the "chaff" he stressed was primarily directed at himself. After all, he did strike an odd figure. With his Texan ten-gallon hat, his English shooting suit and his Turkish lantern, he was an ideal target for that kind of razzing the Rebels enjoyed so much while on the march. They liked, for instance, to tell an officer with a newly waxed moustache, "Take them mice out of your mouth — I see their tails hangin' out."

3. The slower and more harmless a Union officer, the better his reputation with the Confederates. So it was with McClellan, and Major General William S. Rosecrans is another example. Rosecrans moved so slowly that at one point Secretary of War Stanton, in his exasperation, offered a Major Generalship as a prize for Rose-

crans or Grant, whoever should do something first. Rosecrans replied stiffly that he didn't believe in auctioning off military honors — and continued to move as slowly as ever. When he finally did get rolling, he committed perhaps the biggest single battlefield blooper of the war. In the battle at Chickamauga, the center of the Union line was held by the divisions of Generals Wood, Brannan and Reynolds, in that order. Noticing a gap between Reynolds's and Brannan's command, Rosecrans ordered General Wood's division to close it. He forgot that the shift left a tremendous hole in the Union line. The Confederates poured through the gap and Chickamauga became a great Southern victory.

4. General Edmund Kirby Smith was severely wounded as he rushed his troops to the Bull Run battlefield just in time to turn the scales for the South. He spent the fall of 1861 recuperating at Lynchburg and courting the lovely girl who enticed Fremantle to go crayfishing. Her name was Cassie Seldon, and she soon succumbed to the wounded hero's charms. After Kirby Smith's recovery, he put in an uneventful year, and then in early '63 was given command of all the forces west of the Mississippi. After Vicksburg cut the South in two, he became virtually an independent ruler, and the huge area he controlled was facetiously called "Kirbysmithdom."

5. Mr. Edward F. Paine of the Boston Dickens Fellowship agrees with Fremantle that Cairo was the place that Dickens had in mind in *Martin Chuzzlewit*. Certainly Cairo is more appropriate — Dickens had an investment in land there that didn't pay off.

6. A kind of romantic feeling that the South must "earn" recognition ran strong, along with more practical considerations, in Britain's cautious stand on favoring the Confederacy. Little wonder Southerners were now openly asking what had to be done besides winning Bull Run, The Seven Days, Bull Run (again), Fredericksburg and Chancellorsville? They weren't helped by such views as Lord Stanley of the out-of-power Conservative Party wrote Disraeli:

It is premature to recognize the southern confederacy. We can't even get at them. The whole coast is in federal hands. It can hardly be argued that a country which has not a port nor means of ingress or egress is in a position to claim recognition of its independence. (*Stanley to Disraeli,* July 15, 1862.)

To Confederates, this philosophy was depressing indeed. It meant Britain wouldn't recognize the South until the South had done by herself just what she needed British help to do — break the blockade.

7. Chancellorsville was Lee's masterpiece — a perfect example of trapping the trapper. All during the early months of 1863, the Confederate Army under Lee and the Union Army under Hooker had lain quiet, sullenly facing each other across the Rappahannock River. Now it was late April, and Hooker decided to spring a trap. Under cover, he marched most of his army upstream. Then he crossed the river well beyond the extreme left flank of the Southern line, and came marching back down the Confederate side of the river, hoping to fall on Lee from behind. Lee was alerted just in time, swung his army around, and set a trap of his own. On May 2, the cream of his troops secretly marched around the extreme right flank of the Union line, and led by Stonewall Jackson, fell on the rear of Hooker's army.

The uproar that accompanied the Confederate surprise attack was a strange contrast to the quiet intimacy of its planning. Lee and Jackson had hatched the plot late the night before, sitting alone together on a pair of upturned cracker barrels in a small pine grove. No one overheard this conversation, but Confederate staff officers long remembered the sight of the two leaders, caught in the light of a flickering campfire, as they hunched over a map and whispered their plans until nearly 3:30 A. M. After they parted, Jackson lay down on the ground to sleep. A young aide covered him with a cloak, but after the aide himself went to sleep, Jackson quietly arose, spread the cloak over the youthful sleeper and again lay down without it. Before another night could pass, Jackson was fatally wounded by his own men.

CHAPTER 5

Natchez to Mobile

1. Confederates everywhere frequently complained about what they considered the injustice of it all. Old Bishop Meade of Richmond was so obsessed with the idea, even as he lay dying, that he called in Robert E. Lee and grimly instructed the general, "Tell your people to be more determined than ever. This is the most unjust and iniquitous war that was ever fought."

2. Almost as soon as Grant whirled into Jackson, Mississippi, on May 14, 1863, he whirled out again. Fremantle says that the Confederates were astonished, but there was nothing impulsive about Grant's move. He was being as deliberate and methodical as ever. As his army advanced northeastward between Vicksburg and Jackson, he reasoned out his tactics carefully: "Pemberton was now on my left [guarding Vicksburg]. . . . A force was also collected on my right at Jackson, the point where all the railroads communicating with Vicksburg connect. All the enemy's supplies of men and stores would come by that point. As I hoped in the end to besiege Vicksburg, I must first destroy all possibility of aid. I therefore determined to move swiftly toward Jackson, destroy any force in that direction, and then turn upon Pemberton." (*Personal Memoirs of U. S. Grant,* 1885 Vol. I, p. 499.)

3. Major General William Wing Loring had better luck in the Egyptian than in the Confederate Army. As one of Jackson's brigadiers, he started on the wrong foot by going behind his commander's back and persuading Richmond to call off Jackson's pet scheme of holding the Shenandoah Valley by occupying Romney, West Virginia. Loring won his point, but Jackson was no man to be crossed. Loring was soon transferred to oblivion. After the Civil War, his military career enjoyed a remarkable rebirth. In 1869, he joined the Egyptian Army as inspector general. In 1870, he was put in charge of all Egyptian coast defenses. By 1875–1876, he was a division commander and did a good job in the Egyptian-Abys-

sinian War. He capped off his Egyptian career by being made a pasha.

4. Pikes were curiously prominent in the thinking of the Confederate military planners. Nor was the reason merely lack of firearms. In Jackson's thinking, for instance, pikes played about the role of a tank. He visualized soldiers armed with pikes sweeping away all before them as in closed ranks they charged the enemy lines. Thus in 1862 he recommended that whole companies be equipped with long steel pikes and trained to smash armadillo-fashion into the opposition. Lee went along with the idea and ordered a thousand pikes sent to Jackson.

As the war continued, pikes became the popular home-guard weapon, at least in theory. Governor Joe Brown, of Georgia, thought that if every citizen had a pike, the Union Armies could not survive intact. He had thousands made and stored in arsenals. They were, of course, never used. But so many were turned out that until recently, the pikes confiscated by Sherman's army could still be bought at surplus outlets.

5. Clothes could betray a Yankee spy in the South. By 1863, most Southerners were reduced to shabby homespun apparel, and good cloth or a decent cut naturally aroused suspicions. Nor were these fears unwarranted. Mary Boykin Chesnut, an indefatigable Rebel diarist, describes a train trip when a Confederate major in the car was unmasked as a Yankee spy, mostly because of his "nice gray uniform." Seen in this light, patriotic Southerners could be pardoned for their interest in Fremantle's Saville Row shooting suit.

6. Lieutenant General John Clifford Pemberton was as unhappy about his superiors as they were about him. Placed in command of the Confederate forces in Mississippi, he found himself receiving some violently conflicting orders. Jefferson Davis told him to hold Vicksburg at all costs, and not to endanger the city by getting too far from it. General Johnston, who commanded the whole military theater, wanted him to cut loose from Vicksburg (which was probably a trap) and link his troops with the other Confederate forces

in the area, where they might do some good operating together. Pemberton himself wanted to take a firm stand on the Big Black River, a good defensive position east of Vicksburg, and fight it out there alone. Desperately, Pemberton tried to work out a compromise which would please everybody. The result was a military abortion that failed miserably.

Pemberton didn't need to guess how his superiors regarded his defeat. The day before Fremantle reported their disgust, Pemberton himself remarked to an aide, "Just thirty years ago I began my military career . . . and today, the same date, that career is ended in disaster and disgrace." (S. H. Lockett, C.S.A., "The Defense of Vicksburg," *Battles and Leaders of the Civil War*, Vol. III, p. 488.)

7. General Joseph Eggleston Johnston was the number two man in the Confederate Army. But unlike Robert E. Lee (who could do no wrong), Johnston was always in difficulties with Jefferson Davis. It seemed almost fate. While students at West Point together, they were rivals for the hand of a tavern keeper's daughter. One night they fought it out and Davis lost. His humiliation was all the greater, since Johnston was a class behind him. No one knows whether this was one of those little incidents that later make big history, but the fact remains, the two men were in conflict almost from the start of the Civil War.

The feud was intensified when Johnston was put in command of Bragg's army in Tennessee, and Pemberton's army in Mississippi late in '62. Johnston constantly complained that his authority was only nominal, that no one would give him any troops, that Pemberton was incompetent. Davis complained that Johnston was much too cautious. Both were right.

After Pemberton's surrender at Vicksburg, Johnston got the job of stopping Sherman. All through late '63 and early '64, he continued retreating to save his forces — and Davis continued to criticise. Johnston said, well, he at least still had his army; Davis said, yes, but Sherman had the country. When Sherman finally reached Atlanta, Johnston was fired; but he was reinstated when Hood, his successor, did no better. By the end of the war, Johnston was confined to a narrow area in North Carolina.

Despite Johnston's dilatory tactics, he enjoyed a high reputation in the Confederate Army. He was extremely popular to the end — perhaps because he could honestly say he had never lost a battle; more likely because any soldier interested in self-preservation found his ideas of strategy extremely appealing.

8. Soldiers captured in the Civil War had brighter prospects than prisoners of war today. As Fremantle points out, surgeons were treated as noncombatants. Any prisoner had a good chance of being paroled or exchanged until the last year of the war. If paroled, he signed a paper agreeing not to fight anymore until "regularly exchanged." He then was free to go home. Grant took the word of 29,000 men at Vicksburg and let them go. If exchanged, a soldier could even fight again. Often prisoners were first paroled and then formally exchanged much later. When this was done, the exchange took the form of a paper releasing the prisoner from his parole and authorizing him to get back into the fight.

The idea of exchanging prisoners developed early in the war. The North liked it because the South had more prisoners. The South liked it because they needed their own men back and Northern prisoners were one more strain on Confederate resources. On July 22, 1862, the two sides accordingly agreed to exchange all prisoners. A regular table of equivalents was established with a private as the "unit measure."

Noncommissioned Officer	=	2 privates
Lieutenant	=	4 privates
Captain	=	6 privates
Major	=	8 privates
Lieutenant Colonel	=	10 privates
Colonel	=	15 privates
Brigadier General	=	20 privates
Major General	=	40 privates
General Commanding	=	60 privates

To carry out the program, two exchange points were set up. Vicksburg was used in the west and City Point in the east. As the operation wore on, so did the haggling. Two captains and a major might equal a brigadier general — but what if the brigadier was unusually good? Should the special objects of Southern hatred (like James Pope and Butler) and the special objects of Northern hatred (like Confederate prison commandants) be included in the agreement at all? Could a paroled prisoner be used to fight Indians until he was exchanged?

Realizing that release of Southern prisoners simply prolonged the war by stretching out Confederate manpower, Grant cancelled the agreement in April 1864. Exchanges were never again resumed on a large scale, although the South became so anxious to get rid of Northern prisoners that in the final months of the war, many were released without any *quid pro quo*.

9. Many a Confederate leader swore he'd never live again under the stars and stripes — and lived to eat his words. Fremantle ascribes such feelings to Johnston, Maury and Beauregard. In due course, however, all three came back into the fold. After the war, Johnston was quickly reconciled to an insurance man's life in Savannah, later to a term in Congress as a Virginia representative, and finally to a Washington job in Cleveland's administration. Maury also turned out to be an easily reconstructed Rebel, living out a life of genteel poverty in Louisiana and Richmond. And Beauregard, who said he'd rather submit to the Emperor of China than return to the Union, had his bluff called when he was offered command of the Romanian Army in 1866 and the Egyptian Army in 1869. He declined, preferring instead to run the New Orleans, Jackson and Mississippi Railroad.

10. Vicksburg's defenses proved unexpectedly strong. This last Confederate link with the west held out from May 18 to July 4, 1863. The grim tenacity of the defenders can be seen from their diet during the final stages — mule meat, acorns, cane roots, grass and weeds simmered in water, and, finally, rats. During a truce at one point in the siege, General Sherman handed a Confederate

officer some mail that had been entrusted to him by Northern friends of the besieged. The Southerner saucily remarked that the mail would have been old indeed if delivery had depended on Federal capture of the place. "So you think, then, I am a pretty slow mail route?" amiably responded the unruffled Sherman.

11. Stonewall Jackson died before Fremantle had a chance to meet him, but the man was obviously fascinating. Fremantle picked up all the anecdotes he could. And they were endless, as Jackson was so colorful, so eccentric, and such a bizarre combination of qualities. He was so pious that he refused even to open his mail on Sunday — yet, he broke the Sabbath to launch some of his fiercest surprise attacks. (But he would keep his accounts straight by designating some day the following week as "Sunday" instead.) He abhorred delicacies and petty luxuries — yet liked to suck on an inexhaustible supply of lemons, which were unbelievably scarce at the time. (Nobody ever knew where he got them.) He was utterly tireless — could push on when everybody else was exhausted — yet he might suddenly fall asleep like a baby at the most incredible times.

When Jackson forced Harpers Ferry to surrender in 1862, the Union commander found his victorious opponent sound asleep by a log. A. P. Hill shook Jackson and said, "General, this is General White of the U.S. Army." Jackson made a courteous gesture and nodded away again. "He has come to arrange the terms of surrender," shouted Hill. Jackson was silent; Hill looked under the old slouch hat and discovered Jackson was once more sound asleep. He was again aroused, raised his head with difficulty, and finally managed to yawn out, "The surrender must be unconditional, General. Every indulgence can be granted afterwards." Needless to say, he was back asleep within seconds, and there was no more interview.

CHAPTER 6

Mobile to Shelbyville

1. Major General Dabney Herndon Maury was an appropriate companion for Fremantle. He came from an extremely distinguished and scholarly Virginia family. As a young West Pointer, he spent four years of glorious adventure on the Texas frontier, chasing buffalo and Indians over the very land that Fremantle had just traveled. He was a brave and courageous soldier — after losing Mobile harbor to Farragut a year after Fremantle's visit, he continued to defend the city until three days after Appomattox with only 9000 troops against an opposing army of 45,000 men. And, although penniless at the end of the war, he declined a figurehead job with the Louisiana State Lottery that paid $30,000 a year. On the other hand, he didn't hesitate to give up a struggling business to serve as a volunteer nurse when New Orleans was stricken by a yellow fever epidemic.

2. Admiral Farragut finally smashed his way through the channel into Mobile harbor on August 5, 1864. His reckless bravery lives on in his famous words, "Damn the torpedoes. Full speed ahead!" But another less romantic remark by Farragut perhaps illustrates better the true excitement and confusion of the attack. As Farragut's flagship, *Hartford,* led the fleet by Fort Morgan into the bay, she was set upon by the Confederate ram, *Tennessee.* Both the *Hartford* and the Union ship, *Lackawanna,* responded by trying to ram the *Tennessee.* In the confusion, the *Lackawanna* rammed the *Hartford* — backed off and seemed about to do it again. This was enough for Farragut. Turning to his signal officer, Lieutenant John Kinney, he cried, "Can you say 'for God's sake' by signal?"

"Yes, sir," replied Kinney.

"Then," snapped the Admiral, "say to the *Lackawanna* 'For God's sake, get out of our way and anchor.' "

3. Fremantle was fortunate in meeting four celebrities at Confederate General Hardee's headquarters in Wartrace, Tennessee. Bishop Stephen Elliott was not only a distinguished clergyman, he was one of the outstanding educators in the South.

Lieutenant General Leonidas Polk was a curious crossbreed of soldier and Episcopal missionary. As Bishop of Louisiana, long before the war he had wandered around the frontier spreading the gospel among the Indians, but his religious inclinations can be traced even as far as West Point, where he astounded the rest of the cadet company by organizing a "praying squad."

Lieutenant General William Joseph Hardee was the opposite extreme. Tough and virile, he was every inch the ladies' man depicted by Fremantle. It was typical of him that when he wanted to establish a special reward for the men in his corps who achieved outstanding valor on the battlefield, he decided that the perfect prize was to introduce them to the ladies who turned up on the parade grounds whenever the army was being reviewed.

But Fremantle's best "catch" at Wartrace was Clement Laird Vallandigham, an ex-Democratic Congressman from Ohio, who was bitterly anti-war. Vallandigham was high spirited in everything he did. At college he quit without graduating after a big fight with the president over some question of Constitutional law. In politics, he was a fiery states' rights man; and when Burnside announced he would no longer tolerate speeches sympathetic to the South, Vallandigham got himself thrown out of the country by denouncing Burnside's order. (This was when Fremantle saw him.) In postwar law practice, Vallandigham defended a murderer so vigorously that in showing how the gun really went off, he shot himself to death.

4. Wigwag signaling is one of the Confederacy's many contributions to warfare. The idea was introduced at the first battle of Bull Run. Early on the morning of the battle, Signal Officer E. P. Alexander was scanning the horizon for any evidence of a Union flanking movement. Suddenly, his attention was arrested by the glint of the morning sun on a brass fieldpiece. Closer observa-

tion revealed the glitter of bayonets and musket barrels moving through a forest around the left end of the Confederate line. At 8:45 A. M. he picked up his signal flags and flashed to Evans, the endangered Southern general, the first semaphore message in history: "Look to the left — you are turned."

5. Major General Ormsby MacKnight Mitchell was a Northern contribution to the Civil War's notable collection of unlikely soldiers. He had been to West Point, hadn't done too well, eventually drifted into law. This bored him too, and in 1835, he became a professor of mathematics and astronomy at Cincinnati College. He knew his math, but astronomy was just something that went with the job. Overnight, it entranced him.

During the next twenty-five years, he not only dedicated himself but interested the whole country in astronomy. He was a thrilling speaker and crowds everywhere flocked to hear him lecture about the stars. Mitchell's enthusiasm was contagious and his listeners donated money for telescopes, observatories and literature on the subject.

Everything ended when war began. Lincoln offered Mitchell a brigadiership. He accepted, but by now he was a pretty rusty soldier and probably never meant to be one anyhow. Stationed in Tennessee, Mitchell ran a sloppy, undisciplined show. He was also far too much of a "character" for the likes of his hard-headed commander, General Buell. In 1862, he was finally transferred to a less crucial post in South Carolina. There, he soon died of yellow fever.

6. Fremantle's week at Shelbyville was the most pleasant break in his long odyssey from Brownsville to Gettysburg. For a change, he was comfortable. As General Polk's guest, he stayed at Beechwood, the estate of Mrs. Andrew Erwin, which served as a headquarters for many of the officers in Bragg's army. But Beechwood was more than a military headquarters, it was a social center where the company of charming Southern belles was readily available. Best of all, Fremantle enjoyed the camaraderie of Polk's cultured,

aristocratic staff. Their gentle kidding was far easier to take than the coarse humor of Confederate soldiers on the march, and he thoroughly enjoyed it when they assured him that "the gumbo filet for dinner would be 'quite *au fait*' . . . made from the tender twigs of a young sassafras bush embellished with the photograph of a chicken that had done service in days gone by." And would he want champagne? Yes, and they had the best — "made in an old molasses barrel containing about three parts water to one part corn and molasses sufficient to sweeten, when, after a few days of fermentation, it could be drawn and served minus the effervescence."

7. More than one high-ranking Confederate exchanged a cassock for a sword. Stonewall Jackson's chief of staff was Major, the Reverend R. L. Dabney, D.D., former professor of Presbyterian Theology. Lee's chief of artillery was General W. N. Pendleton, D.D. The latter made the switch easily, and even found his background helpful in his new job. As captain of the Rockbridge artillery at First Bull Run, young Pendleton had sighted his guns and cried, "Fire, and may God have mercy on their guilty souls!"

8. Confederate General Braxton Bragg won no popularity contests. As a general, he was disappointing; his attacks at Murfreesboro, Perryville and Chickamauga all looked like wasted blood baths. As a person, he was even more disappointing. Hard-working and a tough disciplinarian, he was harsh, sour, irascible, and had an utter lack of tact. Once, during a public dinner, Confederate General Dick Taylor asked Bragg about one of his top men. The answer was snapped back, loud and typical: "That general is an old woman, utterly worthless."

9. Major General Earl Van Dorn was a glamorous, if disappointing, Confederate leader. As an old Indian fighter before the war, he had been wounded twice by bow and arrow on the frontier. During the war, he was involved with Indians again — this time they were on his side at the battle of Pea Ridge in Arkansas in 1862. Northern General Curtis protested the use of these sav-

ages, but Van Dorn (with amazing blandness for a man who had taken a couple of arrow wounds) assured him that his Indians were a highly civilized people.

The Federals won Pea Ridge anyhow and General Van Dorn, after a good victory at Vicksburg, took another licking at Corinth. He now lost his command and had a comparatively minor post when Dr. Peters surprised him and Mrs. Peters in a private room at headquarters. After he was shot, about the only people who remained true were his staff officers. They showed their loyalty by inserting an ad in the local newspaper, suggesting that it was all a big mistake and Dr. Peters had other reasons for murder, merely concocting the story about Mrs. Peters to justify his crime. The ad wasn't too convincing.

CHAPTER 7

The Stay at Shelbyville

1. Murfreesboro was a crucial test of strength as the Northern and Southern Armies jockeyed for the advantage in Tennessee. It was like a fight between a couple of circling alley cats — the South attacked the Northern left and the North attacked the Southern left at the same moment on New Year's Day of '63. When the fur stopped flying, the Confederates slowly and sullenly withdrew, leaving the field to the Union forces. The Union victory was marred by at least one incident. Federal General Ellis McDowell McCook was shaving when the fight opened. Hearing gunfire before he expected the Union cannonade to start, he dropped his razor and cried, "That's contrary to orders!" Calling for his horse, he turned to the owner of the house and inquired, "Who is opposing me today?" The answer came, "Major General Cheatham." At this, General McCook turned ashy pale and trembling, rejoined, "Is it possible that I have to meet Cheatham

again?" Without waiting for an answer, he mounted his horse and rode off. The *Chattanooga Daily Rebel* happily reported that he was so unstrung he never returned to pick up his razor.

2. For the South, Shiloh was a frustrating affair. As Grant felt his way southward in Tennessee during the spring of '62, Confederate General Albert Sidney Johnston bided his time. Then, on April 6, he suddenly struck back, almost hurling the surprised Federals into the river at Pittsburg Landing. But just when victory seemed certain, Johnston was killed. Two hours of leaderless confusion followed. Finally Beauregard took over, but the momentum of the attack was gone. Grant rallied, reinforcements arrived from Buell, and the following day the Confederates were thrown back, losing all their gains.

The South was bitter, especially at Beauregard, who had apparently frittered away a victory almost won. Stories multiplied — that Beauregard had been sick, in a daze, out of his mind, completely mad. Reports spread that he had even spent the battle in his tent, stroking a pet pheasant which he held in his lap. Actually, Beauregard was as sane — and as uninspired — as usual. As for the pheasant, yes, a soldier had brought one to his tent during the course of the battle; but Beauregard hastily assured the world that he had hardly noticed the bird, and certainly had no idea what had become of it.

3. Foreigners far more belligerent than Fremantle flocked to both sides in the Civil War. Fremantle was much taken with the dashing soldier of fortune Colonel St. Leger Grenfell, but there were others equally colorful in the Confederate service. Perhaps the most renowned — and certainly the visitor who made fair hearts beat fastest — was Major Heros von Borck, a huge Prussian serving as "Jeb" Stuart's adjutant. First in either a cavalry charge or a drawing room, he was all that the South wanted in a soldier — brave, bold, handsome and gay. Even a neck wound at Gettysburg didn't stop him. With the bullet stuck in his throat, von Borck wheezed about Richmond, still the best social catch in

town. He stayed on the scene until after Stuart's death in 1864, when he was sent abroad on a mission aimed to get foreign help for the Confederacy.

4. For a man "enervated by matrimony," Major General John Morgan had plenty of life in him yet. The great Confederate raider made the boldest of all his excursions less than five weeks after Fremantle reported Colonel Grenfell's pessimistic views on Morgan's future usefulness. On July 2, Morgan took 2000 men and four cannon on a raid into Union territory that carried him through Kentucky and into Southern Indiana and Ohio. This time he went too far and got trapped. His command was scattered and Morgan himself was finally captured on July 26.

After his capture, Morgan and thirty of his officers were not handled like prisoners of war, but were sent to the Ohio State Penitentiary. There, he showed he was still not enervated by matrimony. Using table knives from the prison dining room, he and several other officers dug a hole through two feet of concrete floor and tunneled under the prison yard to the outer wall. This they scaled with a rope of bedding and fled, leaving a courteous note to the warden.

Morgan finally reached the Southern lines, and in 1864 he was back as a cavalry raider. Finally, his luck caught up with him and that September he was trapped at Granville, Tennessee. This time the Federals made sure. As he tried to hide behind some vines in a garden, he was shot through the heart.

5. No wonder that time passed swiftly when Morgan was amusing himself with wire tapping. His operator, a Mr. Ellsworth, later described this exchange of messages with an unknown Federal station signing itself "Z":

Z: What news? Any more skirmishing after the last message?

MORGAN: No. We drove what little cavalry there was away.

Z: Has the train arrived yet?

MORGAN: No. About how many troops will be on the train?

Z: 500, 60th Indiana, commanded by Colonel Owens.

MORGAN (beginning to wonder who "Z" was): A gentleman here

in this office bets me two cigars you can't spell the name of your station correctly.

Z: Take the bet. L–E–B–A–N–O–N J–U–N–C–T–I–O–N. How did he think I would spell it?

MORGAN: He thought you would put two "b's" in "Lebanon."

Z: Ha! Ha! Ha! He is a green one!

MORGAN: Yes. He certainly is.

6. Major General Patrick Cleburne was one of those military figures who could incite the deepest devotion among his men. It's hard to separate fact from legend, but a story told during the battle at Franklin, Tennessee, is typical of his reputation. While riding along the lines encouraging his men, Cleburne saw a captain of his command, barefoot, with feet sore and bleeding. He dismounted at once, and asked, "Captain, will you pull off my boots?" The captain did so and the general then asked, "Captain, will you see if they fit you?" The captain complied; the general remounted his horse and rode off, saying, "Captain, I am tired of wearing those boots and can do well without them." When Cleburne was carried mortally wounded from the field several hours later, he was barefoot.

7. When Fremantle heard the sound of a Confederate soldier being shot for desertion, he was hearing something quite unusual in the South. The Confederate authorities tended to take a kind view of desertion, which would be rare indeed today. For instance, in the last six months of the war, Lee's army executed only 39 of some 245 convicted deserters. The soldiers took full advantage of this kind of leniency — some 103,400 deserted, according to Ella Lonn, the best authority on the subject. Far more likely punishment was a good stiff term in the guardhouse followed by dishonorable discharge.

8. The Confederate soldiers had firm convictions about who could — and who couldn't — fight on the Northern side. As Fremantle points out, men from the Northwest generally rated high; the German units very low. This view could be expanded to cover most foreign-born troops fighting for the Union. But by '63, the

enemy's poor fighting qualities were no longer much consolation. More than one Confederate pondered over "the English, Irish, German, French, Italian, Spanish, Swiss, Portuguese and Negroes, who swelled the numbers of the enemy. . . . True, there was not much fight in all this rubbish, but they answered well enough for drivers of wagons and ambulances, guarding stores and lines of communication, and doing all sorts of duty, while the good material was doing the fighting." (*Southern Historical Society Papers*, November 1876, p. 229.)

CHAPTER 8

On to Charleston

1. More than one forerunner of the WACs turned up in Confederate service. Fremantle's discovery may have been Madame Loreta Janeta Velasquez, who posed as Lieutenant Harry T. Buford and served in a Louisiana regiment under Bragg about this time. Certainly, the time and place seem about right, and there couldn't have been too many girls fighting beside the Louisiana boys. Another lady in arms was Captain Sally Tompkins, who ran a hospital and held the highest rank the Southern Army ever gave a woman. Still another was Mary McCarty, a fabulous tomboy who was ultimately captured and sent to the Old Capitol Prison in Washington.

2. Colonel G. W. Rains was as fine an appointment as Jefferson Davis ever made. The colonel was one of the few people in the South who were really at home in a factory, and Davis lost no time giving him the job of building a Southern munitions industry. Rains pushed niter mining in Alabama, Georgia and Tennessee. He built a saltpeter plant at Nashville. He designed and built the magnificent powder plant at Augusta, which impressed Fremantle so much. By the end of the war, this plant had turned out 2,750,000 pounds of powder. The quality was top-flight; there

was plenty of it; and it cost only 35 per cent of the going price for English powder.

3. On April 7, 1863, the Union Navy made its great bid to force Fort Sumter and Charleston to surrender. Nine new, supposedly invincible, ironclads were assembled for the effort. At Admiral S. F. du Pont's signal, they moved slowly in single file towards the channel, guarded by Sumter, that led into the harbor. In the lead went the *Weehawken*, pushing a curious raftlike contrivance designed to clear away obstructions. And there were plenty — hawsers and cables stretched across the channel, torpedoes, mines (including one loaded with 5000 pounds of powder), piles, stakes and even nets calculated to ensnarl enemy propellers. There was plenty of warning too, and as the Union ships advanced, the Confederates held their fire, chivalrously dipped their colors, and had their garrison band play "Dixie" from a parapet.

Then all hell broke loose. As the ironclads moved slowly through the obstructions, the Charleston defenses opened a tremendous fire — 160 shots a minute, 3500 during the engagement. The Yankee *Keokuk*, which was closest to Sumter, took 90 hits. The warships did their best to reply; pumped hundreds of shells into Sumter. But the Confederate pounding began popping the bolts that held the ironclads together, and the Union gunners found themselves dodging a hail of metal that flew about inside the turrets. Finally the squadron withdrew; the *Keokuk* sank the next day from its wounds, and the Charleston garrison celebrated another successful defense.

4. The North maintained a successful blockade of the Confederate coast throughout the war, despite spirited Southern efforts to offset the effects. Generally, these efforts were directed at either building ingenious torpedoes and mines to wreck the blockaders, or building ingenious vessels to run the blockade. The resulting give-and-take fighting along the blockade was always colorful, but perhaps the best incident occurred in 1863, when the brigantine *J. P. Ellicott* was captured by the Confederate privateer *Retribution*. The *Ellicott's* officers and crew were taken aboard the *Ret-*

ribution and a prize crew put in charge of the Yankee ship. But the mate's wife was left on board the *Ellicott*, and this was a fatal mistake. A few days later, she succeeded in getting the Rebel crew intoxicated, locked them up, took over the vessel, and piloted it into St. Thomas, where she delivered it and the Rebels to the U. S. Consul.

5. The Union forces tried every conceivable method of taking Charleston, including the idea General Ripley gave Fremantle, but nothing worked. The Confederates hung on and on. Finally, they voluntarily abandoned both the city and Fort Sumter on February 17, 1865. Sherman was sweeping through the Carolinas to join Grant in Virginia; the Confederates realized that if they held Charleston any longer, they'd be cut off from the rest of the South.

So ended three years of successful defense against a harrowing variety of attacks. The record ran like this:

June '62 — Union Army is stopped trying to get in "the back door" at Secessionville, about eight miles south of the city.

April '63 — Union Navy tries to force the harbor with nine ironclads, and is thrown back as Fremantle describes.

July 11, '63 — Union Army switches to the tactics suggested by Confederate General Ripley to Fremantle: Land on Morris Island south of the harbor, work north and seize Fort Wagner at the harbor's entrance and turn its guns on Sumter and Charleston. The idea doesn't work — Union forces fail to take Fort Wagner.

July 18, '63 — Another Union attack on Fort Wagner is smashed.

August 17–23 — New tactics: Seven-day Union bombardment designed to crush Fort Sumter. Sumter pretty well smashed, but Charleston hangs on.

August 21 — Another shift. Terrorize Charleston into surrender by long-range bombardment. Gun called the "Swamp Angel" hurls 36 incendiary shells at the city and then explodes.

September 6 — Another try at Fort Wagner, this time using

siege tactics. Fort Wagner captured, but Confederates have prepared new defenses and Charleston holds on.

September 8 — Union Navy tries to land a force on Fort Sumter and take place by storm. Attackers slaughtered.

Thereafter, all fighting simmered down until finally on the morning of February 18, 1865, the Union soldiers marched triumphant but unopposed into a shattered Charleston.

6. The Confederates were obsessed by the idea of submarine warfare. Like the Germans a generation later, they faced overwhelming surface ship superiority, and their only chance was to offset this superiority through inventiveness and ingenuity.

Their submarines, to say the least, were ingenious. The *Hundley*, for example, was twenty feet long, four feet wide, five feet deep, and was run by a propeller worked by hand. With her seven-man crew, she was meant to "swim" to the side of an enemy vessel and deposit a torpedo (like an egg). The charge, theoretically, would go off as the *Hundley* "swam" away again.

All this required a lot of practice. On one experimental trip down Mobile Bay in early '63, the *Hundley* tried a dive and never came up again; all seven men were lost. She was eventually raised and shipped to Charleston. While preparing to attack the Federal fleet, one night the *Hundley* was swamped by a passing Confederate steamer and sank again — this time with a loss of six men. Shortly afterwards they pulled her up again, she was swamped again, and sank again — this time with a loss of four men. The resurrected *Hundley* made another experimental dive in Charleston harbor — seven men lost this time. Once more the *Hundley* was raised; once more she tried an experimental dive and this time got tangled in the anchor chain of a ship in Charleston harbor — all seven men lost.

For a fifth time, the *Hundley* was pulled up. Volunteers in the city enthusiastically responded to calls for one last try. To the wonderment of all, the *Hundley* finally moved out of the harbor and towards the blockading Federal squadron. In the dead of a moonlit night, she crawled alongside the U.S.S. *Housatonic* and turned to scoot away.

With a shattering crash, the *Housatonic* exploded and sank beneath the waves — taking the *Hundley* with her as she went. All seven men were lost.

7. General Pierre Gustave Toutant Beauregard was in one of the dips of a roller coaster career when Fremantle ran into him. As the man who fired on Fort Sumter, Beauregard's stature soared at the start of the war. As the victor of Bull Run, he soared even higher. Then came months of idleness, which saw the army's organization and morale — and Beauregard's reputation — sag badly. Early in 1862, he was transferred from Virginia to the West, where he became Number 2 man under Albert Sidney Johnston in the fight to keep the Mississippi open. Johnston was killed leading the Confederate attack at Shiloh, and Beauregard took over in mid-battle. When he lost the battle that Johnston had seemingly won, his stock fell to a new low.

Beauregard was then transferred to Charleston, where Fremantle found him in the comparatively unimportant job of garrison commander. But his fortunes rose again the following year. Grant's '64 plan was to squeeze Richmond between himself attacking from the north and General Butler attacking from the southeast. While Lee parried Grant, Beauregard was assigned the job of stopping Butler. He did a great job, bottling up Butler completely at Bermuda One Hundred. When Grant also was halted north of Richmond, and swung around to an attack from the southeast, Beauregard held him too, until Lee could reform his lines. Beauregard was then placed under Lee, but once again he fell short of expectations and was shifted to an administrative job in the West. When the war ended, he had just been shifted back to Number 2 post under Joe Johnston — exactly where he was when Bull Run had been fought nearly four long years before.

CHAPTER 9

Charleston to Richmond

1. Judah P. Benjamin was the smiling enigma of the Confederacy. It seems incredible that so little is really known of the man who served successively as Jefferson Davis's Attorney General, Secretary of War and Secretary of State — the man who was openly acknowledged to be "the brains of the Confederacy."

His childhood in Charleston, South Carolina, remains a mystery — there are no authentic details. His career in the class of 1829 at Yale was suddenly interrupted by expulsion — nobody knows why. His move from Charleston, where he had excellent opportunities, to New Orleans, where he had none and couldn't even speak the language, is inexplicable. His marriage to a French girl from a distinguished Creole family is equally mystifying. The couple lived together for only a few years, before his wife and daughter moved to France, never to return. Yet it was no breach. Benjamin visited his family in France every summer; he lavished money and attention on them all his life; and he never seemed particularly upset by the situation.

Benjamin himself did his best to perpetuate the mystery. He was a charming writer and a delightful conversationalist, but he wrote little and said less, where the subject was himself. He spent much of his last years destroying letters and files. He was so successful that only one biographer, Pierce Butler, has had the courage to tackle him as a subject.

Yet in some respects, there's no mystery about Benjamin. Everybody agreed that he was the period's most remarkable combination of a taste for elegance and a taste for back-breaking work. Everybody agreed on his devotion to the Cause. Everybody agreed about his charm and his persuasiveness. Everybody agreed that he smiled all the time — although there was considerable disagreement as to what it meant.

2. The Mason-Slidell affair was the only time during the Civil

War when Washington really lost face. Late in '61, the Confederate government named James Murray Mason as its diplomatic representative in England and James Slidell for a similar job in Paris. The two "commissioners" ran the blockade to Havana and then caught the British ship *Trent* for Europe. One day out, the U.S.S. *San Jacinto* stopped the *Trent*, removed Mason and Slidell, and took them to jail in Boston.

The British claimed that the incident violated their rights as a neutral and demanded that Mason and Slidell be released. London followed up this demand by rushing troops to Canada "for defense" and ordering the British Ambassador in Washington to come home if the North didn't back down. Lincoln was in no position to take the challenge, and on December 26, 1861, Secretary of State Seward announced that Mason and Slidell were both "cheerfully liberated."

3. "Bull Run" Russell, the ubiquitous correspondent of the London *Times*, succeeded in making himself thoroughly unpopular with both sides in the Civil War. Northern sensitivities were disturbed by the way he belittled the Union military effort. His account of the Federal rout at Bull Run was a classic of scorn for the soldiers he was writing about; in fact, it gave him his nickname. In the South, Russell stirred far more than Judah Benjamin's resentment. He presented a picture of plantation life which had the lady of the house bawling at field hands hundreds of yards away. After he was through with Charleston, people said he had come away with a thorough knowledge of the three P's — pen, paper and prejudices. Desperately, the Southerners tried in vain to appease this scathing observer. Mary Boykin Chesnut told in her diary of one poor man who studied Thackeray for hours in order to be able to talk to Russell on even terms. Russell yawned his way through such occasions as well as he could. (See Ben Ames Williams, ed., A *Diary from Dixie*, p. 39.)

4. Jefferson Davis could put on a smooth courtesy that was initially a godsend in handling the collection of prima donnas that came to Richmond to launch the government. It seemed that al-

most everybody had his own ideas on how to run the country, and with the Confederacy's weak constitution, endless courtesy and patience were necessary to get concerted action. Davis had the courtesy but not the patience. He could put on a great show of tact, but he couldn't keep it up. As a result, the harmony that marked the early stages of his dealings with people all too often disintegrated into wrangling and bitterness if agreement wasn't quickly reached.

Once trouble began, it was quickly compounded by other weak traits. Davis was basically stiff and cold. He had no humor whatsoever. Above all, he was obstinate. It took some time for many people to perceive these dangerous weaknesses, but his wife saw them right away. On the very first day they met, she wrote her mother, "He impresses me as a remarkable kind of man, but of uncertain temper, and has a way of taking for granted that everybody agrees with him when he expresses an opinion, which offends me. . . . The fact is, he is the kind of person I should expect to rescue me from a mad dog at any risk, but to insist upon a stoical indifference to the fright afterward." (Eron Rowland, *Varina Howell, Wife of Jefferson Davis*, Vol. I, p. 48.)

5. Men like Milroy, Butler and Hunter were tough occupation generals, but no tougher than would be expected today. In fact, they often put up with insults and abuse that no self-respecting occupation authority would now tolerate.

Once in New Orleans a woman doused Admiral Farragut with a pail of filthy water. Another lady carefully trained her children to spit on Union officers. A New Orleans belle named Mrs. Phillips stood on her balcony and howled with glee at the funeral of a Northern officer. A Mr. Mumford cut down the U. S. flag flying over the New Orleans Custom House. Butler's patience was exhausted — Mumford was executed and occupation order Number 28 was issued, which declared that any woman who insulted or showed contempt for any U. S. soldier would thereafter "be treated as a woman of the town plying her avocation."

Southerners had always regarded Butler as the worst of these occupation commanders. Shortly after he went to New Orleans, the story quickly spread that he took the spoons whenever he was invited out to dine and he soon became known as "Spoon" Butler. After order Number 28, he became known as "Beast" Butler.

6. Secretary of War Seddon had a full "in-basket" the day Fremantle found so much trouble getting to see him. That morning reports were coming in from Winchester on the results of its recapture by the Confederates (the news was good — 9000 men and 50 guns taken; only 100 Southerners lost). Colonel Gorgas, Chief of Ordnance, had submitted a paper proposing that the army discontinue issuing 20 extra cartridges to each man; instead, he suggested that each be given only three cartridges a month with the rest going to the commanding general on requisition whenever a battle was pending. There were also reports that the navy had lost an ironclad at Savannah. Other memoranda called the secretary's attention to the careless issuance of passports. There was a discouraging report that a man named Jackson had turned in important military secrets to the Federals, enabling them to raid Northern Neck. Another report, which was of greater interest to the President than the War Department, described the destruction of Jefferson Davis's furniture in Mississippi. (See J. B. Jones, *A Rebel War Clerk's Diary*, 1866, pp. 352–353.)

7. During McClellan's Peninsular campaign in the spring of '62, the Union Navy tried to co-operate by sending a fleet up the James River to bombard Richmond. The move caught the Confederates unprepared. They had counted on the ironclad *Virginia* to hold off the whole Union Navy, but the *Virginia* had to be scuttled, and now the river lay wide open. Working frantically for two rain-swept days, the Confederates sank boats in the channel, fortified the best defensive position at Drewry's Bluff and stationed sharpshooters along the banks of the river. When the Union flotilla appeared on May 15, they were ready. Five guns (not three, as reported by Fremantle) poured such a crushing fire on the two ironclads in the lead that after four hours' firing, the Federals returned back down the river.

Richmond to Hagerstown

1. At the end of April '63, Hooker sent Stoneman's Federal cavalry on a raid designed to wreck Lee's communications and soften him up for Hooker's Chancellorsville campaign. Through bad timing, most of the raid was carried out after Hooker had already been repulsed, and to make matters worse, the foray left Hooker without any cavalry when he needed it most to scout the Confederate movements.

But the raid did give Richmond a terrific scare. The alarm bell clanged steadily for several days early in May. Home-guard units, government clerks and bottom-of-the-barrel reserves dashed out to repel the advance. Federal units actually got as close as John R. Young's farm, just two miles from the city limits, before veering off and returning to the main army. It was a close call and nerves were still on edge when Fremantle turned up six weeks later.

2. Fremantle was quite justified if he felt puzzled by the kaleidoscopic changes in the Confederate flag. Few banners have ever changed so much so often. The flag that Fremantle saw with Lee was but one in a series of experiments. The first flag was turkey red with a white star in the middle and a crescent in the upper left-hand corner. It was sewed together by some Charleston ladies when the state seceded in 1860, and flew briefly from the Charleston Custom House.

As secession spread, the Confederate flag became a solid blue banner with a single white star. This was well plugged by an Irish minstrel named Harry McCarty, who toured the Deep South singing a rousing war song called "The Bonny Blue Flag." This was the flag Fremantle saw with Bragg's army, and it remained popular throughout the general area where McCarty did his trooping.

Next came the Stars and Bars, which resembled the U. S. flag, except that there were only eleven stars and three stripes. The resemblance proved too close. Mistakes easily arose in the confusion of battle, and after first Bull Run, General Joe Johnston designed the famous red battle flag with its blue Saint Andrew's cross.

Richmond next adopted the battle-flag design for a new national flag. This was an all-white banner with the battle-flag emblem in the upper left-hand corner. It was the flag Fremantle saw at Fort Sumter.

But this wasn't the end. The new national flag could be easily confused with a white flag unless a stiff breeze was blowing. As Confederate defeats multiplied in the later stages of the war, this resemblance became embarrassing. To avoid confusion, a vertical red bar was added to the edge of the white field. Before any more variations could develop, Appomattox made the matter academic.

3. Lee faced a tough choice in September '62 — whether to rest his army, which was exhausted by ten weeks of steady marching, or push on while the enemy was on the run in hopes that one more victory might bring foreign intervention, or discourage the North from fighting any more. He took the gamble.

As the army moved northward into Maryland, thousands of Lee's soldiers fell out. Ragged, hungry, barefoot, these stragglers were simply unable to take it any longer. They trailed along ten, twenty, a hundred miles behind the army. Many couldn't or wouldn't cross the Potomac, and a huge tent city grew up along the banks, while the soldiers waited to regain their strength. For the most part, they weren't shirkers; they were just too tired to go on.

General Hill's corps lost 2000 stragglers in three days. Whole regiments disintegrated — the 8th Virginia dwindled to 34 men; the Hampton Legion to 77; and so on. At the start of the Maryland campaign, Lee had some 55,000 men; seventeen days later at the battle of Antietam he had only 35,000. The effect of this straggling contributed heavily to the stand-off fight which forced Lee to return again to Virginia.

Notes for Chapter 11

CHAPTER 11

Campaigning in Pennsylvania

1. Everybody behaved like Barbara Frietchie except Barbara Frietchie. When Southern soldiers marched through Northern towns, the local girls outdid each other in tossing jeers and taunts. Usually the Confederates took it in their stride. When Stonewall Jackson passed through Middletown, Maryland, two pretty girls with red, white and blue ribbons in their hair rushed out of the house and with much laughter waved little Union flags in the face of the general. Jackson bowed, raised his hat and smilingly remarked to his staff, "We evidently have no friends in this town."

But one lady who didn't show the Confederates her colors was Barbara Frietchie. Later on, she waved her flag in welcome as the Union troops passed through Frederick, but she never came into contact with the Rebels. The lady in town who did wave the Stars and Stripes at the Confederates remains unsung — her name was Mrs. Mary S. Quantrell.

2. The nameless Austrian officer discovered by Fremantle in Chambersburg was Captain Fitzgerald Ross of the Hungarian Hussars. Ross had recently entered the South by slipping across the Potomac from Maryland. By now, he was a fixture in that odd assortment of foreign "guests" tagging along with Lee. He stayed on after Fremantle went home, and finally attached himself to "Jeb" Stuart, who made a point of collecting characters. Stuart's entourage already included a Prussian adjutant and a banjo player named Sweeney. Ross fitted in well, and spent a lot of time with Stuart until he returned home in April 1864.

3. Robert E. Lee was worshiped and adored throughout the South. The populace gladly accepted a story that once when he fell asleep exhausted by a roadside, 15,000 men marched by on tiptoe so as not to disturb him. The man's obvious virtue and nobility proved quite a problem for Northern propagandists — particularly in explaining him to children. How to square the

[293]

wickedness of secession with this leader, who was so clearly everything you wanted a child to be? Hard, but Fremantle is wrong
when he says no Northern critic ever accused Lee of the "greater
vices." At least one magazine made a good try:

"General Lee — the man who neither smokes, drinks nor chews
tobacco; who has, in short, none of the smaller vices, but all of
the larger ones; for he deliberately, basely and under circumstances of unparalleled meanness, betrayed his country, and, long
after all hope of success was lost, carried on a murderous war
against his own race and kindred." (*Our Young Folks Magazine*,
September 1865, p. 603.)

4. Longstreet's wartime devotion to Lee is ironic in the light of
his later bitterness. While the war lasted — in fact, as long as
Lee lived — they remained on good terms. But once Lee was gone,
the carping began. Lee's admirers blamed Gettysburg on Longstreet — said he was too slow. Longstreet blamed the defeat on
Lee — said Lee should never have attacked in the first place.

As time passed, the breach widened. Longstreet became a Republican; the other Confederate leaders remained Democrats.
Longstreet grew rich; the others stayed poor. By the nineties,
Longstreet found himself pretty much alone. But being outnumbered was an old story with him, and he fought back as stubbornly
as in any of his campaigns. Finally, he really turned against Lee
in his *Memoirs*, harping on Lee's "nervous condition," "uneven
temper," "desperate mood painfully evident." At one point, Longstreet even said that Lee at Gettysburg was "off balance and la-
bored under that oppression until enough blood was shed to appease him." (*From Manassas to Appomattox*, pp. 358, 359, 361,
384.)

People will argue forever whether or not Lee should have attacked at Gettysburg. Less arguable is the question whether in
choosing his plan, Lee failed to weigh factors and considerations
perceived by Longstreet. General Dick Taylor, who knew them
both, summed it up pretty well when he said, "That any subject involving the possession and exercise of intellect should be

clear to Longstreet and concealed from Lee, is a startling proposi-
tion to those having knowledge of the two men." (Richard Taylor,
Destruction and Reconstruction, 1879, p. 231.)

5. Longstreet learned that Meade had been made Union commander from his trusted scout Harrison, who had just slipped
through the Union lines. Harrison also brought some far more
disquieting news — the Union Army was dangerously close at
hand; it had chased after Lee much more quickly than anybody
expected.

Up to this point, Lee had no idea where the Federals were. At
the start of the invasion, he had sent Jeb Stuart's cavalry to screen
his movements and keep an eye on Hooker's forces. But Stuart
wandered off chasing wagon trains and let the Union Army get
between Lee and himself. To rejoin Lee in Pennsylvania, he had
to make a huge looping circle around the Federals, and this took
time. Meanwhile, Lee was "without his eyes." He could only
guess where the enemy was.

As matters turned out, Lee underestimated the marching speed
of the Union Army, and Longstreet's scout warned him just in
time. But for this, there would probably be no chance to argue
over Gettysburg, for Meade could have caught the scattered Confederate units by surprise and beaten them piecemeal before a
major battle could develop.

CHAPTER 12

Gettysburg

1. The firing at Gettysburg had begun some eight hours before Fremantle first heard the rumble of guns. Early that morning,
a corporal, Alphonse Hodges, of the 9th New York Cavalry, had
been reconnoitering on the Chambersburg road, a few miles west
of Gettysburg. In the early light of dawn, he saw some men approaching about a mile away. He sent his own companions back

to notify headquarters and advanced himself to see what was up. He soon saw that the men were Confederates and as he turned to go back, one of the enemy shot at him. The first gun at Gettysburg had been fired.

2. On the whole, both Federals and Confederates were quick to praise any piece of exceptional bravery shown by their enemy. When A. P. Hill told Fremantle that he was sorry to see a gallant Yankee meet his death, his reaction was quite typical. Not so Jackson. Once during the Valley Campaign, Confederate Colonel Patton told Jackson about a charge by three Union cavalrymen, declaring that he admired the gallantry of the participants and wished his troops had not fired upon them.

"Why would you not have shot these men, Colonel?" asked Jackson curtly.

"I should have spared them, General," answered Patton, "because they were brave men who had gotten into a desperate situation where it was as easy to capture them as it was to kill them."

Jackson's reply was brief. "Shoot them all. I don't want them to be brave."

3. Even on such a historic occasion as Gettysburg, Fremantle's Austrian roommate Ross seems unbearably ebullient for so early in the morning. Fremantle makes him look pretty poisonous, waxing his mustache at 3:30 A. M. Ross's own *Memoirs* make him look worse. He happily recalls that as the sound of cannon aroused him from sleep, he bounced out of bed and gaily sang out, *"C'est le sanglant appel de Mars!"* (Fitzgerald Ross, A Visit to the Cities and Camps of the Confederate States, 1865, p. 49.)

4. While Fremantle perched in his tree, the Confederate leaders beneath him reached a momentous decision on this second morning of Gettysburg. The question was whether to attack the strong Union position on Cemetery Ridge, or try to lure the Federals into making an attack instead. Just out of Fremantle's hearing, Lee made his big point: "The enemy is here, and if we do not whip him, he will whip us." Longstreet thought it better to wait until Pickett's division arrived. In an effort to get some backing,

he took Hood aside and said: "The General is a little nervous this morning. He wishes to attack; I do not wish to do so without Pickett. I never like to go into battle with one boot off." But the die was cast, and Lee remained fixed in his determination to attack. (*Southern Historical Society Papers*, October 1877, p. 148.)

5. Fremantle, like everybody else, was fascinated by the Rebel yell — and also like everybody else, found it almost impossible to describe. Attempts to put it down on paper have resulted in a frightening collection of syllables — a high-pitched "Woh-who-ey!" according to one version; "Yai, yai, yi, yai, yi!" according to another; "Y-yo yo-wo-wo!" according to a third. Even Bell Irwin Wiley gave up after a brave effort to pin it down in his wonderfully detailed *Life of Johnny Reb.*

There's equal disagreement as to the yell's origin. But it was standard Confederate "equipment" at least as early as First Bull Run, when Stonewall Jackson shouted to his men, "When you charge, yell like furies!"

Students of the yell, however, do agree on three points: (1) it was a shrill, high-pitched whooping and yipping; (2) it was completely informal, not remotely like an organized cheer; (3) it sent chills down the spine of even the stanchest Yankee defender.

6. Nothing seems more incongruous than Fremantle's description of a Confederate band playing polkas and waltzes while stationed almost between the lines during the battle of Gettysburg. But bad as their music was, the Confederates loved to have bands around, and they were kept playing whenever possible. General Dick Taylor describes how his Louisiana Creoles pulled up after a long march to support Stonewall Jackson, and immediately started their band going with a waltz. They were newcomers or they probably wouldn't have tried such levity directly in front of Jackson, who was perched on a fence watching them and, as usual, sucking a lemon. "Thoughtless fellows for serious work," was his only remark.

7. Longstreet, like most generals in the Civil War, exposed himself under fire to a degree that now seems incredibly rash for

a top commander. He was in his tightest jam at Antietam, where alone with a single cannon and a few gunners, he held the Confederate center against the whole Union advance for a few decisive moments. The wonder is not that the Jacksons and the Reynoldses were ultimately killed, but that so many generals survived. Joe Wheeler, for instance, had sixteen horses killed under him, and even this was small potatoes to Nathaniel Bedford Forrest, who loved hand-to-hand fighting. Forrest once fought six Union troopers single-handed. During four years of war, he killed some thirty individual opponents and liked to say that he had done better than even the score for the number of horses shot under him. (They numbered only twenty-nine.)

8. Exotic uniforms were rapidly disappearing by the time of Gettysburg, but earlier they had been quite the fashion on both sides. At the start of the war little thought was given to a standard, distinctive dress. Many regiments were raised and equipped by private individuals, or from local contributions, and they were clothed according to the tastes of those who organized them. In the North, Colonel Ellsworth turned up with Zouaves, reflecting the current infatuation with French military tradition. Colonel Cameron had a unit of Highlanders, complete with kilts. Colonel d'Utassy went in for Garibaldi Guards, appropriately costumed. The Confederates too had their Zouaves (especially the Louisiana Tigers), and the privately equipped Maryland Line arrived in bright blue and orange.

Among other problems, this haphazard policy produced tragic cases of mistaken identity. At Big Bethel in '61, one Union regiment fired on another, because it was dressed in gray. At Bull Run a month later, another Union regiment failed to fire in time, because the Confederates were dressed in blue. And when both sides used Zouaves, there was invariable confusion — from 200 yards, any soldier in a fez, a huge sash and flowing plus fours looks the same.

9. A battle in the back yard is naturally exciting to any small boy, and the children of Gettysburg were no exception. With

strange indifference to the danger, they innocently wander on stage in many scenes, adding an incongruous touch to the greatest battle ever fought on American soil. Billy Bailey, a twelve-year old at the time, later reminisced how he and his friends stopped berry-picking and sat on a fence to watch A. P. Hill's men charge across the fields. Another child played more than a spectator's role when Sickle's Union troops were feeling for the enemy during the second day. As the Federals cautiously advanced, a small boy rushed out from behind a barn, pointed to a nearby woods, and warned, "There's lots of Rebels in there! In rows!"

10. Longstreet is rather fatherly about Fremantle's ill-timed congratulations on the "success" of Pickett's charge. Recalling the incident years later, Longstreet remarked: "Colonel Fremantle, only observing the troops of Pickett's command, said to me, 'General, I would not have missed this for anything in the world.' He believed it to be a complete success. I was watching the troops supporting Pickett and saw plainly they could not hold together ten minutes longer. I called his attention to the wavering condition of the two divisions of the Third Corps, and said they would not hold, that Pickett would strike and be crushed and the attack would be a failure." (*Battles and Leaders of the Civil War,* 1884, Vol. III, p. 346.)

11. Lee was outwardly cheerful, but inwardly crushed as Pickett's men reeled back at Gettysburg. That night Confederate General Imboden dropped by the general's headquarters. What he saw shows how Lee really felt.

It was one A. M., and when Imboden first arrived, Lee had not yet returned from the battlefield. Soon the general appeared, riding alone, slowly, deep in thought. He reined in his horse and tried to dismount. The effort to do so exhausted him completely and Imboden rushed forward to help him. Once on the ground, Lee threw his arm across the saddle to rest and leaned in silence, almost motionless upon his weary horse. "The moon shone full upon his massive features," recalled Imboden, "and revealed an expression of sadness that I had never before seen upon his face.

Awed by his appearance, I waited for him to speak until the silence became embarrassing, when, to break it and change the silent current of his thoughts I ventured to remark . . . 'General, this has been a hard day on you.' He looked up and replied mournfully, 'Yes, it has been a sad, sad day for us,' and immediately lapsed into his thoughtful mood and attitude."

It was a trying experience for Imboden. His efforts at sympathetic small talk fell flat. At one point, Lee could only say in a loud voice, in a tone almost of agony, "Too bad! *Too bad!* OH, TOO BAD!" (*Battles and Leaders*, Vol. III, pp. 420–421.)

12. Longstreet's supposed capture at Gettysburg was a case of mistaken identity. When his troops were forced back in their attack on July 2, among the wounded left behind was a Colonel Powell of the Texas 5th Regiment. Powell was a short, stocky man with a full beard and looked very much like Longstreet. The report quickly spread among the Union troops that the general himself had been taken, and it was some time before the mistake was cleared up.

13. In later years, Longstreet was heavily blamed for the failure of Pickett's charge — especially the delay in its start. As criticism mounted, so did his estimates of how many men he should have had in order to carry it off. When he talked with Fremantle the day after the battle, he felt 30,000 men would have sufficed. By 1895, he was saying, "40,000 men could not have carried the position at Gettysburg." (*From Manassas to Appomattox*, p. 404.)

CHAPTER 13

Back into Maryland

1. While the Confederate wagon train began its slow, weary retreat from Gettysburg, the infantry stayed behind to hold off any Union pursuit. Miserable as Fremantle found conditions in the wagons, life was even worse for the unprotected forces cov-

ering the retreat. Ross, Fremantle's Austrian tentmate, was among those who stayed behind and he paints a vivid picture of that wretched, stormy night: "When it was dusk we went on a mile or two farther on the Fairfield road, and presently came on a blazing fire, around which were Generals Lee and Longstreet, with all their staff. We were to remain there till the train had passed, when the main body of the army would be withdrawn from its position and join the retreat. . . . It was certainly a dismal night. The fire was kept up and protected from the rain by continuously piling on fresh wood. . . . It lighted the scene with a strange glare.

"Lee and Longstreet stood apart engaged in earnest conversation, and around the fire in various groups lay the officers of their staffs. Tired to death, many were sleeping in spite of the mud and the drenching rain; and I well remember one long log of wood, a fence rail, which was much coveted as a pillow. . . . By eight o'clock next morning the whole wagon train had got past us, and the troops began to move." (Ross, pp. 71–72.)

2. Getting the Confederate wagon train safely out of Pennsylvania was a back-breaking job. When Lee's army first entered Maryland, the wagon train alone, exclusive of artillery, was 42 miles long. Now the wagons and carts confiscated from Pennsylvania made the train much longer, while mud and exhaustion simultaneously made it harder to move. Under the conditions, a loss of only 38 wagons was a miracle.

3. Most of Fremantle's Confederate friends feared for the worst when he set out to cross the lines into Union territory. Some were afraid he'd be treated as a spy; others viewed him simply as a mascot who'd be helpless without the protection of Southern hospitality. But not Longstreet. The general heartily assured his staff, "A man who has traveled all through Texas as successfully as the Colonel, is safe to get through the Yankee lines all right." (Ross, p. 80.)

CHAPTER 14

Hagerstown to New York

1. Major General Benjamin F. Kelley contributed little at Gettysburg. Handling the Union defense of West Virginia, he was pretty well isolated from the battle; and during Lee's subsequent withdrawal, Kelley's single division could do little but hover off to the west, while the main Union Army tried to organize pursuit on the other side of the retreating Confederates.

Kelley, however, contributed a great deal to the Union cause early in the war. In the preliminary skirmishing over West Virginia, his small force beat the Confederates at Philippi on June 3, 1861. The Rebels were so completely routed that the action was called the "Philippi races" and did much to cement Union spirit in the region. The only Northern casualty — and one of the first of the war — was the wounding of General Kelley.

2. Many a Southern sympathizer kidded himself that Gettysburg was not so bad after all. Fremantle's Austrian tentmate Ross, for instance, wrote: "It is obvious that the campaign has not been a fruitless one. The war has not only been carried on in the enemy's country, but enormous supplies have been obtained, which will maintain the army for several months to come. Wagons and horses, which were very necessary, have also been secured in incalculable numbers. The men, whose meat ration for several months past has been a quarter of a pound of bacon, now get a pound and a half of beef. Fifteen thousand cattle have been driven to the rear for the use of the army, which at present requires about 300 head a day. Then, the enemy has had to evacuate a large portion of Southern territory, upon which they were pressing heavily, and that, too, just in time for the harvest to be secured to the Confederacy. There is no doubt, however, that the North will claim Gettysburg as a glorious victory, and there will be great rejoicing over it in Yankee-doodledom." (Ross, pp. 75–76.)

3. Nothing but the best for Fremantle. He could rough it, but

when he came to New York, naturally he stayed at the Fifth Avenue Hotel, newest, plushest hostelry in the city. Its luxuries even included a new convenience hitherto unknown in hotel living — "a perpendicular railway intersecting each story."

4. "Grayback" wasn't as innocuous a description as it now sounds, when applied to the dirty, ragged Confederate soldiers. It was also the current slang for lice.

5. "Remember this: that the bloody, treasonable and revolutionary doctrine of public necessity can be proclaimed by a mob as well as by a government!" These dangerously inviting words came from Horatio Seymour, New York's Democratic governor, who considered the war an outrageous Republican plot. He was denouncing the first draft in American history, which was scheduled to start in New York City on July 11, 1863. No words could have appealed more to the strong antiwar, anti-Republican, anti-Negro sentiments of the immigrants who at this time were pouring into New York from Europe. No words could have been better calculated to start a riot.

It started on July 13 — Fremantle's first morning in New York. Mobs wrecked the draft offices, and then began wrecking the town in general. With weapons seized in their looting, they fought first the police and then the army. Order was finally restored after five days of pillage, during most of which the governor and other antiwar Democrats were smugly silent or absent from town. Meanwhile, some 1200 people had been killed.

Fremantle was in the heart of the uproar. The fire he saw was probably the enrollment office at Broadway and 28th Street; it went up in flames along with the rest of the block about that time. The Negro he saw chased could have been any one of countless thousands. At one point, the mob even stormed and burned the Colored Orphan Asylum, some 200 Negro children escaping just in time.

CHAPTER 15

Postscript

1. Three months and thirteen days after landing in America, Lieutenant Colonel Arthur James Lyon Fremantle set sail again for England. As he pondered his experiences in the snug cabin of the Cunarder *China*, Fremantle came to a conclusion that today seems startling — sooner or later the South was bound to win the Civil War.

How could this intelligent, observant Englishman be so wrong? True, there were many signs of strength — the resourcefulness that produced a tannery in the wilderness, the fighting skill of Lee, Johnston and their tough resilient men, the fiery spirit of those indomitable women.

But there were also many seeds of weakness. These, Fremantle saw and recorded as faithfully as the strong points. He noted how selfish local interests constantly bucked all central authority. He saw the blockade. He noted the evils of weak conscription, electing officers, straggling, poor discipline and rampant politics in the army. He marveled at the South's overconfidence.

Why, then, did Fremantle discount these weaknesses and smoke his pipe dreams? Most probably because three months in the Confederate States were enough to unhinge any romantic Victorian. By the time he left, he was hopelessly under the spell of frontier days, rattling trains, river boats, campfires and close escapes. He had succumbed to the threadbare graciousness of Charleston, the thunder of Gettysburg, the soft breeze of a starlit night at Shelbyville. Fremantle, in short, was in love with the South, and his heart now ruled his mind.